Alternative Dispute Resolution and Peace-building in Africa

Alternative Dispute Resolution and Peace-building in Africa

Edited by

Ernest Uwazie

CAMBRIDGE
SCHOLARS
PUBLISHING

Alternative Dispute Resolution and Peace-building in Africa,
Edited by Ernest Uwazie

This book first published 2014

Cambridge Scholars Publishing

12 Back Chapman Street, Newcastle upon Tyne, NE6 2XX, UK

British Library Cataloguing in Publication Data
A catalogue record for this book is available from the British Library

ISBN (10): 1-4438-5707-6, ISBN (13): 978-1-4438-5707-9

TABLE OF CONTENTS

ACKNOWLEDGMENTS

This publication is primarily the result of the Third International Africa Peace and Conflict Resolution Conference, on the theme of "ADR and Peace Studies in Africa, 15 years later: Lessons and Future Directions". The conference was held on July 26-28, 2011 in Accra, Ghana.

Several additional papers were selected, to enrich the publication and to contribute to the emerging literature on alternative dispute resolution and peacebuilding in Africa, both in practice and policy. Arguably, this publication will continue to benefit from future revisions and critical reviews, as well as related conference conclaves in Africa and elsewhere.

The publication of this volume would not have been possible without the contributions of the respective authors and conference sponsors. Together, we overcame the challenges involved in producing conference proceedings.

Each author is responsible for the contents of her/his contribution. As the editor, I have taken care not to distort the content or meaning of each contribution. I regret any errors or mistakes herein, as they are unintended. The views expressed in this publication remain those of the contributors or authors, and they do not necessarily represent the viewpoints or endorsement of the July 26-28, 2011 conference organizers: Center for African Peace & Conflict Resolution (CAPCR) and Ghana Association of Certified Mediators and Arbitrators (GHACMA).

Please direct inquires or comments to:
Ernest Uwazie
Editor
December 2013
uwazieee@csus.edu.

ABOUT THE EDITOR

Ernest Uwazie is a Professor of Criminal Justice and Director of the Center for African Peace and Conflict Resolution at California State University, Sacramento, California. He teaches courses on comparative justice, dispute resolution and restorative justice, minorities, and justice, among others. He is a renowned ADR (Alternative Dispute Resolution)/ mediation trainer, practitioner, scholar, and system designer. Some of his publications include "Indigenous disputing modes among the Igbos" in the *Journal of Legal Pluralism* (1994); he co-editor with Professors G.N. Uzoigwe and Isaac Albert *Interethnic & Religious Conflicts Resolution in Nigeria(1999*); "Social relations and peacekeeping among the Igbo", in I. W. Zartman Ed., (2000)*Traditional Cures for Modern African Conflicts;* "Political Parties and National Integration in Nigeria" Robert Dibie (Ed.) *The Politics and Policies of Sub-Saharan Africa* (2001*)* University Press of America; *Conflict Resolution and Peace Education in Africa* (2003); *Contemporary Issues in African Studies: A. Reader* (ed.). (2011); "The Role of Higher Education in Conflict Resolution and Peace Challenges and Prospects for African Universities", in *Journal of International Politics and Development* (2010), vol. 8(2); "Alternative Dispute Resolution in Africa…" (2011), in Africa, Security Brief No. 16, by the Africa Center for Strategic Studies of the National Defense University (Washington, D.C.).

FOREWORD

STEVEN GATEMBU KAIRU

I am delighted to provide a Foreword to this publication on ADR in Africa. Some of the challenges that have faced Kenya—and indeed many countries in Africa—in the administration of justice are attributable to overreliance on the courts in the resolution of all forms of dispute, even where the courts are not well suited to the task and where other forms of dispute resolution would be more appropriate. The result is that our courts are overwhelmed by their caseloads; parties have to wait for a long time in the queue before getting service from the courts, access to justice is hindered, substantial justice is often compromised due to the technical strictures of the court system, and it is often the case that outcomes of court proceedings do not satisfy the interests of the parties involved.

It is against this background that Kenya has embarked on legal reforms to integrate alternative forms of dispute resolution—as well as traditional dispute resolution mechanisms—in the administration of justice. A few of these reform initiatives are worthy of mention. Under the Constitution of Kenya, 2010,[1] courts and tribunals are enjoined, in exercising judicial authority, to apply alternative forms of dispute resolution. In its strategy to promote and facilitate alternative forms of dispute resolution, the judiciary has undertaken to develop laws and rules for alternative dispute resolution, and to sensitize court users and communities to alternative dispute resolution options.[2] The Civil Procedure Act has been amended to empower courts, at the request of parties or where the court deems it appropriate, to refer disputes to mediation or other appropriate methods of dispute resolution.[3] An Arbitral Court has recently been established under an Act of Parliament,[4] which is empowered to adopt and implement

[1] Article 159(2)(c) of the Constitution of Kenya, 2010.

[2] Judiciary Transformation Framework 2012-2016

[3] Sections 59B and 59C of the Civil Procedure Act, Chapter 21 of the Laws of Kenya

[4] Nairobi Centre for International Arbitration Act, Act No. 26 of 2013. The Act also establishes Nairobi Centre for International Arbitration.

appropriate means of dispute resolution on its own motion, or at the request of parties, including conciliation, mediation and other means.

Alongside these reform initiatives is the need for capacity building. Happily, many universities, and law schools in particular, have incorporated alternative dispute resolution courses within their curricula. The Centre for African Peace and Conflict Resolution (CAPCR), under Professor Ernest Uwazie, has made a very significant contribution to capacity building in Africa. In 2004, CAPCR invited nine of us from Kenya to the US to train as trainers of trainers in alternative dispute resolution. CAPCR has provided similar training and curriculum development expertise in other countries in Africa. However, the need to create internal capacity remains, and is urgent in Africa, particularly as the use of ADR expands to include commercial cases.

I therefore welcome this publication on alternative dispute resolution, with contributions by a diverse, distinguished, and experienced group of contributors. It provides an invaluable reservoir of intellectual resources on ADR in Africa and beyond. It will greatly assist in better understanding the status of ADR, and help to address the challenges that face Africa in the administration of justice and the pursuit of peace.

PROLOGUE

ALTERNATIVE DISPUTE RESOLUTION (ADR): THE GHANA EXPERIENCE

GEORGINA T WOOD

The history of Alternative Dispute Resolution (ADR) in Ghana, and perhaps in West Africa, begins with Professor Ernest Uwazie and the Center for African Peace and Conflict Resolution at the California State University, Sacramento, US. It is his vision, foresight, tenacity of purpose and relentless pursuit for excellence that, with the assistance of his ADR project partner, Attorney Daniel Yamshon (and others), gave birth to the ADR movement in Ghana. Their intervention did not end at that. To this day, they continue to nurture the effective growth and internal capacity building of ADR in the sub-region, as well as throughout Africa.

Under Professor Uwazie's leadership (I refer to him as the father of ADR in Africa), in 1996 twelve of us from the West Africa sub-region (Nigeria, Ghana and Senegal) were invited to the US, starting in Sacramento, for an intensive one month Training of Trainers (ToT) program on ADR for legal professionals. It was during this landmark project that, as the representative of the Judiciary of Ghana, I first cut my ADR teeth. I did not have much difficulty in recognizing, in those early stages of the program, that ADR held great promise for justice delivery.

Nene Amegatcher (now President of the Ghana Bar Association) was the nominee of the Ghana Bar Association. The third pioneer was Professor Henrietta Mensah-Bonsu, who represented the Law Faculty of the University of Ghana, Legon. (She later served as the United Nations Secretary General's Deputy Special Representative to the Republic of Liberia). Dan Yamshon is among those gallant men and women whose invaluable contribution to the development of ADR in Ghana—and subsequently in The Gambia during my tenure as a justice of the Supreme Court of the Gambia, while in session—will always be remembered.

I would like to pay special tribute to two of my predecessors as Chief Justice: the late Chief Justices Kwame Wiredu and George Kingsley

Acquah, who, under their respective tenures and working with Professor Uwazie, initiated vigorous policies leading to the development of ADR in Ghana.

Last but not least, I would like to pay a special tribute to Ms. Brooks Robinson, who was then Public Affairs Officer of the United States Information Services in Accra. Brooks, as I love to call her, exerted considerable time and energy assisting in entrenching ADR and other democratic values in our dear country. May I reiterate that I remain encouraged by the invaluable support the Judiciary has received from our donor partners, and all of the wonderful friends earlier acknowledged.

Our task, after the initial training in 1996 (that was of course followed by more advanced training) was, though simple, indeed quite daunting. We moved across the entire country in order to spread the ADR message, sharing the knowledge we had acquired with our colleagues—Bench, Bar and Faculty—and the general public. Our goal was to train and retrain other trainers. Even more importantly, we pushed for policies that encouraged the integration of ADR into our legal system. We found the legal terrain pretty difficult. It was steeped in litigation culture and was not ADR friendly, but we persevered.

Judicial Reforms

Ghana has often been lauded for its democratic progress. For its part, the Judiciary has not relented in its efforts to ensure the effective administration of justice—even in the face of successive military interventions. This notwithstanding, the Judiciary has not been without its share of challenges within the emergent Ghanaian polity. A little over ten years ago, the major stakeholders in the administration of justice felt that the system needed a major overhaul if it was to respond effectively to the needs of the business community, in particular. This was at a time when the private sector had, appropriately, been identified as the engine of growth for the Ghanaian economy. The Judiciary itself, the Private Enterprise Foundation, the Ghana Bar Association and the Ghana Investment Promotion Centre called for remedial policies and judicial reform programs based on sound strategic options. In particular, the adjudication of commercial and land cases were marked by frustratingly long delays. The main causes of these delays varied. The Judiciary was at the time contending with such basic issues as poor and inadequate hard and soft infrastructure, outmoded, cumbersome, and non-user-friendly procedural rules of court, difficult enforcement mechanisms, etc. In short, the institution was underfunded and poorly resourced. Unattractive conditions of service were certainly a negative factor, resulting in a poor work ethic. Under such conditions, it was virtually impossible to attract some of the finest legal brains to the Bench. The overall effect was the occasional seeming loss of public confidence in the court system, due principally to the length and expense associated with litigation. It was rightly thought that institutional reform would lead to the transformation of the judicial system, and that this would positively impact upon such critical areas as commercial and investment law. But we have made and continue to make significant improvements in the area of infrastructure.

With the support of the World Bank, the Government of Ghana, under the Private Sector Development Project, commissioned a study that sought to identify those gaps and weaknesses that needed urgent attention. One area which came under consultants' scrutiny was Ghana's "Administrative Law Procedures on Arbitration and other Alternative Dispute Resolution Mechanisms." Their overwhelming conclusion, which enjoyed the full endorsement of the national body tasked to discuss all recommendations under the project, was that ADR must, with minimum delay, be integrated into the justice system.

The year 1998 witnessed the setting up of a Task Force on ADR, by the then Deputy Attorney General and Minister for Justice, Mr Martin Amidu. Mr Nene Amegatcher and I were privileged to serve on that task force. Its major task was to formulate a standalone Bill on ADR for passage into law. Surprisingly, it took almost ten years for the bill to be passed into an act of Parliament, Act 798 (2010). We found the pace of change rather too slow, given the fact that within the African setting, the cultural environment for ADR was not an issue.

Thankfully, the legal system is well resourced in terms of specific ADR statutory provisions. In other words, there was no dearth of a generalised legal framework or specific supportive ADR legislation for ADR practice in Ghana. Therefore, in spite of the delay, we proceeded, under these laws, to have ADR mainstreamed into the formal judicial system.

The Pre Alternative Dispute Resolution (ADR) Act (Act 798) Era

The Courts Act 1993, Act 459 (as amended) served as the basic legal framework for ADR practice. Pertinently, its predecessors all carried the provision which encourages out-of-court settlements, as we are sometimes used to describing them. It vests in the courts the general power to promote reconciliation in civil and criminal cases. In particular sections, 72 and 73, (quoted in part) empowered the court to:

> (1) ... promote reconciliation and encourage and facilitate the settlement of disputes in an amicable manner between and among persons over whom the court has jurisdiction.
>
> (2) When a civil suit or proceeding is pending, any court with jurisdiction in that suit may promote reconciliation among the parties, and encourage and facilitate the amicable settlement of the suit or proceeding.

Section 73: Reconciliation in Criminal Cases

Any court with criminal jurisdiction may promote reconciliation, encourage and facilitate a settlement in an amicable manner of any offence not amounting to felony and not aggravated in degree, on payment cases of compensation or on other terms approved by the court before which the case is tried, and may during the pendency of the negotiations for a settlement stay the proceeding for a reasonable time and in the event of a settlement being effected shall dismiss the case and discharge the accused person.

In terms of specific ADR legislation, we have the following:

The Arbitration Act 1961, Act 38. This made provision for both domestic and foreign arbitrations. An award was final and binding, and could be enforced in the same manner as a judgment or order of the court.

The Matrimonial Causes Act 1971, Act 367. Section 8 enjoined the court, in divorce proceedings, to adjourn proceedings specifically to promote reconciliation when expedient to do so.

The Commission for Human Rights and Administrative Justice Act 1993, Act 456. Pursuant to section 7(d) (i), the Commission is mandated to take appropriate action to remedy a complaint through negotiation and compromise between the parties.

The Children's Act 1998 Act 560. Child Panels are mandated, under section 28, to mediate in civil and criminal matters affecting children.

The Labour Act 2003, Act 651. This Act endeavours to provide a step by step approach to the resolution of industrial disputes so as to avoid self-help and confrontations. Thus, sections 153, 154 and 157 require parties first to negotiate in good faith, proceed to mediation if this fails, and finally to submit to voluntary arbitration should mediation also fail.

Order 58 of the High Court Civil Procedure Rules 2004, CI 47. This constitutes the special procedural rules regulating commercial litigation in the Commercial Courts, a specialized unit of the High Court. The rules mandate Pre-trial Settlement Conference, where parties are obliged to attempt to reach a settlement of the relevant dispute, principally through the use of mediation by a Judge. Parties may request a reference to an external person or institution other than a Judge. Where parties are unable to reach a settlement, the case is assigned to a new Judge, for a full scale trial.

Minerals and Mining Act, 2006, Act 703 – section 27(1) mandates the holder of a mineral right and the Minister, in the event of a dispute, to use Alternative Dispute Resolution procedures to reach an amicable settlement.

Thus, in 2003, under the auspices of the National Governance Programme (GNP), a Judiciary ADR Task Force was established. It was charged with the responsibility of working out the policies and strategies for achieving the goal of mainstreaming ADR in Ghana. Nene Amegatcher and I, together with a few others, as members of this Task Force, developed the first voluntary Court-Connected ADR model in Ghana. Apart from the Commercial Courts, which practice a mandatory model, this model is operational in all Courts in Ghana. Mediation thus serves as the primary alternative to litigation for the many ordinary citizens who access the courts for justice but who lack the financial resources to engage in endless litigation. It thus works well in the lower courts in particular, where the caseload is higher and more amenable to out of court settlement.

In all of this, I would be remiss if I failed to mention the invaluable contribution of our chiefs, queen mothers, religious leaders, heads of families and elders: they use customary arbitration, negotiated settlements, and other informal conciliatory methods on a daily basis in order to settle a large number of disputes in their respective areas of jurisdiction. We have, over the years, shared the knowledge and experience we have acquired in ADR practice to build their capacities to assure substantive and procedural fairness and integrity in their practice.

The most successful model of Court-Connected ADR is to be found in the Commercial Courts. Established in 2005, these courts provide investors, in particular, with the opportunity for the timely disposal of commercial and other investment related disputes. As part of the practice and procedure of the court, parties are mandated at the pre-trial settlement conference to explore the possibility of full or partial settlement of their dispute. Available information shows that we have not done too badly although, admittedly, there is room for improvement. The Court continues to host study visits from other judiciaries from the sub-region and beyond.

Not unsurprisingly, the deployment of ADR within the judicial system of Ghana was set out as one of the key objectives of Ghana's Growth and Poverty Reduction Strategy for 2006-2009 (GPRS II).

On assuming the high office of Chief Justice, I continued in the path my predecessors had trodden. We have continued to offer training to members of the Bar Association. We have recruited and trained private individuals, including retired professionals, chiefs, queen mothers, paralegals, etc., to serve as ADR neutrals for the Judiciary. Judges, magistrates, registrars and other court staff have not been left out of the ADR skill training and education programs.

Within the Judiciary, the establishment of a Court-Connected ADR Unit, under the directorship of a Justice of the Court of Appeal with national and regional ADR Coordinators, has expanded the frontiers of ADR practice. Refreshingly, the Supreme Court has actively promoted ADR at that apex appellate level. I have, from time to time, received encouraging news of successful Supreme Court ordered ADRs. ADR weeks have become an established regime within the judicial system. Under this program, one week in each legal year term is set aside and dedicated to the settlement of cases via mediation. Again, Sena Chambers, of which Nene Amegatcher is the junior partner, deserves special mention. Week after week, the firm has provided *pro bono* services to the Judiciary, to ensure the success of this program. We salute this team and other lawyers and trained Mediators who have actively lent support to our effort.

The Judicial Training Institute (JTI) of the Judicial Service of Ghana is primarily responsible for ADR training programs. The Institute works in partnership with a number of resource persons from ADR-proficient organizations, particularly, the renowned Ghana Association of Chartered Mediators and Arbitrators (GHACMA), which is a product of the 1996 ADR initiative in Ghana.

Private and Community ADR Institutions

The Ghanaian ADR story remains incomplete without mentioning the contributions of private and community institutions. We need to laud the efforts of the few individuals who have braved the odds to form associations that educate, promote and provide ADR services for our people. Aside from GHACMA, other service providers include Gamey and the Gamey Institute (now known as the Pulse Institute), which specialises in labour and industrial issues; the Ghana Arbitration Centre, under the leadership of Dr. S.K.B. Asante; the International Federation of Women Lawyers (FIDA), and the West African Dispute Resolution Centre (WADREC). Ashaiman, a densely populated, very active and yet deprived community near Accra, now has a well-established and functioning community ADR Center. The training of local mediators was carried out under the auspices of GHACMA. At the time, Ashaiman did not have a court house, and residents had to travel a fairly long distance to access justice. In 2008, I inaugurated a Circuit Court in the community and the initial ADR work that we had earlier undertaken under the auspices of GHACMA. WADREC now effectively complements the traditional role of the court system.

Challenges

This is not to say there are no challenges. There are, but we remain confident of success. One central challenge is apathy among the legal fraternity. Owing to the kind of legal education members receive, they tend to prefer litigation to ADR. We do have Judges and Magistrates who, in spite of the effectiveness of ADR as a case management tool, tend not to invest any time in promoting and encouraging its appropriate use. In 2008, we launched a strategic plan to build on the entire ADR program. It addresses the following five key areas of ADR development: Court-Connected ADR Mainstreaming, Recruitment and training of Neutrals, ADR Infrastructure, and ADR Advocacy and Funding for ADR.

Through a combination of strategies, including the restructuring of legal education to cover a full study course in ADR, we are confident of success. Increasing ADR awareness through a variety of programs aimed at engaging the general public in ADR activities such as seminars, workshops and symposia, remains an effective strategy. Ultimately, the creation of college and university educational programs for the training of conflict resolution managers and ADR experts will help to respond to the challenges in Africa, including Ghana.

Conclusion

During the past 15 years, Ghana has been embarking upon a variety of institutional reforms and development initiatives. The introduction of

ADR remains an enduring feature of the legal system in Ghana. As an adjunct to courtroom adjudication, it holds promise for an improved and qualitative access to justice for all Ghanaians, while serving as an attractive feature for economic development.

December 2013

Note: *Excerpts of the Keynote Lecture at the April 2011 CAPCR Peace Awards Dinner, California State University, Sacramento.*

CHAPTER ONE

INTRODUCTION: ADR AND PEACE-BUILDING IN AFRICA

ERNEST UWAZIE (EDITOR)

It is fitting to take stock of the road travelled by or in the name of peace building and conflict resolution in Africa, since it gained new prominence and momentum in the mid-1990s. In particular, I remember our maiden program in 1996, on "promoting alternative dispute resolution in West Africa", with participants from and activities in Nigeria, Ghana and Senegal. It is probably safe to say that the 1996 ADR project in West Africa was a landmark event in the participating countries, if not all of Africa; it certainly provided useful lessons for expansion, legal sector reform, social policy changes, and cultural adaptations. I also remember our first ADR summit in 1998 in Accra, to stimulate the long road toward internal capacity building for program development, service delivery, and institutionalization. In 2008, we met again in Addis Ababa, Ethiopia, in order to elevate the conflict resolution dialogue, expand the network in the Africa sub-region, and discuss the critical importance or need to evaluate what we do, and to assess whether it was working in Africa.

Fifteen years after that initial project, we are attempting to use this medium for a preliminary review of activities, to assess progress, to identify some challenges, and to chart a new, emergent course in the ultimate quest for a culture of peace that promotes development and social justice.

To recap, the conflict landscape in Africa in the 1990s was alarming: In a resonant lamentation, William Nhara (Coordinator of the Conflict Prevention and Research at the OAU) stated:

> The 1990s has so far witnessed events that will remain as serious indictments in the history of African political development. Never before has there been such 'bloody experiences,' leaving well over three million

> dead, more than 10 million refugees and a historical legacy for our children and future generations of democides and ethnocides.[1]

In *Reviewing Events in Africa,* the former OAU Secretary General Salim Ahmed Salim highlighted the troubling state of conflicts in Africa: 67 military coups staged between 1956 and 1996, 16 countries embroiled in intra-state wars or protracted civil conflicts, and 8 million refugees and 14 million internally displaced people.[2] During that same time frame, there were over 120,000 African child soldiers. One need not imagine the adverse impact of the conflicts on every aspect and corner of the African family, community and nation-state, with economic, cultural, political, social, and environmental costs. The immediate and collateral consequences of the conflicts were significant and widespread, with urgent calls for a more strategic and purposeful approach to conflict resolution in promoting democracy and development in Africa.

In response to these sobering conflict reports, various programs and initiatives were developed in the 1990s, especially Alternative Dispute Resolution (ADR),[3] followed soon after (in the early 2000s) by peace and conflict studies programs at many universities. The ADR programs focused on practical skill building and creation of foundational knowledge on interpersonal, community disputes, namely negotiation, mediation, conciliation, arbitration, and some combination of processes. Attention to ADR program development varied across Africa, from the legal or judicial sector, to the civil society organizations and traditional or community leaders, to certain professional and commercial institutions (chambers of commerce, media, public agencies, etc.). More recently, there has been particular interest and experimentation with the place and prospects of ADR in electoral disputes.[4] Common ADR project objectives include the decongestion of the court system, the creation of access to justice, promotion of peaceful out of court settlements, conflict prevention or de-

---

[1] "Early Warning and conflict in Africa," Occasional Paper No. 1, February 1996

[2] OAU Fact Sheet, 1998-2

[3] ADR advocates the use or application of appropriate dispute resolution mode(s); its emphasis on reconciliation reflects the traditional "African dispute resolution" principle and conciliation process.

[4] Jacob Segun Olatunji, "How INEC will resolve election disputes – Jega," *Nigerian Tribune*, November 12, 2010. It is worth to mention that the Independent National Electoral Commission in Nigeria has a functioning ADR unit.

escalation, and timely resolution of conflicts.[5] Most ADR projects have been led by American and European resource persons or organizations.

A review of sample syllabi of ADR training programs by US, including CAPCR (Canadian, Italian and British trainers in sub-Saharan Africa) reveals common themes, including an anatomy and taxonomy of conflicts, ADR techniques of negotiation, mediation (most dominant), conciliation, and a few other international arbitration procedures. Teaching methodology is primarily carried out through a combination of lecture and role plays of interpersonal, family, commercial and community types of conflicts; CAPCR's curriculum is unique in its cultural adaptation of concepts, examples and role plays. The duration of training programs ranges from 2-5 days, with more advanced or training of trainers program lasting an additional 2-5 days.

Most of the training has occurred in Africa, with some in America, Australia and Europe. Training participants include lawyers, judges, magistrates, court registrars, human rights activists organizations, educators, community/traditional leaders (chiefs), police officers, social welfare officers, university student/youth leaders, electoral officers, and religious and women leaders.

ADR organizational structure and programming has plural designs, from court (connected/annexed in Nigeria/Ghana/Tanzania), community (including NGOs, Female Lawyers Association, FIDA-Kenya), and agency, (e.g., National Institute of Peace and Conflict Resolution in Nigeria, and private-for-profit organizations). Some organizations focus exclusively on various ADR services, while others seem to incorporate it into their program profiles, with certain enabling legislations and/or court rules.[6]

The CAPCR ADR experience and lessons from Ghana, Nigeria, Kenya, and Ethiopia demonstrate that well-designed and properly implemented ADR programs in Africa can:

---

[5] Notably, ADR is being adopted by some African countries to promote foreign investment; the creation of special or commercial courts with mandatory ADR (e.g., Ghana) supports the goal of increasing investment and promoting overall economic development.

[6] While ADR is generally permissible, some countries and institutions have deemed it proper to adopt (court) rules or legislation to ensure sustainability and professional status; e.g., The Ghana ADR Act 798; Kenya 2010 Constitution Referendum; similar provisions exist, e.g., in Uganda, the Gambia, Tanzania, South Africa, Lagos state-Nigeria, Rwanda, and they are being considered in many other places.

1. Provide citizens with concrete and satisfying resolutions to their disputes or complaints;
2. Reduce court backlogs while simultaneously improving their ability to resolve disputes more efficiently and effectively;
3. Use the subject matter expertise and the professional skills of mediators, who do not require the extensive training of a lawyer or judge;
4. Increase confidence in ADR mechanisms among lawyers and traditional authorities or chiefs;
5. Create a mutually supportive, collaborative relationship between the formal legal system and out-of-court, non-formal dispute resolution processes;
6. Increase access to justice and promote national economic development efforts.

The jury is still out on the overall impact of ADR in Africa's declining conflict[7] and the ample increase in democratic states[8] since the beginning of the 21st century. However, the success of any ADR system should be measured or evaluated by key qualitative and quantitative data and adjusted accordingly, to capture both macro- and micro-level conflict phenomena. Measurement indicators include the number of ADR uses and the percentage of cases filed and processed via ADR versus court litigation, the average time spent on a case, the number of successful ADR settlements with agreements reached, the number of active/qualified ADR practitioners and trainers, the number of ADR institutions and services in the country, community acceptance, the level of service satisfaction by disputants and practitioners, the results of any ADR legislation or court rules, and the number of ADR publications and the amount of research conducted. The ultimate test of ADR systems will depend on the functionality of each affected country's peace index or conflict mitigation capability, and its positive impact on social development. Any effective ADR system must have a flexible design structure that is rooted in satisfying the interests of the parties in dispute, and in the professional administering of justice in a dynamic yet culturally sensitive manner.

For sustainability and effective internal capacity building of ADR in Africa, the following key policy steps are critical:

---

[7] See further Conflict Trends in Africa, 1946-2004(DFID, 2006).
[8] See also ECA 2005 African Governance Report, part 1.

1. Enact proper legislation to facilitate ADR institutionalization. While most African court rules or policies permit the judge to encourage parties to settle out of court in most cases, enacting legislation will elevate the status of ADR before a skeptical disputant, will build public confidence, and will further increase ADR utilization and promote ethical practice. Legislation will also provide a framework for reference, review and reform, as well as institutionalizing much needed education and professional training.

2. National and local governments and their international partners should invest in capacity building, through training and infrastructural support for the development of ADR networks of providers and advocates, who can continually advance the best practice. In addition to legal professionals, internal capacity building efforts should include the training of local and religious leaders, traditional authorities and chiefs, election officials, police and security personnel, human rights organizations, public complaints bureaus or the office of the ombudsman, and women and youth leaders. Enhancing the ADR negotiation and facilitation skills of these target groups will add further value by increasing each country's conflict mitigation or prevention capacity, and reducing the number of cases that burden the court docket, thereby freeing up time and resources for the courts to focus on the more suitable cases. Particular emphasis should be given to supporting ADR networks in Africa's conflict-prone countries and communities, which can contribute to improved conflict mitigation and the compliance of conflicting parties. Given the high levels of community participation and legitimacy achieved in ADR pilot programs, it is clear that ADR can also play a vital healing and trust-building role in post-conflict transitional justice contexts.

3. Create appropriate incentives for lawyers and judges for ADR development and use. For lawyers, a strategic use or inclusion of ADR provides additional tools for effective case resolution; this leads to efficiency of practice, increase in revenue, and greater satisfaction for both the lawyer and the client/disputant. A judge's performance report should include the number of cases referred or resolved via ADR and the time taken from case filing to mediation. Appropriate awards or other forms of

recognition by the legal profession, including Senior Advocate reviews and national merit honors, will also elevate the support and use of ADR among members of the bar and bench.

4. Create critical synergy between formal/state ADR institutions and the informal/indigenous community sector and networks, to scale up access to justice and to create a sustainable system of peaceful, nonviolent conflict resolution and mitigation. Change will reach many sectors of society, as well as transforming the nature of disputing, albeit at varying speeds. By enhancing and expanding the use of ADR in all modalities of disputes, whether between individuals or groups, people will gain a sense that justice can be achieved and that the need for self-determination or *interest* can be satisfied. A great advantage of ADR is that it adapts to the people and the dispute at hand, and is equally effective in formal legal systems, traditional disputing mechanisms and broad-based multiparty conflicts.

Perhaps the main lesson and achievement of ADR—as well as related conflict resolution initiatives in Africa, with significant increases in the Global Peace Index rankings of many Sub-Saharan African countries (see GPI 2012)—is to have created an enabling environment and framework for a more robust visioning of the desired ultimate goal of a "culture of peace" through "peace education" or peace studies. Arguably, ADR or conflict resolution is a transactional process, altering the human or group behavior of conflicting or disputing parties, whether in the long- or short-term. Peace education or peace studies, however, aims to achieve both attitudinal transformation and structural paradigm shift; it is anchored in the values of positive peace (though not necessarily in the absence of violence or war) and social justice for sustainable human security, promotion of social development, and stability of nation-states, institutions, communities, groups and families. Like ADR, peace studies view war or violence as a fundamental human creation that is solvable, and hence requires preventative and proactive—and overall pro-peace—thinking and action, including development, planning, and implementation of laws and social policies. Achieving the goal of a culture of peace in Africa requires the synergy and complimenting of theoretical research in peace education and the practical skill facilities of alternative dispute; both fields of knowledge and activism are indispensable.

Since the early 2000s, Peace and Conflict Studies programs have been developed in many universities in Africa, with the primary mission of peace education[9] or the cultivation of conflict resolution knowledge and skills. A recent internet search (2013) revealed over 70 peace or conflict studies programs in African universities, with five in Nigeria alone. Although the names of the programs may vary slightly (e.g., Peace and Conflict Resolution, International Peace and Conflict Resolution, Peace and Conflict Management, Human Rights and Peace, Peace and Strategic Studies, Alternative Dispute Resolution, etc.), these programs are clearly devoted to peace education via teaching, training, research, the development of curricula and materials, and direct or intervention services, both in theory and/or practice and across disciplines. Courses range from such common topics as dispute and conflict resolution, peace and conflict studies, mediation, negotiation, arbitration, religion and conflict resolution, human rights and global justice, peace and development and peace and nonviolence, to more esoteric topics such as peace and development, alternative dispute resolution, research methods in peace and conflict studies, scientific analysis of peace and conflict, war, peace and nonviolence and public sector dispute resolution. They are offered at various levels of undergraduate and graduate studies, with a combination of in-class lectures, simulations, practicum/internship experiences, and service-learning modules. Although most of the programs are multidisciplinary, they are housed in colleges or faculties of law, social sciences (political science, justice studies, criminology and social work), arts and humanities (religion, communication and media, ethnic studies) and business. The creation of the University for Peace (UPEACE) in 1980, with headquarters in Costa Rica and locations in various parts of Africa via UPEACE-Africa) is a clear consequence of the recognition of the critical role of the university in peace education.

Through its work and partners in Nigeria, the UPEACE (Africa) program was instrumental in the establishment of the landmark policy of the Nigeria Federal Ministry of Education, which mandated the creation and integration of peace and conflict studies courses or units into the Nigerian university undergraduate curriculum, [10] and required the same for select subjects in secondary schools. Of course, the schools and universities are faced with conflicts, as in wider society, in particular in terms of ethnic and gender value differences, stereotypes, and practices such as vandalism, student unrest/riots, exam malpractice, stealing, cultism, illegal drug use, rape, beating up of teachers and fellow students, school drop-outs, and other forms of lack of discipline.

---

[9] While ADR emphasizes resolution of conflicts, peace education aims for behavioral and attitudinal changes.

[10] www.Un.org/pubs/chronicle/2007/issue1/0107p40.htm.

From sample CAPCR fieldwork survey experiences in East/West Africa, student enrollments (at undergraduate/graduate levels) in peace studies surpass available space; the students come from various backgrounds and interests, across fields such as criminal justice, security, diplomacy, law, business, government, human rights, etc. Most are run as graduate programs. Upon graduation, some go into a teaching/research related field and a few go into practice, while many go into other fields where their skill and knowledge may be used, albeit in a limited way. Peace clubs in the schools, e.g., in Nigeria, serve as the main focus of promoting peace education through peer mediation, dialogues, and community service. Notwithstanding post graduate employment beyond school, peace education or conflict studies knowledge is applicable at all levels of social interaction and decision making, whether in the private/home or public arena. Peace education will add value to the curriculum of the emerging leadership development initiatives in and on Africa, particularly for the youth (as Africa's future leaders), under the promise of peace architecture. As in ADR, peace education prioritizes nonviolence, particularly mediation, as the most effective and desirable response to conflict.

In sum, much has been achieved and learned since the nascent development of peace education in Africa; challenges remain, especially in the development of indicators of success, both short- mid- and long-term,[11] and in the capacity of teachers to develop and deliver effective and flexible/dynamic curricula, [12] plus an outcome or field assessment of African peace and conflict studies graduates. Such data will provide useful guidance on program planning, curriculum development and continuous visioning. For peace education to succeed, it must be integrated within national educational systems, with a focus on the capacity-building of teachers and appropriate curriculum development for the purposes of both teaching and practical student involvement. Peace education programs need to reflect the peculiar circumstances and conditions of each country, and need to be adapted to enhance both cognitive learning and social/life skills, as well as reinforced and harmonized throughout various school or university subjects. Merely gaining knowledge of peace, without the

---

[11] Ernest Uwazie, "Developing Criteria for Assessment and Evaluation of Peace & Conflict Resolution Projects", Presentation at the Annual Africa Conference, California State University, Sacramento, Center for African Peace and Conflict Resolution, Spring, 2007.

[12] Lilian-Rita Audile (2006), "Assessing Peace education component of the Universal Basic Education in Nigeria through social studies curriculum." Paper presented at the 12th World Conference in Education of the World Council for Curriculum and Instruction, Manila, Philippines, August.

conforming practice or the appropriate forms of supportive behavior and attitude, is incomplete. Peace education is central to achieving the overall education mission in Africa of positive social change and positive development. Sustained efforts must be made to respond to or overcome challenges, both internal and external.

The following courses are recommended (though the list is not exhaustive) for universities offering peace and conflict studies:

- *Introduction to* Conflict Resolution (Covers the basic theories, the sources, causes and costs of conflict, options for response, communication, socio-cultural considerations/issues, peace and justice)
- *Negotiation*
- *Mediation and Conciliation*
- *Arbitration*
- *Peace building and Peacekeeping*
- *Dialogues and Reconciliation*
- *War and peace*
- *Environmental justice and peace*
- *Ethnic and Religious relations*
- *Negotiating Energy and natural resources*
- *Managing land conflicts*
- *Managing cultural conflicts: race, ethnicity, gender, class, and age*
- *Hostage negotiation*
- *Managing workplace conflicts: safety, labor/management, employee relations*
- *Managing natural disasters/Crisis*
- *The media in peace and conflict resolution*
- *Violence and Terrorism*
- *Restorative justice*
- *Ethics and Conflict Resolution*
- *Research Methods in conflict resolution*
- *International negotiation, Mediation and Arbitration*
- *Negotiating/Mediating boundary disputes*
- *Partnering and conflict prevention; especially in construction projects.*

The centerpiece of the course pedagogy should be a classroom simulation that educates students in the theoretic analysis and practical knowledge of the nature, management and resolution of various types of conflicts, whether civil, commercial, or criminal, both domestic and international. At all levels of teaching, the curriculum must be based on core values of alternatives to violence, ethics of the profession of peace makers and teachers, continuous research into what works, proficiency of cultural diversity, education for global citizenship, and community service (or *Ubuntu*), as well as respect for human rights, sensitivity to the environment, and the ultimate mission of achieving social justice.

Conclusion

Conflicts in Africa have much in common, and striking parallels can be drawn between them at all levels. Dynamics affecting the most complex war time conflicts, civil unrest and other macro disputes are in play, even in the smallest community conflicts. The converse is also true: lessons learned through community mediation, for example in South Africa, are applicable to the most complex and largest conflicts to be found on the continent.

Just as conflict dynamics are comparable between African conflicts, whether large or small, local or international, so are mediation processes. Effective approaches to resolving large-scale conflicts and civil wars are effective at the community level, and ineffectual techniques at the community level are just as likely to be counter-productive in mediating international disputes. While there may be some differences in mediating macro- and micro-conflicts (such as the time required, the need for negotiation teams, and the complexities of agenda development or pre-negotiations), as far as the mediation process is concerned, the differences are more like variations on a theme than real substantive dissimilarities.

As African conflict dynamics and mediation processes can be seen as analogous, on levels ranging from the community to the international arena, so too are many of the issues and interests affecting countries, political parties, ethnic groups, interest groups, and communities and civil societies. Often these interests are very basic: survival and safety. At other times, they occur on a higher level of interest, such as self-determination and/or securing human rights, but they are of equal importance at all levels.

A major premise of ADR or peace education is that lessons learned from conflict resolution in larger regional or national conflicts are applicable to community mediation, and vice-versa. Approaches that were successful in the Democratic Republic of the Congo may hold keys to resolving the Niger Delta conflict. As civil wars (or any war) affect large cross sections of countries and communities, so do environmental crises.

As all people have fears, hopes, aspirations and similar basic interests, it should be no surprise that the dynamics of meditative conflict resolution also have a level of universal applicability.

The experience of successfully introducing "formal" mediation into traditional disputing has important implications. It is quite possible that in those cultures and locales where traditions have to be reinstated or rebuilt, introducing mediation—and particularly mediation forms practiced in community settings—could be beneficial. Trainers from such cultures as Ghana or South Africa, where people have experience with the various incarnations of meditative approaches, could be utilized within training programs. Once people begin using mediation in places where customary traditions have been lost, and when they experience its benefits, mediation can take root. Once it takes root, it may develop its own local variations or hybridizations, and once again the African Solution will be in play.

Customary dispute resolution has a long and successful history in most parts of Africa, and retains its viability in many places to this day. "Modern" mediation modalities can add considerably to the effectiveness of traditional approaches, particularly at the community level. The converse is also true. Many traditional approaches are cultural variations of western mediation: ergo, there is a good fit.

In places where customary disputing has been undermined or eliminated, the challenge is great. While it is difficult to recreate a lost tradition, mediation can be combined with those traditions that remain—if they are respected. If not, mediation can be the basis for commencing conflict resolution processes that are responsive to the disputants and their needs. The culture will, over time, inevitably overlay its own sensibilities, and an indigenous local variation of dispute resolution will emerge. Peace in Africa is sustainable with strong investment and commitment in peace education and ADR!

Summary of Subsequent Chapters

In his essay on "Electoral Disputes in Africa...," Chapter Two, Karim regrets that electoral processes in most African countries are often accompanied by conflicts and violence. He substantiates this by making reference to some of the electoral crises experienced in Cote D'Ivoire and Nigeria. A major cause, amongst others, of these conflicts is the fact that aspirants to political office often have other concealed personal or group interests, which they intend to actualize through the seizure or usurpation of political power. To this effect, acceptance of defeat becomes almost impossible, or at least problematic. In handling some of these crises, the traditional court systems have left much to be desired. For this reason, Karim proposes ADR methods as a way forward.

In Chapter Three on "Alternative Dispute Resolution (ADR) in Nigeria: A study of the Lagos Multi-Door Courthouse (IMDC)," Ani examines the functioning and achievements of the landmark LMDC, perhaps the first Court ADR in Africa. She assesses the outcomes of the mediation and arbitration caseload of the LMDC, and makes some recommendations for more utilization of LMDC services and for developing greater support for the organization

In Chapter Four on "The interplay of Cross-culturalism in designing a mediation model for the Niger Delta conflict in Nigeria," Ogaji recognizes the Niger Delta as a major hub of business activities, in which both local and international investors with varying cultural backgrounds are expected to interact and work together in the mutual interest. To effectively address the conflicts that often arise in the collective—and often competitive—pursuit of these goals, she proposes a mediation model which would be a hybrid of the Western and African indigenous conciliation processes. The hybrid in question has to be constructed taking by taking into consideration the cultural mindset, background and world views of the parties involved.

In Chapter Five, on "Online Dispute Resolution as a form of Alternative Dispute Resolution in Africa...," Ononogbu argues that every creative judge always seeks to utilize every good means at her/his disposal in order to achieve the best results. While appreciating the efficacy of ADR in resolving disputes, she proposes that serious consideration and wider utilization of Online Dispute Resolution Methods (ODR), through the use of certain applicable modern technological tools and facilities available through the internet. She acknowledges the challenges facing the use of ODR in Africa, but argues for government support, through feasible means (including legislation) of developing the use of ODR.

In Chapter Six, "A Reassessment of the Impact of African women in Conflict Resolution," Njoku states that wars of ethno-religious and political origin are among the major challenges facing most African nations, with the most devastating impact being upon women and children Accordingly, she suggests the need for the increased participation of women in peacebuilding. Capitalizing on the success stories of the Burundian and Nigerian women in resolving conflicts within their various traditional communities, she argues for the necessity of the strategic use of "woman power" or the revered cultural status of women in the peacebuilding processes.

In Chapter Seven, "Civil Society and Conflict Resolution in the Niger Delta of Nigeria," Dibie examines the nature and causes of conflict in the Niger Delta of Nigeria, and the role of civil society groups therein. He argues that the resolution of the Niger Delta conflict rests on the extent to which conflicting interests can be mediated, perhaps through ADR methods and related peacebuilding initiatives.

In Chapter Eight, "Institutionalizing Dispute Resolution Training and Practice...," Musah-Khaleepha discusses the relevance of ADR methods. Furthermore, he proposes the establishment of ADR professional bodies that would oversee the training, accreditation and the quality of services rendered by dispute resolution experts for each country. He provides some guidelines for the institutionalization of ADR, especially in Ghana.

In Chapter Nine, Uwazie and Yamshon analyze the salient features of two landmark "ADR legislations in Ghana and Uganda," revealing their key common elements, and examining their implications for the fundamentals of ADR conceptualization and practice. Overall, the Ghana and Uganda ADR legislations provide key insights for the recognition of the traditional indigenous justice institutions, and their dynamic relationship with the more formal justice system. The Ghana and Uganda experiences will serve as useful lessons for similar efforts in other parts of Africa, especially as the need (or the push) from both internal and external influences for uniformity and formalism gain steam and irresistibility in the atmospherics of peace and development in Africa, through meaningful legal sector reform.

In Chapter Ten, "Toward Sustainable Peace," Albert examines the Ghana National Peace Council (Act 818) and its implications, both in terms of sustainable peace in Ghana and as a model for internal conflict resolution mechanism in the West Africa sub-region. Although Ghana is a relatively peaceful country, ranking 50th of 158 nations in the GPI (2012) Act 818, there has been a conscious effort to consolidate the peace process and to promote a dynamic structure for conflict resolution in this country.

The final chapter, Chapter Eleven, on "Restorative Justice...," explores the use of ADR principles of interest satisfaction and the process of reconciliation in societal responses to crime and punishment, particularly in Nigeria. Obiora discusses the key elements and types of restorative justice, and their prospects for achieving crime prevention while serving the needs of the victim, the community and the offender. She suggests that restorative justice needs to be incorporated into prison reform efforts in Nigeria.

CHAPTER TWO

ELECTORAL DISPUTES IN AFRICA: CAUSAL ANALYSIS AND PROPOSAL FOR ADR MECHANISM FOR RESOLUTION

A.A. KARIM

Introduction

Elections are a very vital component of democracy in any country that wishes to be considered as part of the comity of democratic states in the world today. Indeed, elections have been part of the very process of democracy since time immemorial (Karim and Albert, 2010). In ancient African societies, the elective principle operated in similar fashion, wherein particular responsibilities devolved to particular individuals and groups of individuals in society, in relation to given tasks and for a given duration of time.

The fact that electoral disputes have come to be infused into political processes in Africa cannot be over-emphasized. According to one Amnesty International Report (2008), the violent struggle for power, even in states which do not descend into armed conflict, still remains a worrisome component of political life in Africa. The violence that accompanied elections in Nigeria in 2003 and 2007, Lesotho in 1998 and 2007, Kenya in 2007 and Zimbabwe in 2008, lend credence to this observation (Japhet, 2009). More recently, in Cote D'Ivoire in 2010 and Nigeria in 2011, according to the disclosure of the Inspector General of Police, in Bauchi and Niger States alone there were 520 deaths (and 157 churches, 46 mosques, 1435 houses, 78 cars and 219 motorcycles were burnt, and about 21,500 people were internally displaced) during the three-day mayhem that greeted the announcement of President Goodluck Jonathan as the winner of the 2011 presidential election (Babalola, 2011).

In essence, elections have become periods during which both the stability and security of African states hang in the balance. They are events that lay bare the political fragility of the majority of African states, even those that have long been considered stable and touted as bastions of peace. This is a clear negation of what elections stand for. An election is the process by means of which a democratic polity is able to effect peaceful change of the personnel and/or the direction of political leadership. The character of a modern democracy often shows itself in the kind of electoral system that is operant in the given society (Franck, 1992).

In many African countries, elections are struggles over access to the resources controlled by the state, and these resources are often society's greatest prize. Given these high stakes, politicians resort to a variety of means, whether fair or foul, to attain public power and office. Election related disputes are an intrinsic part of the electoral process, and the credibility of that process is determined to a large degree by the capacity of the State to effectively resolve these disputes (Electoral Dispute Resolution Discussion Paper, 2009). Against this background, this paper offers a causal analysis of electoral disputes in Africa, and proposes the use of Alternative Dispute Resolution in the peaceful resolution of electoral disputes before they degenerate into violence.

Conceptual Clarifications

A. Election

One of the most significant features of democracy is the provision that citizens should decide for themselves who will govern them and represent their interests. Though the processes of selecting representatives and those who will govern have varied across times and societies, modern states have come to focus on elections as one of the most critical elements in the selection of leaders. Beyond this, elections are also considered to be a significant feature of democracies, for without them, competition for power would be much more chaotic. Furthermore, one of the most significant functions of elections is to legitimize a political system, in order to ensure the accountability of leaders and to reinforce people's participation in the political process. Elections are generally conceived as a means of implementing peaceful change of leadership in societies. In democratic societies, elections empower ordinary citizens to choose among contestants for political offices, and promote or encourage participation in governance (Balogun, 2003). Competitive elections are both an integral feature of democracy and a way of dealing with issues of governance (Höglund, 2006). Ideally, they allow for the peaceful transfer of power, and make it possible to demand accountability from those who govern. Elections facilitate communication between politicians and citizens, and also serve symbolic purposes by giving voice to the public. In fact, the right to elections has been enshrined in international law (Franck, 1992).

B. Electoral Dispute

Electoral dispute is an amalgam of election and dispute. Hornby (2000) defines *dispute* as an argument or a disagreement between two people, groups or countries. An *election dispute* is the climax of the election process, and refers to arguments or disagreement between political parties over the conduct and outcome of elections. At times, these can lead to violence; thus, *electoral* violence emerges out of *disputes* over the election. Electoral violence is violence perpetrated in the course of political activities before, during, and after election periods. It includes the following acts: thuggery, the use of force to disrupt opponents' political meetings or voting at polling stations, the use of dangerous weapons to intimidate voters and other electoral processes, or the causing of bodily harm or injury to any person connected with electoral processes. Some writers have associated electoral violence with the process of democratic transition (Afolabi, 2003).

C. Alternative Dispute Resolution (ADR)

Alternative Dispute Resolution (ADR) is a collection of processes used for the purpose of resolving conflict or disputes informally and confidentially. The rising popularity of ADR can be explained by the increasing caseload of traditional courts, the perception that ADR imposes fewer costs than litigation, a preference for confidentiality, and the desire of some parties to have greater control over the selection of the individual or individuals who will adjudicate in their dispute (Totaro, 2010). ADR provides alternatives to traditional processes such as grievances and complaints; however, it does not displace those traditional processes. ADR is generally classified into at least four types: *negotiation*, *mediation*, *collaboration*, and *arbitration*. Sometimes a fifth type, *conciliation*, is also included, but for present purposes this can be regarded as a form of mediation.

Electoral Dispute: A Causal Analysis

While frequent dispute in Africa does not generally occur spontaneously and is not an intractable problem, electoral dispute does not follow normal historic ethno-religious or sectional dividing lines. In most African countries, especially in Nigeria, an electoral dispute can be both intra- and inter-party and can cut across religion and sections, though it might transform into ethno-religion conflict without initially aiming to do so. There are many reasons behind electoral disputes in Africa. The following are just a few:

Illiteracy and Ignorance: The lack of adequate knowledge or information on politics, particularly electoral processes, coupled with low levels of education and high levels of deprivation and impoverishment among youths, force many to take the readily available "job opportunity-implementers" of electoral violence. These conditions easily play gullible youths into the hands of unscrupulous politicians, who manipulate these youths by dangling irresistible bait for them to undertake electoral violence, despite the attendant aftermath of violence. The aftermath could be the denial of education and other capacity development training for the youths, a vicious circle that leads to further rounds of electoral violence.

Proliferation of Political Parties: The proliferation of political parties has been a contributory factor in electoral disputes in African countries, especially in Nigeria. The number of political parties has increased sharply since the 1999 elections in Nigeria. From the 3 political parties who stood in 1999, the number of parties had increased to 63 in 2010 (Karim and Albert, 2010).

Sit-tight Syndrome: Having enjoyed the plums and paraphernalia of office, as well as the immunity attached to their positions, incumbents use the state resources and machinery at their disposal to maintain power. Everybody is seen as a resource or as an enemy. All the Election Management Bodies (EMBs) are influenced and maneuvered to rig elections in favour of the government of the day. Security operatives, the most effective instrument of coercion in accomplishing this selfish ambition, are brazenly implored or bribed. They are deployed to harass, intimidate, arrest and physically terrorize opponents. For this—and other reasons—the opposition does take this lying down. Thus, clashes and electoral violence are the result.

EMBs are electoral umpires. In the case of Nigeria, the Independent National Electoral Commission (INEC), States' Independent Electoral bodies, the security forces, the political parties, the media, civil society organizations, and judicial officials are all EMBs. The EMBs are responsible for providing election security. Election security is the process of protecting electoral stakeholders such as voters, candidates, poll workers, the media and observers, electoral information such as vote results, registration data and campaign material, electoral facilities such as polling stations and counting centres, and electoral events such as campaign rallies against death, damage or disruption. In all respects—the rule of law, respect for human rights, democracy, good governance, morality—the EMBs should discharge their duties and responsibilities honestly, transparently, fairly, and impartially with respect to all electoral stakeholders, without fear or favour. Unfortunately, this is not always the case, and almost all the EMBs are found wanting in the discharge of their constitutional and civic responsibilities. Their brazen approach to electoral matters is a significant cause of electoral violence (Usman2009).

The Media: The role of the media goes a long way towards either preventing or triggering electoral violence. So, media sources can become a source of conflict generation if they succumb to the influence of selfish politicians, who may want to use media outlets as propaganda launch pads. The media is a causative instrument for electoral violence if it indulges in campaign of calumny, mudslinging, defamation or slanderous attack on political actors. This is a sure cause of electoral violence. According to Isola (2010), the mass media, as an important institution in the democratic process, has contributed significantly to both the successes and the pitfalls witnessed in the various elections in Nigeria.

Religious and Ethnic Sentiment: Religion and ethnicity are two very sensitive issues, which unpatriotic elements can make effective use for their selfish purposes. Either one or both religious or ethnic cards are used, depending upon which is more favourable to the instigator. Sometimes places of worships are turned into campaign grounds for candidates. The support of religious and community leaders is sought, and once this is achieved, their followers fall into place like a pack of cards. These practices pose a great threat to the very fabric of a country's national unity and integration, and to qualities such as competency, honesty, integrity, trust and credibility.

Rigging: Rigging is generally a causative factor in electoral dispute. Election rigging is the criminal act of subverting an entire electoral process through organized fraud, usually with the active participation and support of officials of the electoral body, sometimes including state security officers. Rigging is usually perpetrated for the purposes of gratification, and can take the form of stuffing the ballot box with fake ballot papers before the day of the election; it can also take place on the day of the election itself, through the falsification of results and the forgery of figures at polling units and collation centres, voting by unregistered and under-aged persons, and the publication of false statements concerning the withdrawal of an opposition candidate (Karim, 2010).

Role of the Elites: The political manipulation of the electorate by political elites has also generated violent competition at elections. Political elites in Nigeria for instance have sponsored and promoted electoral violence. Essentially, these elites represent capitalists who depend on the state machinery for their survival (Joseph, 1999). According to Nweke (2005), the political elites have always convinced the youth that violent struggle at elections will ensure the victory of their tribesman, religious man or party man, and that this is a struggle in their favour and against marginalization or other forms of socio-economic discrimination. Thus, the political elites use ethnic and religious sentiment to achieve their political goals.

Theoretical Underpinning

A theory is an attempt to explain a phenomenon such as electoral dispute. In the social sciences, theories are propounded very tentatively, owing to the nature of the subjects that social scientists study—namely, human beings (Bechhofer, 1992). Peace scholars explain why events occur the way they do, and it is therefore imperative, in this section of the study, to state the theoretical orientations that will underpin the explanation of electoral dispute in Africa. To this end, the institutionalism-functionalism theory will be analyzed, in order to explain the reasons underlying electoral dispute.

If elections reflect the dynamics and functioning of a society, then it follows that stories of electoral dispute and fragility can only be understood within their societal contexts. Just as societies are varied in their dynamics and their modes of functioning, so there are varied factors and conditions that lead to electoral dispute in these societies.

The theory of institutional-functionalism explains the phenomenon of fragility or instability by focusing on the interface between institutionalization and political participation. According to Huntington, political disorder is more likely to occur in societies marked by high levels of political participation but with slow or weak processes of political institutionalization, such as in Nigeria. In essence, institutional-functionalism draws a direct correlation between fragile or weak states and the phenomenon of electoral dispute. Thus, electoral dispute is likely to erupt where the state fails to meet popular demands. The "high level of political participation" which Huntington (1968) refers to is not present in countries such as—among others—Nigeria, Kenya and Zimbabwe, and yet there remains a high incidence of electoral violence in these countries. The explanation in these cases would lie in the highly competitive way members of the political class contend for the perks of office. According to Nathan (2000), where underdevelopment is coupled with inequality, electoral dispute and violence may occur as expressions of anger, frustration and fear.

Institutional functionalism is intricately connected to structuralism, which gives pride of place to social stratification and the configuration of power relations among social forces—within and without the ambit of the state—in explaining fragility or instability. Thus, the structural explanation of electoral dispute suggests that society and politics are organized in a manner that generates conflict (Friedrich, 2001). Here, the causal factor of electoral dispute and violence is the structure of the political economy of the state. In other words, where the state is organized in such a way that significant elements of the population are excluded from meaningfully participating in and benefiting from economic and political life, then such segments are bound, at some point, to resort to violence to reverse the effects of this exclusion. In essence, such exclusion increases a state's level of fragility. Friedrich observes that:

> […] a common cause of election dispute is that the stakes of winning and losing valued political posts is in many situations, and especially in conditions of high scarcity and underdevelopment, incredibly high. When winning a state office is the key to livelihood not just for an individual, but for their entire clan, faction, or even ethnic group, then the electoral contest becomes a battle for survival in which all manner of forces and resources can be mobilized to ensure success. (Kirschk, 2000)

Essentially, when an election becomes a contest between the "included" and the "excluded," the stakes of winning such an election are raised, to a point where violence is the real outcome, in the event of disappointment for either group (Silntb, 2008). The stakes are raised even higher when it is assumed that the likelihood that resources will be channeled to a particular group is directly related to whether the politician who controls those resources is a member of the group in question. In such a situation, those in power will seek to retain control at all cost, including the use of foul means. Conversely, if those outside power have long been excluded from mainstream state political power, they will seek to attain it by all means, including violence. In essence, electoral violence may be ignited by a disputed election, but its root causes may lie in historical marginalization and exclusion. According to Sisk, when parties are quite certain of loss or exclusion in an electoral contest, especially when they expect to be "permanent minorities" (to lose not just once but again and again), the certainty of outcomes is also a strong causal driver of violence. When a very insecure party or faction expects to be systematically excluded from political power, that party or faction may well turn to violence, to either prevent their exclusion or to prevent the election process itself (SiIntb, 2008).

With so many fragile states in Africa, it is easy to understand why electoral processes have often been tainted with violence, given what has been said above. In the majority of these countries, the development of political institutions lags behind social and economic change. As such, these countries have often failed to respond to popular demands: in consequence, the legitimacy of the state and the moral claim of the state to rule over the citizenry are diminished. In addition, political power in a majority of these countries is personalized rather than embedded within political institutions (Van de Walle, 2003). As a result, the political playing field is skewed in favour of those in power who, in their resolve to cling to power, use this opportunity to manipulate elections in order to win them at any cost. Moreover, the political manipulation of ethnicity in African countries has come to mean that politics in the continent is understood as revolving around the transfer of state resources by politicians in return for securing voters' political allegiance. All these factors (election manipulation, unsettled grievances, weak political institutions and political ethnicity) come together to render almost inevitable the recourse to violence as a means of expressing grievances and reconciling social differences.

Overview of Electoral Disputes in Africa

There is clear evidence that electoral violence is a global problem, because it cuts across all democratic societies. In the aftermath of electoral defeat, the emotional reaction could be waves of destruction, even if polling has been free and fair. In point of fact, such violence is enacted precisely because the vote has been free and fair! From a conflict management perspective, dispute has a negative impact in polarizing the electorate along conflict lines and, in extreme cases, leading to a chain reaction of violence covering the entire landscape of society, and involving persons who become partisan on one side or another, without understanding what is really at stake (Höglund, 2006).

The case of Uganda is instructive in this light. Various means were used to perpetrate electoral violence in Uganda on March 12, 2001, the presidential election day. These included torture, extrajudicial executions, arbitrary detention, abductions and kidnappings, arrest without warrant, beatings, personal humiliation by stripping to nakedness, killings, shootings, death threats, the threat of beatings (using phrases such as "you will see us," "we are bad," and "we shall burn you"), chasing away voters from polling stations on the pretext that they were non-Ugandans or underage, and malicious damage to property. In Kenya, political and electoral violence has manifested itself in various forms, including assassinations, attempted assassinations, confinement, battery, threats of violence, torture, arson, looting, rape, sexual harassment, hate speech, hijacking, character assassination and insult, political thuggery, destruction and damage to property, economic repression/sabotage, eviction/displacement, closure of party/campaign offices or premises, and the violent or physical disruption of public meetings and campaign rallies (Friedrich Ebert Stiftung and Centre for Conflict Research, 2001).

Over the years, this violence has varied both in terms of its manifestations and its intensity. The most recent Cote D'Ivoire election (2010)—including its re-run presidential election which the opposition leader Alhassan Quattara won, and the incumbent Lourent Bagbo declined to hand over power before being forced out by the UN-led forces in April 2011 and the winner was finally installed—is a case in point. These events came at great cost: the colossal loss of life, the creation of factions, damage to property and social infrastructure, and many internally displaced persons who were forced to seek refuge in neighbouring states. In the case of Nigeria, Omotosho (2008) noted that events in the fourth republic showed that the major ethnic groups and leading political parties were deeply enmeshed in an internal crisis with a high level of violence, which led to the assassination of some party leaders. Scores of such incidents were reported across the country. Between June and August 2006, three gubernatorial candidates were assassinated (Omotosho, 2007). The run-up to the April 2007 elections was violent, and campaigning in many areas was punctuated by political killings, bombings and armed clashes between supporters of rival political parties. The violence formed part of a broader pattern of violence and abuse that is inherent in Nigeria's still largely unaccountable political system (Ibrahim and Egwu, 2005).

Local and international observers in the 2007 elections were in agreement that fraud and violence had occurred in most parts of the country, and that these acts were perpetrated by supporters of the political parties involved. However, official election results were announced, and a majority of the incumbent state governors were re-elected. In some places, there was no pretense of even staging elections. For example, many polling stations closed almost as soon they opened, or they postponed voting until the following day, for instance in the Niger Delta. As a result, angry youths burnt down INEC offices in protest at the postponement of the elections. In other locations, armed thugs snatched ballot boxes or vandalized election materials. An election observer described vehicles full of PDP thugs screeching into polling stations and large numbers of youths jumping out and leaving the doors open, to show that the vehicles were full of guns and ammunition (Omotosho, 2008).

Proposal for ADR Mechanism for Resolution

At times, people attempt to resolve their disputes without going to court through various methods called Alternative Dispute Resolution (Maduewesi, 2001). One of the most widely used forms of ADR is *arbitration*. In arbitration, people submit their disputes to a third party (not a judge in a court) to make a decision. Arbitration has the advantage of being a simpler procedure and leading to a quicker resolution of disputes, than a lawsuit in court. On the other hand, many procedural protections that are present in court proceedings may not be present in arbitration or other forms of ADR. Another widely used form of ADR is *mediation*. In mediation, a third party works to help the parties agree to a settlement of their dispute. An arbitrator usually has the power to decide the matter; a mediator lacks this authority and acts to facilitate a compromise between the parties (Maduewesi, 2001). The outcome of mediation is that if an agreement is reached, the mediator will help to draft a resolution agreement that all parties will then sign. When signed by the parties, the agreement is binding. If the parties are unable to reach agreement, the issue may be referred to another dispute mechanism, such as the EEO or grievance process, since the statutory entitlement to use these traditional mechanisms is not affected by use of ADR processes (Office of the Director, Alternative Dispute Resolution and Conflict Prevention, 2002).

It is no longer news that violent struggle for political power, the rising spate of electoral disputes and the daunting challenges posed to the administration of justice remain central components of the political development of African countries. In Nigeria for instance, since the attainment of political independence in 1960, elections and electioneering campaigns have often been characterised by thuggery, violence, fraud, corruption, and other forms of malpractice. The statutory framework and judicial approach by the courts and tribunals to this malaise have often left many people disappointed.

It is in the light of the above that ADR is seen as a veritable mechanism for the peaceful resolution of electoral dispute in Africa. Corroborating this fact, the Chairman of the Independent National Electoral Commission (INEC), Professor Attahiru Jega, recently proposed ADR to politicians, as a means of reducing pre-election cases and court orders served on the commission (Punch, 2011). The idea, according to the INEC chairman, would be to institute a culture of resolution of political and election disputes through ADR methods. He decried the number of court cases instituted by politicians against INEC, adding that the ADR was a direction which stakeholders should be tapping into. According to Professor Jega:

> This will enable every stakeholder in the political and electoral process to see it as an obligation to commit to a new attitude to losing, a new attitude to violence and a new attitude to electoral integrity. (Punch, 2011)

> Our courts have been overburdened and sometimes overwhelmed by the magnitude of cases placed before them for adjudication. Even the decisions of the courts are not respected. It has become a common practice for litigants to exploit the multiplicity and the hierarchy of court to either delay or frustrate the course of justice. The issuance of court orders could also affect timelines for crucial electoral activities. While this constitutes a major but different challenge for the judiciary and INEC, the consequence of unresolved disputes and conflicts affect all spheres of our national life (This day, 2011).

Similarly, the former Ghanaian President John Kufuor stressed the need for well-meaning Nigerians and Africans to embrace ADR, saying that it "offers flexibility to the regular court system; it's cost effective, time-saving and offers a multi-dimensional approach to remedy justice" (This day, 2011). He noted that building mechanisms for effective election dispute resolution is a necessary part of the process of ensuring that peaceful elections are held in Africa, and that the gains of democracy are consolidated.

In adopting ADR as a mechanism of electoral disputes in Africa, the following steps, adapted from Maduewesi (2001), could be implemented:

1. Introduction: The mediator sets the political parties at ease and explains the ground rules. The mediator's role is not to make a decision but to help the political parties reach a mutual agreement. The mediator explains that he or she will not take sides.

2. Telling the Story: Each political party says what happened, and the person bringing the complaint tells his or her side of the story first. No interruptions should be allowed. Then, the other political party explains their version of the facts.
3. Identifying Facts and Issues: The mediator attempts to identify agreed upon facts and issues. This is done by listening to each side, summarizing each party's view, and asking if these are the facts and issues as each party understands them.
4. Identifying Alternative Solutions: Everyone thinks of possible solutions to the problem. The mediator makes a list and asks each party to explain his/her feelings about each possible solution.
5. Revising and Discussing Solutions: Based on the expressed feelings of the parties, the mediator revises possible solutions and attempts to identify a solution that both parties can agree to.
6. Reaching Agreement: The mediator should help the parties reach an agreement that both can live with. The agreement should be written down. The parties should also discuss what would happen if either of them breaks the agreement.

It is important to note that ADR is particularly useful in internal democracy or during party primaries in arriving at a consensus candidate among the various aspirants. Using ADR in the post-primary elections may not be achieved, especially in Nigeria, where the electoral act hinders the application of ADR, with the establishment of tribunals to resolve electoral disputes. Besides, there is still low-level awareness concerning the practice of ADR in most African countries, coupled with low numbers of ADR practitioners and organizations.

Conclusion

We have discussed the role of ADR as an alternative means of electoral dispute resolution. Electoral violence and disputes arising from elections have often been seen as a major threat to democracy in African countries, including Nigeria. A cursory inquiry into electoral history reveals that violence has been the bane of democratic stability, with adverse effects on peace and stability in most African countries. ADR would complement court proceedings in settling election disputes, and would also provide another platform for enriching our knowledge, taking the discourse further, from dialogue towards action. On this note, it is recommended that serious efforts should be made—through organizing seminars and enlightenment programmes for stakeholders in Africa—to increase awareness of the import of ADR in resolving electoral disputes. In addition, more people should be trained in the art of ADR. It is also important that many ADR practitioners should be engaged in partisan politics, so as to influence the adoption of ADR in the resolution of electoral disputes.

References

Afolabi, A. A.., (2003) "Electoral Violence and the Democratisation Project: The Nigerian Experience", Olasupo, B. A. (ed.), *Electoral Violence in Nigeria: Issues and Perspectives*. Friedrich Ebert Stiftung. p. 79.

Amnesty International Report (2008), The State of the World's Human Rights.

Babalola, J., (2011) "520 died in Kaduna, Niger violence, says Ringim" *The Nation* .June, 2 p.1

Balogun, T. A. (2003) "Electoral Violence and National Security," A paper presented to the Security Agencies in Preparation for 2003 General Elections on Electoral Violence and National Security in Nigeria, held at National Conference Centre.Abuja.pp.1-11.

Bechhofer, F., (1992) "The Research Process," in Worsley, P (ed), *The New Sociology*, London: Penguin Books, pp. 78-115.

Electoral Dispute Resolution Discussion Paper (2009) Experts Meeting, Atlanta GA – February.

Franck, T. M., (1992) "The Emerging Right to Democratic Governance." *The American Journal of International Law*, Vol. 86, No.1, pp. 46-91.

Friedrich Ebert Stiftung (FES) and Centre for Conflict Research (CCR) (2001) "Political and Electoral Violence in East Africa." Working Papers on Conflict Management No.2.

Höglund, K., (2006) "Electoral Violence in War-Ravaged Societies: The Case of Sri Lanka." Paper prepared for the Workshop on Power-sharing and Democratic Governance in Divided Societies, Center for the Study of Civil War, PRIO August 21–22.

Hornby A. S., (2000) *Oxford Advanced Learner's Dictionary of Current English*. Oxford: Sally Wehmeier.

Huntington, S., (1968) Political Disorder in Changing Societies in Matlosa, K., (ed.) Managing Post-Election Conflict in Lesotho. Lesotho: *Global Insight*. p.47.

Ibrahim, L. and Egwu, S., (2007) "Nigeria Elections 2007: Defending the People's Mandate," *Global Rights*, Abuja.

Isola, O., (2010) *Mass Media and Election Violence-1965 and 1983 Experiences in Western Nigeria.* Ibadan: John Archers.

Japhet, B., (2009) "Electoral violence and fragility in Africa: drawing lessons from Kenya's experience in the 2007/2008 post election violence." Paper for presentation at the poster session of the conference on "Financial Markets, Adverse Shocks and Coping Strategies in Fragile Countries", Accra, Ghana, 21-23 May, 2009.

Joseph, R., (1991) *Democracy and Presidential Politics in Nigeria: The Rise and Fall of Second Republic.* Ibadan: Spectrum Books.p.74.

Karim, A. A., (2010) "Youth and Electoral Violence: Implications for Human Security in Nigeria" in Albert, I. O, Danjibo, N. L.

Isola, O.O. and Faleti, S. A. (eds.) *Democratic Elections and Nigeria's National Security,* Ibadan: Peace and Conflict Studies Programme Institute of African Studies, University of Ibadan.

Karim, A. A. and Albert, O., (2010) "Electoral Violence and Its Implications for National Security in Nigeria's Fourth Republic" in Albert, I. O, Danjibo, N. L. Isola, O.O., and Faleti, S. A. (eds.) *Democratic Elections and Nigeria's National Security.* Ibadan: Peace and Conflict Studies Programme Institute of African Studies, University of Ibadan.

Kirschke, L.., (2000) "Informal Repression, Zero-sum Politics and Late Third Wave Transitions," *The Journal of Modern African Studies,* Vol. 38, No. 3, pp. 383-405.

Maduewesi, E., (2001) Introduction to Legal Literacy in Nigeria (Understanding the Nigerian Legal System). System, 2001 and reprinted by permission of The State Bar of California, State of California, United States of America.

Nathan, L.., (2000) "The Four Horsemen of the Apocalypse: The Structural Causes of Crisis and Violence." *Peace and Change,* Vol. 188, No. 191, p. 17.

Nweke, N. N.., (2005) "State, Youth and Electoral Violence in Nigeria", in Onu, G. & Momoh, A. (eds.) *Elections and democratic consolidation in Nigeria.* Lagos: Educational Publishers and Printers, pp. 386-387.

Nwoke, C.N., (2010) "Electoral Violence, Democratic Misadventure, Governance Failure: The Deepening Crisis of Nigeria's Underdevelopment." Paper presented at Roundtable on "Democracy and the 2011 Elections in Nigeria," organized by the African Centre for Peace-Research, Empowerment and Documentation (ACPRED), Ilorin, 21–23 September.

Office of the Director Alternative Dispute Resolution and Conflict Prevention (2002), What is ADR? March 6 Atlanta.

www.cdc.gov/od/ADR/about.htm.

Omotosho, M., (2007) "Political Assassinations and the Prospects of Democracy in Nigeria," a Paper Presented at the 1st International Conference, Faculty of Administration, Obafemi Awolowo University, Ile-Ife, Nigeria, 5th-7th September.

—. (2008) "Electoral Violence and Conflict in Nigeria: The 2007 Elections and the Challenges of Democratisation." A paper presented at the 27th Annual Nigerian Political Science Association (NPSA) Conference at Benue State University, Makurdi, 16th-19th.

Punch (2011) Election petition: INEC proposes alternative dispute resolution. Thursday 31 March.

SiIntb, T., (2008) International Studies Association Annual Meeting, March 24-28, 2008, p. 9.

ThisDay (2011) "Kufuor, Others Proffer Solution to Nigeria's Electoral Disputes." November, 8.

Totaro, G., (2010), "Avoid court at all costs" *The Australian Financial Review* Nov. 14 April 19.

Usman, S. M., (2009) "Causes and Consequences of Youth Involvement in Electoral Violence," A Paper presented at a One-Day Workshop On "Youths Against Electoral Violence," Organised by Arewa Patriotic Vanguard In Collaboration with Independent National Electoral Commission (INEC) For Youths in the Northwest Zone Nigeria 12th November.

Van de Walle, N., (2003) "Presidentialism and Clientelism in Africa's emerging Party Systems," *Journal of Modern African Studies* p. 297.

CHAPTER THREE

ALTERNATIVE DISPUTE RESOLUTION (ADR) IN NIGERIA: A STUDY OF THE LAGOS MULTI-DOOR COURTHOUSE (LMDC)

COMFORT CHINYERE ANI

Introduction

The Lagos Multi-Door Courthouse (LMDC) was established in June 2002. The name "Multi-Door" is derived from the Multi-Door Courthouse concept, which envisions one courthouse with multiple dispute resolution doors or programs. Cases are referred for resolution through the appropriate door.[1] The traditional courthouse offers only one "door" to the public for resolving disputes—namely, the litigation process. The Multi-Door Courthouse concept arose out of the realization that litigation is not the best choice for resolving many disputes.[2] In addition to adjudication, parties should be offered a range of alternatives, such as Mediation, Arbitration, Case Evaluation, Med-Arb, Private Judging and Mini-Trials. Parties should also have access to assistance in "screening" their cases, or evaluating their cases to determine which dispute resolution process is the most appropriate. Cases are referred, through the appropriate door, for resolution.[3] The goals of a multi-door approach are to provide citizens

---

[1] See Superior Court of D-C.–Multi-Door Dispute Resolution Division, available at: www.dccourts.gov/../index.jsp. Last accessed on 19/6/2011

[2] Ani, C. C.., "An Appraisal of Alternative Dispute Resolution (ADR) Mechanisms", article awaiting publication in: *University of Benin Journal of Public Law*.

[3] Stuart K. K., & Savage C. A., "The Multi-Door Courthouse: How It's Working". Available at: http://74.6.238.254/search/srpcache?ei=UTF8&p=multi+door+courthouse+and+frank+sander&fr=yfp-t-892. Last accessed on 1/10/2010.

with easy access to justice, to reduce delay, and to provide links to related services, making more options available through which disputes can be resolved.[4]

Objectives, Significance and Methodology of the Study

The objective of this study is to highlight the activities of the LMDC and, in so doing, to assess its case settlement ability by analyzing the empirical evidence concerning its activities. The study is significant in that it provides an insight into the goings-on the LMDC insofar as they affect ADR, in terms of the information that may influence stakeholder preference for ADR processes at the Federal and State levels both in Nigeria and across Africa. Further, it provides the evidence necessary to develop appropriate policy reengineering for the entire justice delivery system, both in Nigeria and beyond.

For the purpose of this study, data was obtained from the LMDC regarding the ADR services it rendered. Given the peculiarity of the subject, and the need for simplicity and precision, a simple percentage was adopted in analyzing the data obtained from the LMDC, which comprises its ADR activities from January 2007-June 2010, and two settlement weeks held in 2009 and 2010.

What is Alternative Dispute Resolution (ADR)?

Alternative Dispute Resolution (ADR) is a term that refers to several different but philosophically linked methods of resolving disputes outside traditional judicial process in formal courts.[5] It has been defined as the methods and procedures used in the resolution of disputes: these are alternatives to taking legal action in court and its attendant complications, as a result of requiring strict compliance with the rules and procedures of legal practice.[6] According to Shedrack Best, ADR is about the search for and the application of "non-Conventional" peaceful methods of settling

---

[4] Available at: http://www.dccourts.gov/dccourts/superior/multi/index.jsp. Last accessed on 28/9/2010

[5] Ani, C. C.., "An Appraisal of Alternative Dispute Resolution (ADR) Mechanisms", *op. cit.* note 2

[6] Coker, S. A. & Adeleke M. O., *et al,* "An Appraisal of Alternative Dispute Resolution as an Antidote to Delay of Judicial Proceedings In Nigerian Courts", in Yusuf F.A. (Ed), *Issues in Justice Administration in Nigeria* (Lagos: VDG Intl. Ltd., 2008), p. 102.

disputes and resolving conflict situations, using the least expensive methods in ways that satisfy the parties involved, in ways that preserve relationships after a settlement might have been reached.[7]

These alternative methods help people to resolve legal problems before or without going to court. With the exception of Negotiation, which sometimes involves a third party, other ADR mechanisms typically involve an independent third person, called a "neutral", who tries to help to resolve or narrow down the areas of conflict. Other acronyms that have been proffered for ADR include: Additional Dispute Resolution, Appropriate Dispute Resolution, Assisted Dispute Resolution and Amicable Dispute Resolution.[8] The choice of available options or mechanisms may depend on the type and nature of the conflict (e.g., the degree of seriousness or complexity), the customs/laws that inform or require certain processes and outcomes, the relationship of the parties (long-term, etc.), prior experience, cost (time/money), available remedies, and the expectations of the grievant/complainant).[9]

ADR is seen as possessing some advantages over traditional litigation because it has the ability to do the following:

1. Strengthen judicial modernization efforts;
2. Reduce delay by unclogging courts;
3. Increase access to justice for the poorest disputants;
4. Reduce costs of justice for all users;
5. Preserve, improve or restore relationships among disputants;
6. Support economic development by reducing the transaction costs of disputes and by increasing the certainty of investments;

[7] Best, S. G.., "The Methods of Conflict Resolution and Transformation", in Best, S. G.., (Ed.) in *Introduction to Peace and Conflict Studies in West Africa*, (Ibadan: Spectrum Books Ltd. 2006), p. 96.

[8] Astor H., and Chinkin C.., *Dispute Resolution in Australia* (2nd ed, 2002), 77-78, cited in Lewis M., and McCrimmon L.., The Role of ADR Processes in the Criminal Justice System: A view from Australia. A paper presented at ALRAESA Conference 4-8 September, 2005, at the Imperial Resort Beach Hotel, Entebbe, Uganda. Available at: http://74.6.238.254/search/srpcache?ei=UTF8&p=ADR+in+the+criminal+justice+system&fr=yfp-t-. Last accessed on 5/10/2010.

[9] Uwazie, E. & Yamshon, D., *The Conflict Resolution Manual for the Training of Trainers (ToT) Program*, organized by ADR Centre Italy and the NCMG College, 2009, p. 15.

7. Increase the satisfaction of users.[10]

Rationale for ADR in Nigeria

It is an acknowledged fact of human existence that disputes are perennial, and disperse energy, time and finances, whereas amity is the foundation for progress and development. While conflicts cannot be completely eliminated in human relations, it is desirable not to allow conflicts to escalate, but rather to resolve them in an amicable manner. Nigeria[11] is a country where the adversary system of civil Justice has dominated the judicial landscape; it is practiced as received from its colonial masters, Britain.

This adversarial court based approach sometimes results in acrimony and frustration, due to inordinate delays arising from undue attention to procedure and combativeness and gamesmanship by lawyers, at the expense of parties and true justice.[12] The problems besetting the procurement of justice through adversarial adjudicatory process in Nigeria have been described as multifarious and multidimensional. They include: court congestion as a result of too many cases for trial in the courts, delays and denial of justice, insufficiency of judicial personnel, an archaic system of court adjudication, corruption,[13] and a lack of modern court management

[10] United Nations Office on Drugs and Crime, Training Manual on Alternative Dispute Resolution and Restorative Justice, October 2007, p. 20.

[11] Nigeria is the most populous country in Africa and, with a population of 140 million, people accounts for approximately one-sixth of Africa's people. See: http://www.nigeriamasterweb.com/Nigeria06CensusFigs.htmlhttp://www.nigeriamasterweb.com/Nigeria06CensusFigs.html.
Last accessed on 10/7/2011
See also Nigeria Strategic Conflict Assessment Methodology, Key Findings and Lessons Learnt in Social Development notes, no. 11, May, 2003, available at: http://siteresources.worldbank.org/INTCPR/214578111751313696/20480272/SDN83CPR11.pdf
Last accessed on 10/7/2011

[12] Excerpts from a speech delivered at the launching of the LMDC on Tuesday June 11, 2002, by the former Governor of Lagos State, Ashiwaju Bola Ahmed Tinubu, read on his behalf by Prof. Yemi Osinbajo, the former Attorney-General of Lagos State. Available at: http://allafrica.com/stories/200206180151.htm. Assessed on 15/6/2011

[13] See: Peters, D. "Alternatives to Litigation: The Multi-Door Court House Concept" in Yusuf, F. A. (Ed), *Op. cit.* note 6, p. 437.

techniques, etc.[14] Delays engender the frustration of litigants and the reluctance of investors to do business.[15] An example of the ugly face of delay in the Nigerian judicial system is the case of *Ariori v. Elemo*:[16] proceedings in this case commenced in October 1960 but took almost two decades to reach the Supreme Court of Nigeria.[17] Several other cases have followed the path of delay, and the courts have been quick to frown upon such delays.[18] The consequences of delaying a case unreasonably before judgment are far reaching. The judge may lose sight of the impressions of all the witnesses at the trial, which occasions miscarriages of justice and contravenes the fair hearing provisions of the Constitution,[19] thereby giving credence to the saying "justice delayed is justice denied."

Expectedly, like any other problem confronting man, efforts were made at reforming the justice system to make access to justice timely and cost efficient by overhauling the nation's procedural laws: these were obsolete, and constituted an impediment to the administration of Justice in the country. The reforms led to the enactment of the High Court of Lagos

---

[14] Some other factors identified as causes of the perpetual delays in civil justice delivery include: Lawyers capitalizing on scheduling too many cases for the same day, knowing that they will not go on, so they do not prepare; not using cogent parts of the rules of procedure available to narrow down the issues like admissions; settlement of issues and discovery, and some cumbersome rules of procedure that left room for delay, etc. See Owasanoye B. O., "Case Flow Management Procedure" A Paper presented at the Nigerian Institute of Advanced Legal Studies Advanced Course in Practice and Procedure, 15th June, 2009, p. 1.

[15] See the Daily Trust Newspaper, Wednesday April 6, 2005, p. 5 where former President Olusegun Obasanjo blamed court adjournments and delays in the judicial process for low foreign investment in the country. See also, Ani, C. C. "Towards Eradicating the Problem of Delay in Criminal Justice Administration in Nigeria," in Yusuf F. A. (Ed.) *Issues in Justice Administration in Nigeria, op. cit. note 3*, pp. 136- 153.

[16] (1983) 1 SCNLR 1. The case was filed at the High Court of Lagos in 1960 and part heard in 1964. It stared *de novo* before another judge in 1972. Evidence was concluded in 1974. Judgment was delivered in 1975. Appeal got to the Supreme Court and it was decided that the case be sent back for retrial.

[17] See also, *Obioso v. Okoye* (1989) 5 NWLR (P.119) 80, which suffered 33 adjournments.

[18] *Awobiyi v. Igbalaiye* (1965) 1 ALL NCR 163; *Kakarah v. Imonikhe* (19740 4 SC 157; *Obioso v. Okoye, ibid.*

[19] Section 36 of the 1999 Constitution (Cap. C23 LFN 2004) deals with the right to a fair hearing.

State Civil Procedure Law, 2004, with its accompanying rules.[20] The rules introduced new, radical and far reaching innovations, and expunged many orders and rules, deemed to be out of keeping with the spirit of speedy administration of Justice in the State.[21] One of the innovations in these new rules is that Judges now assume the role of Managerial Judges and encourage alternative means of dispute resolution. Another innovation in the administration of justice is the establishment of the Lagos Multi-Door Courthouse (LMDC) and Citizen's Mediation Centres.

Although there is a renewed interest in ADR, it is to be stressed that ADR is not an entirely new phenomenon in Nigeria. This explains why ADR is also considered to be an acronym for African Dispute Resolution. This buttresses the fact that traditional African societies settled disputes and differences through Conciliation and Mediation, with the major aim of reconciling the parties in a manner that engendered a good and friendly relationship, post-settlement, achieved through compromise and reparation for the wrong committed.[22]

In the pre-colonial era, Nigerians had a culture of compromise and peaceful resolution of their disputes, and regarded the involvement of the king's, Emir's, Oba's, Obi's or Eze's Court as a last resort.[23] What we have in contemporary ADR is simply a repackaging of the Nigerian traditional system of dispute resolution. Our indigenous judicial system, as noted by Hon. Justice Ademola, was characterized by simple and informal procedures, where compensation rather than judgment was the end result

---

[20] Many Nigerian states are modernizing and updating their civil procedure rules. Several states have modeled their revisions after those of Lagos and Abuja, who led the momentum in this area. See: http://www.fias.net/advisory-services /regulatory-simplification/subnational-doing-business/doing-business-in-nigeria-2010.cfm. Last accessed on 11/7/2011

[21] Mohammed, S., "The High Court of The Federal Capital Territory, Abuja, Civil Procedure Rules, 2004: Can the New Rules Lead to Just, Efficient and Speedy Dispensation of Justice?" available at: www.gamji.com/article4000/NEWS4652.htm. Last assessed on 19/6/2011

[22] Sokefun J. A.., "Dynamics of Customary Arbitration in Nigeria", in Osipitan T. A.., (Ed.), *Perspectives on Contemporary Legal Issues: Essays in Honour of Justice Dolapo Akinsanya,* (Lagos: Text-Royale Law Publishing Ent. 2006), pp. 29-30.

[23] Olufokunbi, F. "Illusions and Realities of ADR in Nigerian Civil Justice System" in Yusuf, F. A., (Ed), *Issues in Justice Administration in Nigeria*, *op. cit.* note 6, P. 89.

of dispute resolution. The procedure was reconciliation and mediation—and in some cases arbitration—not trial of issues.[24]

ADR Practitioners in Nigeria

In Nigeria, ADR is practiced institutionally and individually, both within and without the court system. Institutions that practice ADR are: the court annexed Multi-Door Courthouses, the Citizen's Mediation Centres, the Chambers of commerce, and industry groups and private enterprises. Individuals that practice ADR include: Judges, specially trained practitioners (arbitrators and mediators), elders, and religious or other traditional leaders recognized by their communities. Some ADR practitioners are industry specific, or have technical expertise in specific areas like environmental disputes, labour disputes, family law, etc.[25]

Legal Framework for ADR in Nigeria

Current Nigerian laws have ample provision on the use of ADR methods in resolving disputes. These laws are briefly discussed below.

The 1999 Constitution[26]

The Constitution, which is the supreme law of the land, endorses arbitration. Section 19(d) of the Constitution states that part of Nigeria's foreign policy objective is respect for international law and treaty obligations, as well as the seeking of settlement of international disputes by negotiation, mediation, conciliation, arbitration and adjudication.[27]

Arbitration Laws

Nigeria, like other progressive countries, subscribes to some international ADR Laws and Rules. *The United Nations Commission on International Trade Law (UNCTRAL Model Law of 1985)* and *UNCITRAL Arbitration Rules* have been domesticated in Nigeria through the *Arbitration and*

---

[24] Ademola, A., "Court Decongestion: Arbitration, Conciliation, Mediation & Reconciliation, p. 164, cited in Femi Olufokunbi, *ibid.*

[25] *Op. cit.*

[26] Cap. C. 23 LFN 2004.

[27] See Ani, C. C.., "The Role of the Courts in Arbitration, in Nigeria", in Azinge, E. & Aduba, N., (Eds.) *Law and Development*, (Lagos: NIALS, 2010), P.1041.

Conciliation Act (ACA),[28] which is a federal and principal enactment on arbitration, applicable throughout Nigeria. The Act provides a unified legal framework for the fair and efficient settlement of commercial disputes by arbitration and conciliation, and makes applicable the *Convention on the Recognition and Enforcement of Arbitral Awards (New York Convention)* to any award made in Nigeria or in any contracting State arising from international commercial arbitration.[29] The Act not only inaugurated an effective legal framework for the conduct of arbitration in Nigeria, but also made possible the enforcement of arbitral awards rendered elsewhere or in Nigeria, for the international enforceability of awards rendered in Nigeria.[30]

Other Federal Acts

Nigeria's body of laws is replete with statutes that provide for the application of arbitration or other ADR mechanisms. For want of space, it will suffice to mention the laws and the applicable sections: sections 11 and 30 (4) of *Matrimonial Causes Act* [31]; section 2 of the *Consumer Protection Council Act*; [32] sections 29 and 33 of the *Environmental Impact Assessment* (EIA) Act [33]; Sections 4, 8, 9, 20, and 22 of the *Trade Disputes Act* [34]; section 11 of the *Petroleum Act* [35]; section 26 of the *Nigerian Investment Promotion Commission Act* [36]; section 27 of the *Public Enterprises (Privatization and Commercialization) Act* [37]; section

---

[28] Cap. A 18, LFN, 2004. This Act replaced the Arbitration and Conciliation Decree No. 11 of 1988, which replaced The Arbitration Act of 1914. See Dakas C. J. "The Legal Framework for the Recognition and Enforcement of International Commercial Arbitral Awards in Nigeria Dilemmas and Agenda for Action," *Journal of International Arbitration* 15(2): 95-116, 1998.

[29] See the Long Title of the ACA. See Adaralegbe A., "Challenges in Enforcement of Arbitral Awards in Capital-Importing States: The Nigerian Experience," *Journal of International Arbitration* 23(5):401-426, 2006.

[30] Ibid. Part III of the ACA contains provisions relating to International Commercial Arbitration and Conciliation. See also, Ani C. C. "The Role of the Courts in Arbitration, in Nigeria, *op, cit.* note 26, P.1041.

[31] Cap. M7 LFN 2004.

[32] Cap C25 LFN 2004.

[33] Cap. E12 LFN 2004.

[34] Cap. T8 LFN 2004.

[35] Cap. PI0 LFN 2004.

[36] Cap. N17 LFN 2004.

[37] Cap. P38 LFN 2004.

22 of the *Nigerian LNG (Fiscal Incentives, Guarantee and Assurance) Act* [38]; section 49 of the *Nigerian Co-Operative Societies Act* [39]; section 5 of the *National War College Act* [40]; sections 3 and 6 of the *National Boundary Commission, Etc. Act* [41]; section 3 of the *Advisory Council on Religious Affairs Act* [42]; section 4 of the National *Office for Technology Acquisition and Promotion Act*[43]; section 4 of the *Nigerian Communications Commission Act* [44], etc.

Court Laws and Rules

Section 17 of the Federal High Court Act,[45] dealing with reconciliation in civil and criminal cases, provides that in any proceedings in the Court, the Court may promote reconciliation among the parties thereto and encourage and facilitate the amicable settlement thereof. Order 25 of the High Court of Lagos State (Civil Procedure) Rules 2004 introduced pre-trial conferences. The pre-trial conference is, among other things, fashioned to enable the judge to give directions as to the future course of action that appears best adapted to secure the just, expeditious and economic disposal of the matter, and to promote the amicable settlement of the case or the adoption of alternative dispute resolution. Order 17 of the High Court of the Federal Capital Territory (Abuja Civil Procedure Rules 2004) provides that a Court or judge, with the consent of the parties, may encourage settlement of any matter(s) before it by Arbitration, Conciliation, Mediation, or any other lawfully recognized method of dispute resolution.

Rules of Professional Conduct (RPC) for Legal Practitioners, 2007

Rule 15 of the RPC makes it mandatory for a lawyer to inform his client of the option of ADR mechanisms before resorting to or continuing litigation on behalf of his client. Lawyers are also barred from fomenting strife or

---

[38] Cap. N87 LFN 2004.
[39] Cap. N98 LFN 2004.
[40] Cap N82 LFN 2004.
[41] Cap. N10 LFN 2004.
[42] Cap. A8 LFN 2004.
[43] Cap. N62 LFN 2004.
[44] Cap. N97 LFN 2004.
[45] Cap. F12 LFN 2004.

instigating litigation and, except in the case of close relations or of trust, he shall not, without being consulted, proffer advice or bring a law suit.[46]

The Lagos Multi-Door Courthouse

The concept of the Multi-Door Courthouse was the idea of a Harvard Law School Professor, Frank Sander. He made proposals for a variety of processes that might provide more effective forms of conflict resolution.[47] The proposals made by Sander are regarded as a blueprint for the drastic changes that were to occur later on how the courts in the United States and around the world administered justice, approached case backlogs, and revolutionized how disputes are resolved.

The LMDC is the first Multi-Door Court-house to be established in Nigeria. It was set up in Lagos State on 11 June 2002, and is the brain child of a legal practitioner, Mr. Kehinde Aina. Mr. Aina keyed into the concept enunciated by Frank Sander. To actualize his vision of a Multi-door Courthouse in Nigeria, in 1995 he founded the Negotiation & Conflict Management Group (NCMG), a non-profit private organization. In 2001, he brokered collaboration between the NCMG and the Lagos State Judiciary through a public private partnership, to establish the Lagos Multi-Door Courthouse (LMDC) as the first court-connected ADR centre in Africa. The former Chief Judge of Lagos State, Hon. Justice Sotiminu, made the following remark during the official launch of the Lagos Multi-Door Courthouse (LMDC):

> The advantages of the LMDC are numerous, but suffice to say that it will not only create a congenial environment, but also encourage foreign investments in Nigeria. It will on the whole provide the needed support for our nascent democracy.[48]

Also commenting on the purpose of the LMDC, the Chairman, LMDC Governing Council, Justice Opeyemi Oke said:

---

[46] Rule 47 of RPC.

[47] French R.., "Perspectives on Court Annexed Alternative Dispute Resolution", available at: http://74.6.238.254/search/srpcache?ei=UTF&p=multi+door+courthouse+and+frank+sander&fr=yfp-t-892- Last accessed on 5/10/2010

[48] Aina, K., The multi-Door Concept in Nigeria: The Journey so Far" P. 10. Available at: www.ainablankson.com/pdftemp/pdf_AB Last accessed on 19/6/2011

> The courthouse was established to provide and enhance access to justice, which does not only mean access to the courts, lawyers and the judicial process,... providing opportunity for a just, economical and timely outcome of justice. It is backed by the LMDC Law 2007 and remains the first court-connected ADR centre in the country. It was specifically established to take care of the frustrations from the traditional courts which are bogged down by allegations of corruption, manipulations and procrastination.[49]

The objective of the LMDC is to enhance access to justice by providing timely and cost effective alternative mechanisms to supplement litigation in the resolution of disputes, and to minimize citizens' frustration, and delays in justice delivery, by providing a standard legal framework for fair and efficient settlement of disputes through ADR.[50] The operations of the LMDC are backed up by a Law enacted in May 2007.[51] The Federal Capital Territory of Abuja and other States like Kano, Kwara, Ondo, Delta, Rivers, Abia, Akwa-Ibom, and Kaduna have established Multi-Door Courthouses.

The LMDC maintains a panel of neutrals made up of accredited Mediators, Arbitrators and Neutral Evaluators from every field of endeavour. They are approved by the Chief Judge of Lagos State, on the recommendation of the Neutrals' Screening Committee.[52] The LMDC handles cases of varying types, including banking, business/commercial, construction, maritime, telecommunication, energy, administrative, civil rights, education, employment, environmental, matrimonial causes, insurance, intellectual property/technology, labour, personal injury, probate, product liability, professional malpractice/negligence, real property, securities, and shipping/transportation.[53] While the LMDC's main focus is Commercial ADR and the design and development of sector specific dispute resolution mechanisms for commerce and industry, the LMDC has followed global trends in ADR development with very keen interest, such

[49] Available at: http://www.independentngonline.com/DailyIndependent/Article.aspx?id=29387. Accessed on 10/7/2011

[50] *Ibid.*

[51] See A Law to Establish the Lagos Multi-Door Courthouse and for other Connected Matters 2007, No. 56, vol. 40 Lagos State of Nigeria Official Gazette.

[52] Aina, K., "The multi-Door Concept in Nigeria: The Journey so Far" *op. cit.* note 48, P. 10.

[53] Available at: http://lagosmultidoor.org/index.php?option=com_content&view=article&id=120&Itemid=59.

as the introduction and growth of Peer Mediation in campuses, to equip young people with the techniques of dispute resolution.

Commencing a Case at the LMDC

Action may be commenced at the LMDC in any of the following ways:

A. **Court Referrals:** A High Court Judge may refer a matter pending before him to the LMDC for possible settlement.

B. **Walk-Ins:** A party or both parties to a dispute can initiate mediation, arbitration, or other ADR service by writing to the Director of the LMDC or visiting the LMDC to initiate action.

C. **Direct Intervention**: The LMDC may intervene in a dispute in the public domain, where public interest or the interest of the disputing parties so demand. The parties are approached with a view to assisting in the resolution of their dispute.[54]

Procedures at the LMDC

Cases that go to the LMDC for settlement undergo, where possible, some procedures from intake to settlement. The ADR process at the LMDC comprises five major stages: Case Initiation, Intake Screening, Pre-Session, ADR Session, and Closure.

1. **Case Initiation:** In a nutshell, when parties get to the LMDC through any of the above-mentioned ways, the initiating party completes and submits for filing a Request Form (Form 1), attaching four copies of a brief Statement of Issues. Upon receipt of a Request Form or receipt of a Referral from the court, the LMDC sends, within seven days of such receipt, a Notice of Referral to the other party, along with a Submission Form (Form 2) and a copy of the Applicant's Statement of Issues. Within 7 days, the Responding Party is expected to return the duly completed Submission Form (Form 2) to the LMDC, along with four copies of a brief Statement in response.[55]

---

[54] See the *Lagos Settlement Week Information Brochure*, (Lagos LMDC, 2009), p. 10.

[55] *Op. cit.* note 53.

2. **Intake Screening Stage:** The LMDC Registrar evaluates the matter for case classification and allocates the file to a Dispute Resolution Officer (DRO) for Intake Screening. The DRO carefully studies the parties' Statement of Issues and Statement in Response, and determines the nature of the claim and the underlying interests, as well as the appropriate "door" for possible resolution.[56] This provides a unique opportunity for individual case needs assessment and litigation/ADR management.[57]

3. **Pre-Session Stage:** After assigning the appropriate door for settlement, the DRO convenes a Pre-Session Meeting, during which he explains the ADR processes to the parties. The Neutral, (Mediator, Arbitrator or Neutral Evaluator) considered suitable for the case is recommended by the Registrar from the LMDC Panel of Neutrals, to assist in resolving the dispute. A date for the session is scheduled, and the Parties then sign a confirmation of attendance form and a confidentiality agreement (Form 5).[58] An ADR Session Notice is subsequently sent to the parties after the Neutral has completed the Disclosure Form, clarifying his relationship with either of the disputing parties. Where a party, after being served with the notice of the matter involving him/her, refuses to submit within the stipulated time to Mediation, the DRO notifies the ADR Judge, who may then order the recalcitrant party to appear before him, and afterwards make requisite orders and give necessary directives.

4. **Closure, Evaluation and Enforcement**: An ADR process must come to an end at some point, whether the matter is settled or not. Where the matter is settled, a settlement agreement is executed by the parties. If parties fail to reach a settlement of any or all of the issues during mediation proceedings, they may submit such issue(s) to advisory arbitration, binding arbitration or any other ADR process considered suitable. A Neutral may, by written declaration, terminate the mediation process where efforts at further mediation are deemed no longer worthwhile.[59] At the close of the process, the

---

[56] *Ibid.*
[57] Aina, K., "The multi-Door Concept in Nigeria: The Journey so Far" *op. cit.* note 48, pp. 5-6.
[58] *Op. cit.* note 53.
[59] Article 18 the of the LMDC Practice Direction on Mediation.

LMDC issues a questionnaire entitled "Feedback Form" to the parties, to assist with its quality control, assessment of the skills of the Neutrals and development of the LMDC. By virtue of Section 19 of the LMDC Law, settlements reached by parties at the LMDC become enforceable once they are reduced into writing, signed by the parties and endorsed by the Referral Judge or an ADR Judge. Such agreements are deemed to be enforceable as a consent judgment of the High Court of Lagos State, under section 11 of the Sheriffs and Civil Processes Law.[60] Arbitrator's Awards are also enforceable by leave of a Judge, in the same manner as a consent judgment.[61]

5. **Expenses and Fees:** A subsidized fee rate has been devised at the Lagos Multi-Door Courthouse, in order to be self-sustaining, affordable, and to maintain a standard of service rooted in independence, quality and professionalism. Parties are required to pay a non-refundable administration fee. Parties are also required to pay Session Fees before the commencement of Mediation, or as they may be directed to do so by the LMDC. All other incidental expenses are borne equally by the parties, unless they agree otherwise.[62]

Brief Definition of Methods Applicable at the LMDC

By section 3 of the LMDC Law, the LMDC is to apply Mediation, Arbitration, Neutral Evaluation and any other ADR mechanisms in the resolution of such disputes as may from time to time be referred to it from the High Court of Justice, Lagos State, Courts of other jurisdictions outside Lagos State, Federal Courts, private persons, corporations, public institutions, and dispute resolution organizations.

Early Neutral Evaluation Door: This is an impartial assessment of the merits of a case, with the evaluator providing an advisory opinion as to settlement value, strengths and weaknesses, and/or assistance with settlement negotiations.[63] In this process, a Neutral Evaluator is employed,

---

[60] Article 17, *ibid.*
[61] Order 39, rule 4 (3) of the High Court of Lagos State Civil Procedure Rules.
[62] See Article 19 of the LMDC Practice Direction on Mediation.
[63] Alternative Dispute Resolution- Multi-Door Courthouses Security, Justice and Growth, (DFID and British Council, 2010), available at:

who may be a retired judge, an experienced lawyer or a person with the required background and expertise in a given field.[64] Neutral Evaluation Proceedings are initiated to guide the parties towards resolution. The process is mostly adopted prior to or in the course of a Mediation session, with a view to assisting the parties in their negotiation.

Mediation Door: Mediation is negotiation carried out with the assistance of a neutral third party referred to as a Mediator, Conciliator, Facilitator or a Neutral, who assists the parties in coming to a mutually satisfying resolution. [65] It is a voluntary and confidential process that offers disputants meaningful and creative solutions at a fraction of the cost of the litigation system.[66] Mediators assist parties in communicating with each other, clarify issues, developing options and encouraging everyone to collaborate in solving the problem and reaching a mutually satisfying agreement. Mediators usually abstain from suggesting outcomes or solutions, and hence mediation places control and ownership of the process with the parties: the parties control the outcome. To date, mediation has proved to be the most popular form of ADR at the LMDC.

Arbitration Door: This is the reference of a dispute or difference between not less than two parties for determination, after hearing both sides in a judicial manner, by a person or persons other than a court of competent jurisdiction.[67] The difference between Mediation and Arbitration is clear-cut. While mediation is voluntary, and the parties mutually agree upon a fair settlement, arbitration is mandatory. Arbitration proceedings are governed by the Arbitration and Conciliation Act. [68] The Arbitrator makes

---

http://www.j4anigeria.org/joomdocs/Multi_door_Courthouse.pdf
Last accessed on 10/7/2011

[64] Peters, D., "The Multi-Door Court House Concept" A paper presented at the Nigerian Institute of Advanced Legal Studies Advanced Course in Practice and Procedure, 2006, p. 6.

[65] Aina, K., "Alternative Dispute Resolution: The Practice and Procedure" A paper presented at the Nigerian
Institute of Advanced Legal Studies Course in Practice and Procedure, June, 2008, p. 6.

[66] Macforlane, J., "An Alternative to What?" in Macforlane (Ed.), Rethinking Disputes: The Mediation
Alternative, p. 4.

[67] See Mustill M. & Boyd S., *The Law and Practice of Commercial Arbitration in England,* (London: Butterworths, 2nd ed., 1989), p. 39.

[68] Cap. A 18, LFN, 2004.

a ruling known as an "award" which is final.[69] Arbitration is similar to court, except that it is quicker and cheaper. Arbitration clauses are included in many contracts and business agreements.

Hybrid Door: The Hybrid Door is the creative mix of various ADR mechanisms, like mediation, arbitration and neutral evaluation, in order to obtain a settlement or resolution that is best suited to the particular case. Some of the Hybrid models of ADR include: Arb-Med (Arbitration and Mediation), Med-Arb (Mediation and Arbitration), Med- ENE (Mediation and Early Neutral Evaluation).[70]

Data Analysis and Findings

The table below shows that of the 313 cases handled, 111 (35.46 percent) resulted in a resolution. The year 2009 recorded the highest number of matters filed over the period, with mediation matters being the highest. Court referred matters and walk-ins were also at their highest in the same year. Generally, it can be seen that arbitration and other ADR processes—apart from mediation—are very minimal for the period under consideration. This shows clearly that mediation is the preferred method of ADR at the LMDC. It can also be observed from the data that walk-in matters (219) surpassed court referred matters (113) by 106 (48.0%).

Table 1. ADR Services- Performance Indicators from January 2007-June 2010[71]

Performance Indicators	**2007**	**2008**	**2009**	**Jan-June 2010**	**Total**
No. Mediation filed	36	62	152	65	315

[69] However, the Courts may intervene in several circumstances. Courts have the powers to enforce and to set aside arbitral awards. See Ani, C. C. "The Role of the Courts in Arbitration in Nigeria", *op. cit.* note 27. See *Baker Marine Nig. Ltd. v. Chevron Nig. Ltd. (2000)* 12 NWLR (Pt. 681) at 393 and *Kano State Urban Development Board v. Fanz Construction Co. Ltd.* (1990) 4 NWLR (Pt. 142) 1.
[70] See the Lagos Multi-Door Courthouse Brochure, p. 6.
[71] Source: Etuk, C. Report of the Lagos Multi-Door Courthouse (LMDC) to the Governing Council of the LMDC, April, 2011.

No of Arbitrations and other ADR matters filed	2	8	4	3	17
No of Court-Referred matters	4	30	59	20	113
No of Walk-In matters	34	40	97	48	219
No of cases discontinued	5	4	10	-	19
Total No of Cases Resolved	16	15	58	22	111

Note: *Total number of cases handled is 313 (315 mediation matters + 17 arbitration matters, 19 matters discontinued).*

The LMDC Settlement Week

The Settlement Week is a week set aside by the Chief Judge of Lagos State for specific Courts to clear the backlog of cases, through means which include referral to the LMDC for possible resolution through Mediation, Arbitration, Neutral Evaluation or any other ADR procedure.[72] In 2009 (November 2-6), the LMDC held the first ever Settlement Week in Nigeria, with the training of mediators and some preparation and supervision by Professor Ernest Uwazie. The Settlement Week has become an integral part of the Lagos State Judicial calendar, and an annual event.

The objectives of the Lagos Settlement Week include

- To impact the Justice System of Lagos State through a gradual but definitive reduction of the case load of the courts, while providing satisfying, timely and cost effective Justice to litigants.
- To encourage the use of non-adversarial dispute resolution mechanisms as far as possible, especially for Commercial and General Civil matters.
- To create widespread awareness of the benefits and effectiveness of Mediation as a dispute resolution method.

[72] Section 31 of the LMDC Law.

- To provide the platform to raise public awareness of ADR, and showcase the services of the LMDC.[73]

Statistics of Cases before the Hon. Judges of the High Court of Lagos State, 4th Quarter 2009:

- Total number of cases brought forward from 3rd quarter, 2009: 12,547
- Total number of cases assigned in the last quarter of 2009: 12,108
- Total number of matters disposed of by the courts in the last quarter of 2009: 1,825
- Total number of pending cases on court docket as at December 2009: 13,376
- 12.5% settlement rate in the existing court system.

Statistics of the 2009 Settlement Week:

- Court referrals: 34
- Cases referred from other sources: 235
- Cases admitted after screening: 145
- Cases mediated: 83
- Cases settled: 37
- Settlement rate: 44.58%[74]

During the week, the LMDC mediated a total of 83 cases. Of the 83 cases mediated, 37 (44.58%) were settled within the week. This is a fair success rate, when compared to the settlement rate of 12.5% in the existing court system in Lagos State. This success rate is laudable, considering that it was the first attempt at the initiative.

The 2010 Settlement Week

- Court referrals: 34
- Cases referred from other sources: 217
- Cases admitted after screening: 173

---

[73] See Etuk C., "The Lagos Settlement Week, Process, Actors and Challenges", paper presented at the LMDC Settlement Week Neutral's Workshop, October 19th, 2010.

[74] Source of Data: Etuk C., ibid.

- Cases mediated: 77
- Cases settled: 14
- Settlement rate: 24 (31.17 %)[75]

In 2010 (November 1-5), the LMDC's target was to settle 400 cases through time bound mediation. However, only 217 cases were referred from the courts. At the completion of the case screening, 173 matters were selected as suitable for time bound mediation. Confirmation of attendance was received for 91 cases. Fourteen of the cases were settled before the settlement week, leaving 77 cases for mediation. Twenty four (31.17%) out of the 77 cases were settled during the week.[76]

On the basis of above statistics, it can be observed that there is a remarkable increase in the number of cases referred from the courts in the 2010 Settlement Week, though many of them were not suitable for mediation. The increase in court referred cases may perhaps be attributed to better reception of the scheme by the judges. When compared with the 2009 Settlement Week, there is a difference of 13.41% below the settlement rate of 2009. Nevertheless, the percentage of success recorded during the LMDC Settlement Weeks still far exceeds the settlement rates at the regular High Courts, which makes ADR very desirable as a viable option for court decongestion.

Partnership, Collaboration and Support

For its effective functioning within the Justice Sector, the LMDC has sought to create collaborations with other organizations and stakeholders, both locally and internationally. It also receives support from organizations. Some such partnerships, collaborations and support are discussed below.

Security Justice and Growth Programme of DFID and the British Council

By way of support, the Security Justice and Growth Programme contributed the following to the LMDC:

- Refurbishment of the LMDC office space

---

[75] Ibid.

[76] Ibid, p. 16.

- Training of Magistrates in ADR
- Training and international accreditation by the Centre for Effective Dispute Resolution (CEDR) of LMDC staff and other stakeholders
- Computer equipment
- IT consultants to implement a website and internal network
- A generator for the exclusive use of the LMDC
- Training and workshops for the senior staff of the LMDC in the construction of the Network of Multi-Door Courthouses.[77]

The LMDC-NBA Forum

The LMDC collaborates with the Nigeria Bar Association (NBA) Forum to promote ADR within the legal community and to generate awareness among lawyers of the workings of the LMDC.

Citizens Mediation Centre (CMC)

Collaboration exists with the Citizens Mediation Centre and Ministry of Justice, Lagos State. The Citizens' Mediation Centre (CMC) provides alternative dispute resolution services through the process of mediation. By the provisions of the *Citizens' Mediation Centre Law,*[78] the CMC is empowered to mediate on disputes relating, *inter alia,* to landlord and tenant, employer and employee, family, and debt recovery.[79] Memoranda of Understanding reached at the CMC are registered at the LMDC for the enforcement through the machinery of the Lagos High Court. *The Association of Multi-Door Courthouses of Nigeria* is an organization set up to promote the Multi-Door Courthouse concept and to spearhead their replications nationwide and standardization of its practice in Nigeria.

---

[77] Alternative Dispute Resolution- Multi-Door Courthouses Security, Justice and Growth Programme, (DFID and British Council, 2010), available at: http://www.j4anigeria.org/joomdocs/Multi_door_Courthouse.pdf. Last accessed on 10/7/2011

[78] The *Lagos State Citizens' Mediation Centre Law, 2007*

[79] At its inception, the CMC was the first of its kind in Nigeria as a government institution exclusively devoted to providing free mediation services. See Oluyemi Atinuke, "History," in *A Decade of Mediation* (Lagos: CMC, 2009), P. 4, cited in Comfort C. Ani "Access to Justice in Nigerian Criminal and Civil Justice Systems," in Azinge E. & Owasanoye B. O. (Eds.), *Rule of Law and Good Governance* (Lagos: NIALS, 2009), p. 417.

Banks

The LMDC has, in recent times, partnered with Chartered Institute of Bankers, Nigeria, (CIBN) for the promotion of ADR awareness within the Banking sector. The LMDC facilitated the Entrepreneurial Development Programme, which involved an ADR workshop on Dispute Resolution in the Banking Sector. It contributed to the Proposed Amendment of Banks and Other Financial Institutions Act (BOFIA) 1991, as amended. It also made contributions to the review of the regulatory and operational challenges in the implementation of BOFIA.[80] The LMDC has a Banking Track (BT) project, which involves a Dispute Resolution Survey of the entire sector, and the selection of some banks for a Dispute Resolution Audit, with a view to developing a Dispute Resolution Guideline for the industry.[81]

Training Programmes

The LMDC has done a lot through its resolve to train, create awareness, educate, and sensitize lawyers, judges and the entire legal community on ADR, with a view to securing their interest and patronage. Hence, it has been involved in the following programmes:

1. **LMDC Neutral's Parley:** The LMDC occasionally holds parleys for its Neutrals. These meetings provide a forum for deliberation on a myriad of issues concerning ADR and the LMDC. During the meetings, insightful and highly educative presentations are given, followed by interactive sessions where several issues affecting ADR, the LMDC and the neutrals are raised and addressed.[82]

2. **Case Management Workshops for Judges**: This is a workshop for Judges of the High Court of Lagos State, held to review the Settlement Week Procedure (Practice Directions) and the Guidelines for Referrals.[83]

3. **Train the Trainer Program:** The LMDC collaborated with the World Bank to facilitate Intensive *Train the Trainer* courses.

[80] Op. cit. note 53.
[81] Ibid.
[82] Ibid.
[83] Ibid.

Participants were drawn mainly from the LMDC Panel of Neutrals. This group of mediators was listed for participation in the Settlement Week conferences.

4. **Mediator Skills Training Courses**: The LMDC organizes Mediator Skills Training courses for the training of Assistant Mediators on Time Bound Mediation.

5. **NBA LMDC'S Continuing Legal Education:**[84] The LMDC gives presentations at the Nigerian Bar Association's (NBA) Continuing Legal Education Workshops and Annual General Meetings of the NBA.

Challenges

Femi Olufokunbi has identified what he termed "the Nigerian Factor" as the major obstacle to the progress of ADR.[85] The Nigerian Factor, according to him, embraces issues like the lack of a culture of obedience, low levels of development, and the starvation of funds for the judiciary to build ADR methods into the judicial system, as in the US.[86] Nigerian disputants are easily caught up in the tension of hostility, preferring to win outright rather than compromising their rights, and preferring to consult their lawyers first to ascertain their rights.[87]

Although mediation and other ADR processes are claimed to be cheaper than traditional litigation, the costs involved in ADR processes are also a cause of the low patronage of ADR processes, especially among low income earners. The Director of the LMDC, Mrs. Caroline Etuk, enumerated the challenges confronting LMDC as follows:[88] low referral rates and marginal increase in referrals, low settlement rates, inadequate awareness creation and funding to ensure capacity building etc., inadequate manpower, poor buy-in of the legal community, and

---

84 Director of the Lagos Multi-Door Court House, Mrs. Caroline Etuk was appointed as a member of the Continuing Legal Education Committee of the NBA, Lagos Branch.

85 Femi Olufokunbi., "Illusions and Realities of ADR in Nigerian Civil Justice System," pp. 97-98.

86 In the U.S., Arbitrators and Case-Evaluators are paid by the courts or work on pro-bono basis.

87 Femi Olufokunbi., *ibid.*

88 Etuk, Caroline, Report of the Lagos Multi-Door Courthouse (LMDC) to the Governing Council of the LMDC, April, 2011, p. 20.

inadequate research base. Despite these challenges, the LMDC is certain that as a dispute resolution mechanism, ADR has etched its relevance into justice administration, but the comprehension of the phenomenon by stakeholders and consumers of justice will be gradual.[89]

Suggestions and Conclusions

ADR mechanisms have become firmly rooted as legally recognized modes of justice administration in Nigeria. Besides the growing statutory enactments compelling the use of ADR methods, the spread of Multi-Door Courthouses in the states of the federation also makes it obvious that ADR has come to stay. What is lacking is the requisite patronage, which may be linked to the lack of awareness of ADR processes among the wider populace.

The LMDC has, through its activities, demonstrated impressive commitment towards the spread and acceptance of ADR in Nigeria. Though settlement rates are not on the high side, they may still be considered impressive, because the LMDC is still in its early stages. However, a comparison of available data reveals that its settlement rate surpasses that of the High Courts.

ADR is currently not taught as a subject in most of our universities, either at undergraduate or graduate level. The Nigerian law school only recently added it as a subject. It is important to include ADR in the university school curriculum. This will help create awareness and understanding of the processes involved and will dispel inhibitions about ADR. This translates into the need for lecturers with adequate skills to teach ADR at undergraduate and post-graduate levels. There should be training and continued education for teachers in this new area that most were not given the opportunity to study in school.

There is an urgent need for the legal community—and indeed other stakeholders in the ADR industry—to keep abreast with the growing best practices in the field. Vigorous involvement of legal practitioners through the Nigerian Bar Association in the crusade for ADR is necessary in order to curtail apathy towards ADR among legal practitioners.

The LMDC deserves better funding from government and local and foreign organizations. This will make it possible for it to train its staff better, and to continue to vigorously pursue the training of judicial personnel, lawyers, court registrars and judicial assistants. Enhanced

---

[89] Ibid, p. 2.

funding will also enable it to carry out mass enlightenment through media publicity.

The judiciary has a vital role to play in the sustenance of ADR in the following respects: planning and execution, case referral, case filtering and selection, review and approval of agreements, enforcement of agreements, monitoring and evaluation of programs and people, and professional development and discipline of mediators.[90] It is imperative for judges and magistrates to let go of some of the cases pending before them which are appropriate for ADR and to refer such matters to LMDC, either at the pre-trial conference stage or when the matter comes up for hearing (if it is already in court). Statistics disclose that walk-in matters far outnumber court referred matters. The reverse should be the case, as judges and magistrates ought to be more aware than ordinary disputants of the efficacy of ADR.

References

Adaralegbe, A., "Challenges in Enforcement of Arbitral Awards in Capital-Importing States: The Nigerian Experience," *Journal of International Arbitration* 23(5): 2006.

Aina, K., "The multi-Door Concept in Nigeria: The Journey so Far". Available at: www.ainablankson.com/pdftemp/pdf_AB. Last Accessed on 19/6/2011.

—. "Alternative Dispute Resolution: The Practice and Procedure." A paper presented at the Nigerian Institute of Advanced Legal Studies Course in Practice and Procedure, June, 2008.

Alternative Dispute Resolution: Multi-Door Courthouses Security, Justice and Growth Programme, (DFID and British Council, 2010), available at: http://www.j4a-nigeria.org/joomdocs/Multi_door_Courthouse.pdf. Last assessed on 10/7/2011.

Ani, C. C., "Towards Eradicating the Problem of Delay in Criminal Justice Administration in Nigeria", in Yusuf F. A. (Ed.) *Issues in Justice Administration in Nigeria,* (Lagos: VDG Intl. Ltd., 2008).

—. "The Role of the Courts in Arbitration, in Nigeria, in Azinge, E. & Aduba, N.., (Eds.) *Law and Development*, (Lagos: NIALS, 2010).

—. "Access to Justice in Nigerian Criminal and Civil Justice Systems", in Azinge, E. & Owasanoye. B. O. (Eds.), *Rule of Law and Good Governance* (Lagos: NIALS, 2009).

[90] See: United Nations Office on Drugs and Crime, Training Manual on Alternative Dispute Resolution and Restorative Justice, October 2007, p. 21.

Astor, H., and Chinkin C., *Dispute Resolution in Australia* (2nd ed, 2002).

Best, S. G., "The Methods of Conflict Resolution and Transformation," in Best, S. G. (Ed.), *Introduction to Peace and Conflict Studies in West Africa,* (Ibadan: Spectrum Books Ltd. 2006).

Coker, S. A. & Adeleke M. O. *et al*., "An Appraisal of Alternative Dispute Resolution as an Antidote to Delay of Judicial Proceedings In Nigerian Courts," in Fassy Adetokunbo Yusuf (Ed), *Issues in Justice Administration in Nigeria,* (Lagos: VDG Intl. Ltd., 2008).

French R., "Perspectives on Court Annexed Alternative Dispute Resolution," available at: http://74.6.238.254/search/srpcache?ei=UTFulti+door+courthouse+and+frank+sander&fr=yfp- Mustill, M., & Boyd S., *The Law and Practice of Commercial Arbitration in England,* (London: Butterworths, 2nd ed., 1989).

Dakas, C. J., "The Legal Framework for the Recognition and Enforcement of International Commercial Arbitral Awards in Nigeria Dilemmas and Agenda for Action," *Journal of International Arbitration* 15(2): 1998.

Etuk, C., Report of the Lagos Multi-Door Courthouse (LMDC) to the Governing Council of the LMDC, April, 2011, p. 20.

—. "The Lagos Settlement Week, Process, Actors and Challenges." Paper presented at the LMDC Settlement Week Neutral's Workshop, October 19th, 2010.

Lewis M., and McCrimmon L., "The Role of ADR Processes in the Criminal Justice System: A view from Australia." A paper presented at ALRAESA Conference 4-8 September, 2005 At Imperial Resort Beach Hotel, Entebbe, Uganda. Available at: http://74.6.238.254/search/srpcache?ei=UTF8&p=ADR+in+the+criminal+justice+system&fr=yfpt. Last assessed on 5/10/2010

Olufokunbi, F., "Illusions and Realities of ADR in Nigerian Civil Justice System," in Yusuf F. A. (Ed), *Issues in Justice Administration in Nigeria* (Lagos: VDG Intl. Ltd., 2008).

Owasanoye B. O., "Case Flow Management Procedure," A Paper presented at the Nigerian Institute of Advanced Legal Studies Advanced Course in Practice and Procedure, 15th June, 2009.

Mohammed, S., "The High Court of The Federal Capital Territory, Abuja, Civil Procedure Rules, 2004: Can The New Rules Lead to Just, Efficient and Speedy Dispensation of Justice?" Available at: www.gamji.com/article4000/NEWS4652.htm. Last accessed on 19/6/2011.

Peters, D., "Alternatives to Litigation: The Multi-Door Court House Concept" in Fassy Adetokunbo Yusuf (Ed), *Issues in Justice Administration in Nigeria*, (Lagos: VDG Intl. Ltd., 2008).

—. "The Multi-Door Court House Concept." A paper presented at the Nigerian Institute of Advanced Legal Studies Advanced Course in Practice and Procedure, 2006.

Sokefun J. A., "Dynamics of Customary Arbitration in Nigeria", in Osipitan T. A., (Ed.), *Perspectives on Contemporary Legal Issues: Essays in Honour of Justice Dolapo Akinsanya*, (Lagos: Text-Royale Law Publishing Ent., 2006.

Stuart K. K.., & Savage C. A., "The Multi-Door Courthouse: How It's Working". Available at: http://74.6.238.254/search/srpcache?ei=UTF-frank+sander&Fr+yfp-t-892, accessed on 1/10/2010.

United Nations Office on Drugs and Crime, Training Manual on Alternative Dispute Resolution and Restorative Justice, October 2007.

Uwazie E. & Yamshon D. The Conflict Resolution Manual for the Training of Trainers (ToT) Program, organized by ADR Centre Italy and the NCMG College, 2009.

Superior Court of D-C.–Multi-Door Dispute Resolution Division, available at: www.dccourts.gov/../index.jsp. Last accessed on 19/6/2011.

http://www.lagosmultidoor.org/index.php?option=com_content&view=article&id=135:2009-in-retrospect&catid=38:news-items&Itemid=174.

CHAPTER FOUR

THE INTERPLAY OF CROSS CULTURALISM IN DESIGNING A MEDIATION MODEL FOR THE NIGER DELTA CONFLICT IN NIGERIA

JOY O. OGAJI

Introduction

Debates have resonated, especially within academia and among practitioners, on the viability and efficiency of mediation in multicultural settings. This argument was further elaborated in a study conducted by Gehm (1998.[1] The outcome of his findings among the 555 eligible victims willing to participate in Victim-Offender Mediation showed that 47% of them were more willing to participate if, like them, the offender was white.[2] Consequently, Bottoms (2003, 110)[3] argued that restorative justice is unlikely to work as well in contemporary (urban/multicultural) societies as it does in more traditional ones. This is because, according to him, restorative justice, even in traditional societies, only works well if the victim and offender have either a "thick" (family) or "thin" (culture) relationship with each other.[4] In multicultural modern societies, where there may be no relationship at all other than that related to the conflicting event, it may be that as, Bottoms (2003, 110) argues, any attempt to use a

---

[1] Gehm, J.R., (1998), "Victim-offender mediation programs: An exploration of practice and theoretical frameworks," *Western Criminology Review*, vol.1, pp.1-36.
[2] Ibid Gehm.
[3] Bottoms, A. E., (2003). "Some sociological reflections on restorative justice," In von Hirsch, A., Roberts, J., Bottoms, A.E., Roach, K. and Schiff, M. (eds.), *Restorative Justice and Criminal justice: Competing or Reconcilable Paradigms?* Oxford: Hart, pp. 79-113.
[4] Ibid Bottoms.

"blanket" delivery of restorative justice will always achieve modest and/or patchy results.[5]

Similarly, Umbreit (2001, 66)[6] warns that in a multicultural society, the cultural background of victims, offenders and mediators is often different. If not carefully handled, this carries a risk of miscommunication, misunderstanding or, worst of all, of re-victimization.[7] Furthermore, Smith (1995, 157)[8] argues that "for re-integrative shaming to work, a broad moral consensus must exist on what is good and bad conduct, on right and wrong."

In furtherance of the above assertions, it appears that the interplay of multi-culturalism (or cross-culturalism) is very fundamental, and hence should be dealt with in order to design and implement a viable mediation model for the Niger Delta, a hub for investors where local people and expatriates from different cultures interact, produce, and innovate together.

In addition, according to research findings, cross cultural mediation may not be as easy as it sounds, because pursuing a negotiation process is often more difficult than imposing a settlement. This fact was corroborated by Avruch & Black (1991), [9] who asserted that "[t]rying to lump all of these together as one common group is obviously not very feasible. Each group has unique considerations which must be taken into account for any service planning." To overcome this, Avruch & Black proposed a cross-cultural perspective on conflict and conflict resolution. A major component of this perspective involves culture-specific mapping, in order to get at how local groups have traditionally made sense of conflict, and dealt with it, which Avruch & Black label *ethno praxis*.[10]

The Proposal for Writing a Hybrid Model

The proposal to develop a hybrid mediation process in the Niger Delta conflict emerged from the findings of a field trip of a PhD researcher, conducted by the researcher from July-August 2011, in the three core states of the Niger Delta states in Nigeria.[11]

---

[5] Ibid Bottoms.

[6] Umbreit 2010.

[7] Ibid.

[8] Smith, D., (1995) *Criminology for Social Work*, Basingstoke: Macmillan.

[9] Avruch, K.; and Black, P., (1991). The culture question and conflict resolution. *Peace & Change*, 16(1), 22-45.

[10] Ibid.

[11] Rivers, Delta and Bayelsa states of Nigeria.

The study found a high level of support for indigenous mediation. This overwhelming support for the indigenous process was due to its amenability to the people, and the fact that they have faith in the system, having seen its success and weaknesses. This finding was corroborated by recent empirical research which showed that Nigerians prefer to resolve conflicts through informal modes, particularly mediation.[12] Following these findings, the researcher further explored the viability of the indigenous process, bearing in mind both the interplay of cross culturalism in the parties in the region, and the fact that in most contemporary/urban societies, communitarianism has been questioned and in some cases is giving way to urbanism.[13]

The need for a hybrid model is becoming imperative. The hybrid model[14] is intended to take care of not just one party's views, but a fusion of both, which is fundamental to building cross-cultural bridges and the integration of cultures, as it challenges the stereotypes that justify segregation in most multi-cultural societies.

In addition, the hybrid model proposed will enable issues to be settled by any among a range of given models, depending on the choice of the parties involved. If, for instance, a conflict occurs within the indigenous community,[15] the invocation and application of the indigenous process becomes imperative, due to a common sense about what is required for relationships of social equality to exist.[16]

On the other hand, what will happen when conflict ensues, between, say, a Niger Delta community and any of the multinational oil companies? Whose culture is distinctive in terms of ideas about how social equality is to be achieved? In such a setting, the hybrid model, which is an integration of the western and the indigenous mediation model will apply, taking into cognizance the culture and value system of both parties.

The central aim here is to restore, as much as possible, the relationship of the parties prior to the occurrence of the incident. Hence, what is

---

[12] Khaminwa, A., *Peacebuilding and Co-existence in Nigeria*, in The Afrobarometer- *Violent Social Conflict resolution in Nigeria*, Briefing Paper No.2, August 2002.

[13] Marshall, T, F., (1999) *Restorative Justice: An Overview*, London: Home Office Research and Statistics Directorate.

[14] The main framework of the hybrid model is not stated in this chapter, due to lack of space and time. Instead, what this study deals with is the impact of inter-culturalism in the proposed model.

[15] Between two Nigerians who are conversant and amenable to the traditional dispute resolution process.

[16] Guarded by Ubuntu values.

needed in order to restore the relationship cannot be dictated by one party, for this would exclude the other party from the process. Furthermore, research has shown that bringing people face to face with one another (as is the case in Victim-Offender Mediation) helps to dispel the myths and stereotypes each has of the other.[17] It allows the offender/perpetrator to meet and to hear the victim's story, experiencing it in his/her own words; it also allows the victim to see the offender or wrongdoer as a person, instead of as an evil or heartless criminal, and allows the community to see that neither the victim nor the offender/wrongdoer are unlike the rest of the community.[18]

The Interplay of Cross Culturalism in the Proposed Model

As has been elaborated above, cultural differences may arise due to a variety of factors. Individual differences in goals, expectations, values, proposed courses of action, and suggestions about how to best handle a situation, are unavoidable.[19] In view of the fact that conflicts are inevitable, a proper understanding and appreciation of the diversity in cultures, values and styles of people involved is vital. This is because, if they are not managed properly and speedily,[20] the effect could be devastating, as in the current case of the Niger Delta.[21]

[17] Omale, D.J.O., (2006) "Justice in History: An Examination of the African Restorative Traditions and the Emerging Restorative Justice Paradigm." *African Journal of Criminology and Criminal Justice*, vol.2 (2), pp. 30-60.

[18] Omale, D.J.O., (2006) "Justice in History: An Examination of the African Restorative Traditions and the Emerging Restorative Justice Paradigm." *African Journal of Criminology and Criminal Justice*, vol.2 (2), pp. 30-60.

[19] Darling JR, Fogliasso C.E., (1999), "Conflict management across cultural boundaries: a case analysis from a multinational bank," Eur. Bus. Rev. 99(6): 383-392; Baba K., (1996), "Development of construction management based on regional culture," in Langford D.A, & Retik A., (Eds). *The organization and management of construction: Shaping theory and practice*, Vol.1. London: E&FN Spon.

[20] Suen H, Cheung S.O., and Mondejar R., (2007), "Managing ethical behaviour in construction organization in Asia: How do the teaching of Confucianism, Taoism and Buddhism and Globalization influence ethics management?" Int. J. Project Manage. 25(3): 257-265.

[21] Zhou YQ, Lu L, Jiang B (2005). "Study on staff management practice of multinational company," Manage. Decis. 43(4): 516-522.

Major Cross-Cultural Differences Likely to Impact Mediation in the Niger Delta Setting

Before exploring these differences, it will be pertinent to start by defining culture, which many authors have argued is difficult and daunting to define. This, we believe, is due to the fact that there are over 400 definitions of "culture".[22] However, a definition of culture can, for present purposes, be drawn from Carley H. Dodd, who defined it as "the total accumulation of an identifiable group's beliefs, norms, activities, institutions, and communication patterns.[23]

Culture, it is argued, is both pervasive and largely invisible, and is quite different from what we think it is.[24] This definition implies that culture is an attribute of a group, and also contemplates the fact that there may be as much variation within the group as between different groups.[25] We often associate culture with a national group; however, culture includes ethnic groups, clans, tribes and organizations.

An important dimension of culture in the Niger Delta is the fact that two groups exist; the extent to which members identify with a particular group (collectivism) rather than with themselves as individuals (individualistic) is of significance in designing any model. LeBaron says that cultures affect the ways we name, frame, blame, and attempt to tame conflicts. Whether a conflict exists at all is a cultural question.[26] A culture is like the water fish swim in, unaware of its effect on their vision. Cultures are a series of lenses that shape what we see and don't see, how we perceive and interpret, and where we draw boundaries. In shaping our values, cultures contain starting points and currencies.[27]

---

[22] MalinAquilon, *Cultural Dimensions in Logistics Management: A Case Study From the European Automotive Industry* http://www.emeraldinsight.com/Insight/ViewContentServlet

[23] Carley H. Dodd, *Dynamics of Intercultural Communication* 36 (3d Ed. 1991).

[24] Carley H. Dodd, *Dynamics of Intercultural Communication 36* (3d Ed. 1991).

[25] The variation even between the 300 Niger Delta communities is enough diversity.

[26] LeBaron, Michelle, "Culture and Conflict." *Beyond Intractability*. Eds. Guy Burgess and Heidi Burgess. Conflict Research Consortium, University of Colorado, Boulder. Posted: July 2003 <http://www.beyondintractability.org/essay/culture_conflict/

[27] Ibid.

In an interview conducted in Canada, an elderly Chinese man indicated that he had experienced no conflict at all for the previous forty years.[28] This was largely due to his particular conception of what conflict is. People of other regions (in America for instance) may say different things when asked the same or a similar question.

Reminiscent of the manifold definitions of "culture," there are dizzying arrays of lists of cultural differences.[29] These norms, beliefs, traditions and institutions and communication patterns, as described by Carley, will have some impact, whether negative or positive, on any proposed mediation process:

1. **The Place of Harmony:** Research has shown that collectivists place a high value on harmony, getting along, and "face saving". Thus, for collectivists conflict is seen as a sign of social failure; while individualists also feel discomfort with conflict, they acknowledge conflict as an inevitable part of life that must be dealt with, and hence do not see it as something to be ashamed about.

2. **Labeling Behaviour:** Another area in which cross-cultural disparities show themselves is in labeling behavior that may be interpreted by a person from another culture as strange, if not as insulting or offending.[30] Paul Pedersen, describing cross cultural disparity, says that "behaviours have no meaning until they are placed into a cultural context."[31] Individuals from different cultural settings, when together, expect certain forms of behavior, and interpret the behaviours of people from other cultures as if those people were from their own culture.

---

[28] LeBaron, Michelle & Bruce Grundison, (1993) *Conflict and Culture: Research in Five Communities in British Columbia, Canada*. Victoria, British Columbia: University of Victoria Institute for Dispute Resolution.

[29] HAMPDEN-TURNER (1981); MAPS OF THE MIND Andre Laurent, *The Cultural Diversity of Western Conceptions of Management*, 13 INT. STUD. OF MGMT. & ORG. 75 (1983); Shalom H Schwartz & Anat Bardi, *Value Hierarchies Across Cultures: Taking a Similarities Perspective*, 32 J. of cross-cultural psychol. 268 (2001).

[30] The flamboyant lifestyle of oil workers and their frivolity has been frowned upon by the indigenous people, who have argued it impacts on their norms and socio-cultural perspectives. Youths engaging in drugs, possessing fire arms, prostitutions and other vices.

[31] Paul Pedersen, Lecture to John Barkai's class (Feb. 15, 2006).

3. **A Rational and Linear Decision-Making Process.** Another cultural difference that may impact on the model of mediation is a rational and linear decision-making process. The mediator guides the parties through a fixed series of problem-solving stages. While this model works well for some groups in society, other groups tend to operate best with different patterns of communication: for example, circular thinking or passionate discussions (LeBaron, 1997,[32] Lederach, 1986).[33] To ask people from such backgrounds to talk about only one issue at a time, or to speak without emotions, contradicts their traditional patterns of interaction and conflict resolution.

4. **Differences in Conflict Processing.** Research has shown that the Western model of conflict resolution is problematic, because it asks people to separate the people from the problem. In many cross-cultural conflicts, such as in the Niger Delta, people and problems are deeply intertwined. One cannot separate them. For some groups, harmony is highly valued; they cannot experience conflict with others and maintain a positive relationship (Duryea, 1993).[34]The difference must be resolved in order for the relationship to be reconciled. This Western notion will, in the Niger Delta setting, pose a major problem, since the conflict in question involves cross cultural and identity-based conflicts, involving parties whose opinion differs: each party sees the other through the prejudices, myths, and biases of his or her cultural group (Rothman, 1997).[35] In order to arrive at a resolution that does not hinder the successful implementation of the proposed model, the problem must be confronted and dealt with.

---

[32] LeBaron, J...P., (1997). "Mediation, conflict resolution and multicultural reality: Culturally competent practice" In E. Kruk (Ed.). *Mediation and conflict resolution in social work and the human services.* Chicago: Nelson Hall.

[33] Lederach, J. P., (1986). Mediation in North America: An examination of the profession's cultural premises. Unpublished Comprehensive Examination Paper. University of Colorado, Denver.

[34] Duryea, M. L., (1993). Conflict and culture: Research in five communities in Vancouver, British Columbia. Victoria, BC: UVic Institute for Dispute Resolution.

[35] Rothman, (1997): Source: Etuk, C. Report of the Lagos Multi-Door Courthouse (LMDC) to the Governing Council of the LMDC, April, 2011.

Yet another factor to be borne in mind is the issue of power, since the predominant model of mediation assumes a relatively equal balance of power between the parties. There exist significant power imbalances in society, particularly between people from minority and majority groups. The Niger Delta host communities are deemed a minority in this sense, due to the fact that the Nigerian government and the multinational companies are seen and viewed as the majority group and the more powerful party, who may have greater influence because of greater financial resources, better negotiation skills, better language skills, etc. If the mediator tries to re-balance power in favour of the weaker party, the stronger party may object. The question that then poses itself is: how can the mediator redistribute power and still remain neutral? It has been argued that this issue can be dealt with by applying non-violent mechanisms (without resorting to violence).[36]

A good example is the Gandhian[37] tactic of "speaking truth to power,"[38] influencing and persuading the power-holders,[39] furthering the tactics of mobilizing popular movements, increasing solidarity, making demonstrations of resolve and establishing a demand for change.[40] Raising awareness of the conflict among those who are external or internal supporters of the top-dog may start to weaken the regime (as it did, for example, in the case of the opponents of apartheid in South Africa).[41]

Another area that may lead to conflict in a cross cultural setting, such as the Niger Delta, is that of *Individualism* versus *Collectivism*. The focus on the individual versus the collective is another "great divide" in the Niger Delta, which hosts investors from world cultures. This fact can be both a source of friction and also an opportunity to come to an agreement, since the parties have different interests. The Niger Deltas (Collectivists) act predominantly as members of their group or organization, and emphasize obligations to the group. They take responsibility for fellow

[36] Using the Gandhian process.

[37] Pyarelal, Mahatma Gandhi, Vol 1, The Early phase: Navajivan Publishing House.

[38] http://dspace.vidyanidhi.org.in:8080/dspace/bitstream/2009/1345/11/UOM-1996-169-10 Accessed on 10.6.11

[39] The Nigerian policy makers and multinational oil companies.

[40] Ibid Etekpe, "The history of the Niger Delta resistance movement is fraught with peaceful demonstration which received a violence response", Boro. Isaac. A (1982). *The Twelve Day Revolution, Benin City* Indoho Umeh publishers.

[41] Graybill, L.., (1998). "South Africa's Truth and Reconciliation Commission: ethical and theological perspectives." *Ethics and International Affairs*, 12, 43-62.

members of their group.[42] Collectivists seek mediators who are already "insiders."

Further, in collectivist cultures there is more of a focus on the ongoing relationships of the parties than on the tasks at hand or the issues being negotiated. In this sense, it may be impossible to "separate the people from the problem." The people and their relationships are intertwined with the problem and may even *be* the problem.

In contrast, in the (individualist) culture of the Multinational oil companies, there may be a focus on individual achievement and interpersonal relationship.[43] This may be the measure of the identity of a culture.[44] Their central value is "respect my freedom."[45] Individualist cultures have a "task focus" when they want to get down to business quickly. The interests of the individual prevail over those of the group. Individualistic cultures value self-sufficiency, personal time, freedom, challenge, as well as extrinsic motivators such as material rewards, honesty, "talking things out," privacy, and individual rights.[46] Individualists seek neutral and impartial mediators: the aim of "separating the people from the problem" arises within the perspective of individualism.[47]

Remedial Measures

Cultural fluency[48] is the only key to unlocking the hidden complexities of culture in developing a viable model for the Niger Delta. Generalizations about how people from a specific culture may think or act may lead to rigid notions about a group's cultural patterns, which may result in

---

[42] Geert Hofstede, Homepage, www.geert-hofstede.com.
[43] Geert Hofstede, Culture Dimensions, http://www.geert-hofstede.com.
[44] EXPLORING CULTURE, *supra* note, at 35–36.
[45] Ibid, Geert.
[46] Aaron Marcus, Cultural Dimensions and Global Web User-Interface Design: What? So What? Now What?
Available at http://wwmr.org/ip-marcom/hofstede-ad.htm
[47] Catherine H. Tinsley, Jenifer J. Curhan and Ro Sung Kwak, (1999), "Adopting a Dual Lens Approach for Examining the Dilemma of Differences," in *International Business Negotiations*, 4 INT'L NEGOT 5(7).
[48] *Cultural fluency* means familiarity with cultures: their natures, how they work, and ways they intertwine with our relationships in times of conflict and harmony. Cultural fluency means awareness of several dimensions of culture, including Communication, ways of naming, framing, and taming conflict, approaches to meaning making, identities and roles.

inaccurate stereotypes, gross injustice to the group and inaccurate, and (possibly disastrous) assumptions or actions.

In addition to cultural fluency, it has been argued that the following measures will manage the interplay of cross culturalism in the Niger Delta conflict:

1. Learning the cultural stereotypes about the culturally different parties to the mediation
2. Investigating the actual people involved, as well as the problem, before jumping to conclusions or hasty generalizations

In other words, be flexible: keep an open mind, and understand that the parties may well act differently than the stereotypes, but that the stereotypes may be useful to bear in mind during the mediation process.

Conclusion

In conclusion, the relevance of cross culturalism in mediation, as proposed by the researchers, is premised on the fact that understanding cultural differences is crucial to the development of an approach to cross- cultural mediation. The fact that culture is key in designing any conflict-management model, including mediation, cannot be overemphasized, as research into cultural differences in mediation has shown.[49]

There is a Chinese marital proverb, which translates as "same bed, different dreams." This "same bed" may mean, in the context of this chapter, the same region (Niger Delta), but different dreams.

The Niger Delta region is a hub for investors, where local people and expatriates from different cultures must interact, produce and innovate together. Aligning these dreams may be difficult, but it is not impossible.

---

[49] Julia Ann Gold, ADR Through A Cultural Lens: How Cultural Values Shape Our Disputing Processes, 2 J. DISP. RESOL. 289 (2005); Julie Barker, International Mediation—A Better Alternative for the Resolution of Commercial Disputes: Guidelines for a U.S. Negotiator Involved in an International Commercial Mediation with Mexicans, 19 LOY. L.A. INT'L & COMP. L. REV. 1, 52 (1996); Daniel Q. Posin, Mediating International Business Disputes, 9 FORDHAM J. CORP. & FIN. L. 449 (2004); Paul B. Pedersen & Fred E. Jandt, Culturally Contextual Models for Creative Conflict Management, in CONSTRUCTIVE CONFLICT MANAGEMENT (1996). See also Walter A. Wright, Cultural Issues in Mediation: Individualist and Collectivist Paradigms,
http:// www.mediate.com/articles/wright.cfm (last visited Mar. 11, 2006.

Ray Block, et al.,[50] asserted that mediation can resolve conflicts more effectively when it enhances shared, if initially less salient, aspects of the disputants' identities.[51] In other words, when the disputants possess a shared identity aspect, mediation can enhance its salience, particularly when the mediator shares the same identity.[52] The identity mentioned here does not relate to the needs of the parties, nor does it relate to ethnic affiliation: rather, it relates to the perceived values or histories that bind all the parties together.[53] That is, it looks towards a point of commonality. The point of commonality in the Niger Delta context is the oil in the region. The key here is for parties[54] to engage, as joint problem solvers, seeking to resolve the dispute, and to try and "enlarge the pie" rather than to act as adversaries and thereby aggravate the situation.

In addition, the identification of common ground will afford parties a deeper understanding of the fluidity of conflict, will provide insight into how mutually exclusive identities develop, and will provide a mechanism for an understanding of how history can be re-interpreted to suit the demands of developing identities.

The Beagle Conflict of 1978 [55] offers an example of a third party resolving a conflict by appealing to an aspect of the claimants' identity that, though seemingly unimportant to the conflict itself, became a point of common interest.[56] It was argued that Pope John Paul II appealed to the Christian sensibilities of the claimants.[57] Garrett (1986)[58] further notes that

---

[50] Ray Block Jr.., Paul R. Hensel and David A. Siegel, "The Impact of Social Identity on Third-Party Mediation":
http://www.paulhensel.org/Research/BHS09.pdf accessed on 20/5/11.

[51] Ibid.

[52] Ibid.

[53] Ibid.

[54] The Nigerian Government, Niger Delta host communities, and multinational oil companies operating in the Niger Delta region of Nigeria.

[55] United Nations. (1977). "Dispute between Argentina and Chile concerning the Beagle Channel." Reports of International Arbitral Awards (XXI): 53-264.

[56] Ibid.

[57] The Papal mediation in the Beagle conflict followed the failure of negotiations between Chile and Argentina when, on 22 December, 1978, the Argentinean Junta started Operation Soberanía to invade Cape Horn and the islands awarded to Chile by the Beagle Channel Arbitration Soon after the event, Pope John Paul II offered to mediate and sent his personal envoy Cardinal Antonio Samoré to Buenos Aires, Argentina. In acceptance of the authority of the Pope over the overwhelmingly Catholic Argentine population, the military operation was called off and the mediation accepted. On 9 January 1979, Chile and Argentina signed the Act of

the Pope knew that this shared denominational identity, if made salient in the context of the negotiations, could overshadow Chile and Argentina's secular grievances and play an important role in resolving the Beagle Channel conflict.

Finally, we can glean from the foregoing that cross culturalism will not hamper the proposed model for either the diverse communities of the Niger Delta or the multinational companies. They can all live and interact with each other through recognition, respect and appreciation of the diverse cultures and belief systems that exist amongst them all. This notion was well expressed by Marsden, when he said: "Balance is based on the understanding that all forms of life and all peoples are intrinsically complementary, and will flourish if the domain of each is perceived and respected".[59]

Fritz Scharpf[60] argues that "[t]he criterion is mutual compatibility, and the characteristic outcome is not the displacement of one jurisdiction by the other, but the obligation of both to choose mutually acceptable means when performing the proper functions of government at each level".[61]

References

Aaron Marcus, "Cultural Dimensions and Global Web User-Interface Design: What? So What? Now What?" Available at http://wwmr.org/ip-marcom/hofstede-ad.htm.

Avruch, K.; & Black, P. (1991). "The culture question and conflict resolution." *Peace & Change*, 16(1), 22-45.

Baba K., (1996). "Development of construction management based on regional culture," in Langford DA, Retik A, editors, *The organization and management of construction: Shaping theory and practice,* Vol.1. London: E &FN Spon.

Bottoms, A. E., (2003). "Some sociological reflections on restorative justice", In von Hirsch, A., Roberts, J., Bottoms, A.E., Roach, K. and

Montevideo, formally requesting mediation from the Vatican and renouncing the use of force. (Catholicism is the national religion of both nations).

[58] Garrett, James L. (1985). "The Beagle Conflict: Confrontation and Negotiation in the Southern Cone." *Journal of Inter-American Studies and World Affairs.* 27(3): 81-109.

[59] Marsden, as cited in Oman (2004:83).

[60] Scharpf, "Community and autonomy: multi-level policy-making in the European Union," 1 *Journal of European Public Policy* 219, 225 (1994).

[61] Ibid.

Schiff, M (eds.) *Restorative Justice and Criminal justice: Competing or Reconcilable Paradigms?* Oxford: Hart, pp. 79-113.

Dodd, Carley H., *Dynamics of Intercultural Communication 36* (3d ed. 1991).

Darling J.R, & Fogliasso C.E., (1999). "Conflict management across cultural boundaries: a case analysis from a multinational bank," *European Business*, Rev. 99 (6): 383-392.

Duryea, M. L., (1993). Conflict and culture: Research in five communities in Vancouver, British Columbia. Victoria, BC: UVic Institute for Dispute Resolution.

Garrett, James L. 1985. "The Beagle Conflict: Confrontation and Negotiation in the Southern Cone." *Journal of Inter-American Studies and World Affairs.* 27(3): 81-109.

Geert Hofstede, Culture Dimensions, http://www.geert-hofstede.com.

Gehm, J.R., (1998). "Victim-offender mediation programs: An exploration of practice and theoretical frameworks", *Western Criminology Review*, vol.1, pp.1-36.

Hamden-Turner, (1981). "Maps of the Mind," Andre Laurent, *The Cultural Diversity of Western Conceptions of Management*, 13 International Studies of Management and Organization, 75 (1983); Shalom H Schwartz & AnatBardi, *Value Hierarchies across Cultures: Taking a Similarities Perspective*, 32 J. of cross-cultural psychol. 268 (2001).

Gold, Julia Ann, ADR Through A Cultural Lens: How Cultural Values Shape Our Disputing Processes, 2 J. DISP. RESOL. 289 (2005); Julie Barker: International Mediation—a Better Alternative for the Resolution of Commercial Disputes: Guidelines for a U.S. Negotiator Involved in an International Commercial Mediation with Mexicans, 19 LOY. L.A. INT'L & COMP. L. REV. 1, 52 (1996); Daniel Q. Posin: Mediating International Business Disputes, 9 FORDHAM J. CORP. & FIN. L. 449 (2004); Paul B. Pedersen & Fred E. Jandt: Culturally Contextual Models for Creative Conflict Management, in *Constructive Conflict Management* (1996). See also Walter A. Wright: Cultural Issues in Mediation: Individualist and Collectivist Paradigms, http://www.mediate.com/articles/wright.cfm (last visited Mar. 11, 2006.

Khaminwa, A.., *Peacebuilding and Co-existence in Nigeria*, in The Afro-barometer- *Violent Social Conflict resolution in Nigeria*, Briefing Paper No.2, August 2002.

LeBaron (1997). "Mediation, conflict resolution and multicultural reality: Culturally competent practice." In E. Kruk (Ed.), *Mediation and conflict resolution in social work and the human services*. Chicago: Nelson Hall.

LeBaron, Michelle & Bruce Grundison, 1993. *Conflict and Culture: Research in Five Communities in British Columbia, Canada*. Victoria, British Columbia: University of Victoria Institute for Dispute Resolution.

LeBaron, Michelle, "Culture and Conflict." *Beyond Intractability*. Eds. Guy Burgess and Heidi Burgess. Conflict Research Consortium, University of Colorado, Boulder. Posted: July 2003 <http://www.beyondintractability.org/essay/culture_conflict/

Lederach, J. P., (1986) Mediation in North America: An examination of the profession's cultural premises. Unpublished Comprehensive Examination Paper. University of Colorado, Denver.

Malin, Aquilon, "Cultural Dimensions in Logistics Management: A Case Study from the European Automotive Industry." http://www.emeraldinsight.com/Insight/ViewContentServlet?

Marsden, as cited in Oman, 2004:83.

Marshall, T, F., (1999) *Restorative Justice: An Overview*, London: Home Office Research and Statistics Directorate.

Omale, D.J.O., (2006) "Justice in History: An Examination of the African Restorative Traditions and the Emerging Restorative Justice Paradigm," *African Journal of Criminology and Criminal Justice,* vol.2 (2), pp. 30-60. Paul Pedersen, Lecture to John Barkai's class (Feb. 15, 2006).

Ray Block Jr., Paul R. Hensel and David A. Siegel, "The Impact of Social Identity on Third-Party Mediation" at: http://www.paulhensel.org/Research/BHS09.pdf. Accessed on 20/05/11

Reports of International Arbitral Awards (XXI): 53-264.

Scharpf, "Community and autonomy: multi-level policy-making in the European Union," 1 *Journal of European Public Policy* 219, 225 (1994).

Smith, D., (1995). *Criminology for Social Work*, Basingstoke: Macmillan.

Suen H, Cheung S.O.; Mondejar R. (2007), "Managing ethical behaviour in construction organization in Asia: How do the teaching of Confucianism, Taoism and Buddhism and Globalization influence ethics management?" Int. J. Project Manage. 25(3): 257-265.

Tinsley, Catherine H. Jenifer J. Curhan & Ro Sung Kwak, "Adopting a Dual Lens Approach for Examining the Dilemma of Differences," in *International Business Negotiations,* 4 INT'L NEGOT. 5, 7 (1999).

United Nations. (1977). "Dispute between Argentina and Chile concerning the Beagle Channel."

Zhou, YQ, Lu L and iang B., (2005). "Study on staff management practice of multinational company," *Management. Decisions,* 43(4): 516-522.

CHAPTER FIVE

ONLINE DISPUTE RESOLUTION IN AFRICA: PRESENT REALITIES AND THE WAY FORWARD

IJEOMA ONONOGBU

Introduction

Traditionally, disputes were solved through litigation, and because of its popularity, people found it a lot easier to identify than any alternatives. With time, the situation has begun to change, and as a result people have started seeking inexpensive, faster and more economical means of resolving their disputes. The dissatisfaction felt by litigants in the use of litigation gave birth to the emergence of ADR. This concept of the resolution of disputes has been embraced by litigants because of its obvious advantages, which include its speedy nature, its cost, and the privacy its accords to the parties involved. There is no doubt that Alternative Dispute Resolution (ADR) has come to stay. However, as ADR has grown in strength and popularity, litigation has suffered a couple of setbacks, from ADR being preferred in certain cases to lawyers training as ADR experts, as well as laymen training professionally in mediation, which is an important aspect of ADR. The emergence of ADR and its methods (such as arbitration, mediation, negotiation, conciliation, and various hybrid forms) has resulted in a great many people opting for ADR as a form of dispute resolution rather than litigation.

Interestingly, as ADR has grown, so has the concept of Online Dispute Resolution (ODR). It goes without saying that online dispute resolution is a rather recent concept, and is a revolutionary concept in Africa. The commonly used forms of ADR in Africa are mediation and arbitration. The type of mechanism used will largely depend on the type of dispute in question. International disputes are mostly settled by litigation and sometimes by arbitration, which is a form of ADR, although it is notable that arbitration practitioners are keen to stress its exclusivity, thereby distinguishing arbitration from other forms of ADR.[1] The attraction of alternative dispute resolution as opposed to litigation as a form of resolving commercial disputes is mostly due to its speed, its flexibility and its privacy. A significant number of disputants will state their admiration for alternative dispute resolution (ADR) mechanisms without reservations, because of their ability to protect disputants from prying eyes, which is not possible in litigation. However, another avenue of resolving disputes through online dispute resolution (ODR) is also guaranteed.[2]

I. The State of Online Dispute Resolution (ODR) in the Resolution of Disputes

Marshall McLuhan[3] made an emphatic statement concerning ODR, when he said that "when a new technology comes into a social milieu it cannot cease to permeate that milieu until every institution is saturated."[4] What McLuhan did not envisage was how fast the effect of electronic age would be on the resolution of disputes.[5] Although he predicted the effect of the electronic age on every aspect of the human race, and importantly on the resolution of disputes, he cautioned and raised the issue of culture.[6] Insofar as technological advancement alone cannot change people's way of life instantly,[7] other factors, such as the willingness of the people to embrace change, are fundamental for the effect of change to be seen.[8] There is no

---

[1] Anthony Connerty, Manual of International Dispute Resolution, Commonwealth Secretariat 2006, p. 13.

[2] Ethan Katsh & Janet Rifkin, *Online Dispute Resolution: Resolving Conflicts in Cyberspace* Jossey-Bass, 2001, p. 4-5.

[3] Marshall McLuhan (July 21 1911 to December 31 1980): A Philosopher, Scholar and Professor of English literature. He is widely regarded as the father of the electronic age. His views on media are regarded as the bedrock of some electronic theories today. Marshall McLuhan is known for his expressions notably, "the medium is the message," "global village" and the prediction of the term "World Wide Web."

[4] Marshall McLuhan, *Understanding Media,* McGraw- Hill New York 1964, p. 161.

[5] Ethan Katsh & Janet Rifkin, *Online Dispute Resolution: Resolving Conflicts in Cyberspace*'. Jossey- Bass, 2001, p. 21.

[6] Ibid.

[7] Ethan Katsh & Janet Rifkin, *Online Dispute Resolution: Resolving Conflicts in Cyberspace*, Jossey, Bass, 2001, p. 26.

[8] Faye Fangfei Wang, *Online Dispute Resolution; Technology, management and legal practice from an international perspective,* Chandos Publishing 2009, p. 67.

mystery in the growth of the electronic age; even the forces of culture have been observed to have been pulled down by that growth, and in some circumstances relegated to the background.[9] Although technology is often used to create new tools, which in turn create new environments in which the tools can be used effectively, the success of technology in the electronic age has been due to the willingness of people to accept it, regardless of their old ways.[10] The resolution of disputes has also undergone a transformation, through ODR. It is fair to say that ADR moved matters away from the courts, and ODR expressly moved matters further away from the courts. This, for sure, makes ODR less mysterious and highly dependable for disputants, who over the years have seen litigation as burdensome. On the other hand, ADR was seen as too stressful and jurisdiction-based, just like litigation itself. With all the challenges facing litigation and the conventional methods of ADR, such as jurisdiction, privacy became one of the factors that drew disputants towards ADR. Inasmuch as ADR mechanisms provide for privacy, they still function under strict guidelines and the due processes of the law.[11] The Freedom of Information Act 2000 provides for access and routes to information and assistance, within the reasonable degree expected of the authority.[12]This provision extends to all persons seeking information that would assist in their dispute, irrespective of its specific nature. Therefore, a person seeking information that would enable him/her to resolve a dispute through ADR is more or less protected under the law, and to a large extent assured that the matter will be dealt with in private.[13] Internationally, the well-established freedom of information legislation (FOI) is one which many countries—including common law countries—have adopted.[14] This legislation makes freedom of information of paramount importance, and guarantees access to data as well as information held by the State.[15] It follows that people seeking information that would enable them to resolve their dispute through ADR mechanisms,

[9] Ethan Katsh & Janet Rifkin, *Online Dispute Resolution: Resolving Conflicts in Cyberspace*, Jossey- Bass 2001, p.26.
[10] Ibid.
[11] Lee Bygrave & Jon Bing, *Internet Governance: Infrastructure and institutions*, Oxford University Press 2009, p. 92.
[12] Michael Superstone Q.C. & Timothy Pitt-Payne, The Freedom of Information Act 2000 Section 16: Butterworths LexisNexis 2001, p.87.
[13] Michael Superstone Q.C. & Timothy Pitt-Payne, The Freedom of Information Act 2000 Section 16: Butterworths LexisNexis 2001, p. 87.
[14] Ibid, p 3.
[15] Ibid, p 87.

by the use of online dispute resolution processes, are entitled to such information where and when it is needed.[16]This may pose a challenge in Africa, where most governments have yet to enact such legislation.

However, countries such as South Africa in 2000, Kenya in 2008, and, most recently, Nigeria, which enacted a Freedom of Information Law in June 2011, have all shown some transparency in the use and dispensation of information. Therefore, it would be a grave mistake, if not contradictory in substance, to claim that the enactments of governments—or even global institutions and organizations—are transformed into tools for the use of only a few.[17]Thankfully, these enactments are for the growth and development of the larger population, because it is the people make up the community.[18] Not only is the global economy failing the least developed and worst governed states, but, evidently, they are abjectly neglecting to protect their own people.[19] Although there are a number of organizations interested in implementing the enacted legislation, the onus lies with the populace to advocate for laws that would lead to transparency, accessibility and freedom, as seen in the use of online dispute resolution mechanisms (ODR) by eBay.[20]

II. The Emergence and Growth of ODR

Every litigant expects the creative judge to employ all the tools at their disposal to accomplish their desired result. This includes a thorough evaluation of the best method of resolving disputes, proper research into the matter and, most importantly, less expensive forms of resolving the dispute.[21] This is precisely where ADR comes in, because the absence of attributes associated with litigation (such as costliness) has made ADR attractive. As ADR grew in strength, so the emergence and growth of ODR came to be recognized. ODR was born as a result of the shortcomings of conventional methods of ADR, such as arbitration,

---

[16] Ethan Katsh & Janet Rifkin, *Online Dispute Resolution: Resolving Conflicts in Cyberspace,* Jossey-Bass 2001, p. 11.

[17] David Kinley, *Civilising Globalisation Human Rights and the Global Economy,* Cambridge University Press 2009, p. 217.

[18] David Kinley, *Civilising Globalisation Human Rights and the Global Economy,* Cambridge University Press 2009, p. 217.

[19] Ibid.

[20] Ethan Katsh & Janet Rifkin, *Online Dispute Resolution: Resolving Conflicts in Cyberspace,* Jossey-Bass 2001, Page 97-98.

[21] Ijeoma Ononogbu, "The growth and impact of ADR and the vanishing court trials," QMUL 2011.

mediation, conciliation and negotiation, which can be traced to the 1970s, when ADR was formally established at the Pound Conference.[22] However, some would argue that ADR has always existed, and this assertion does have some legitimacy. Although ADR did exist prior to the Pound Conference, its nature was not fully established until the end of that Conference, when delegates were able to come up with guidelines which, in effect, put many ideas into perspective and the concept of ADR as we know it today was formed. ADR had operated mostly within the family structure, especially amongst children when there was a disagreement, and parents sought to negotiate, and still more so when couples had misunderstanding and relatives stepped in to seek a compromise; these are exemplary ways in which ADR was practiced prior to the Pound Conference and in which it is still practiced today,[23] notably in African communities. ADR addresses some of the methods of resolving disputes which are slightly removed from traditional legal and administrative forums.[24] These methods, which include various types of arbitration and mediation, have grown stronger and more popular in recent years, simply because companies and courts have become exceedingly frustrated about the cost, time, and emotional torture required in order to resolve disputes through normal legal avenues.

The failings and inaccessibility of ADR in certain situations, such as in e-commerce, resulted in the birth of Online Dispute Resolution (ODR), which is a form of dispute resolution that uses technology to facilitate the resolution of disputes between parties.[25] The emergence of ODR was the result of the failures and inadequacies of litigation and alternative dispute resolution.[26] For many disputants, ODR seems favourable because of the challenges encountered in the conventional methods of ADR, such as geographic distance, time and scheduling concerns, or other obstacles normally envisaged as arising in face-to-face meetings.[27] Quite a

---

[22] Simon Roberts and Michael Palmer, *Dispute processes: ADR and the primary forms of decision making,* Cambridge University Press 2005, p. 55.
[23] Ibid.
[24] Dennis Sandole, Hugo van Der Merwe Scimecca, `*Conflict Resolution Theory and Practice Integration and Application,* New York, Manchester University Press 1993, p. 211.
[25] Ethan katsh & Janet Rifkin, '*Online Dispute Resolution: Resolving Conflicts in Cyberspace*'. Jossey-Bass 2001 p. 29.
[26] Ibid.
[27] Ethan Katsh & Janet Rifkin, *Online Dispute Resolution: Resolving Conflicts in Cyberspace.* Jossey- Bass, (2001), p. 29.

significant number of ADR practitioners and programs are moving part of their dispute resolution process online.[28]

III. Current Safeguards Attributed to the Success of Alternative Dispute Resolution

Every State requires a justice system in which aggrieved disputants can seek reparations through the legal enforcement of their rights.[29] Traditionally, litigation served this purpose, mostly because the natural inclination of parties to settle disputes arose only under compulsion, even where dialogue or mutual agreement would have served them adequately.[30] The concept of ADR seemed far-fetched until the 1970s and the Pound Conference, which formally introduced ADR and made the concept legitimate for legal practitioners as well as litigants.[31] The historical bias towards litigation is now giving way to consensual processes, principally ADR as the first recourse in the settlement of these disputes and, to ODR more recently. The legal profession has always placed paramount importance upon the resolution of disputes, whether through litigation or through alternative means in the form of ADR. What matters is not only that justice must be done, but that it must visibly be seen to be done. The resolution of disputes by means of litigation was, for centuries, the disputants' sole option in the due court process, until the emergence of ADR. The emergence of ADR has been attributed to the dissatisfaction experienced by a significant percentage of disputants over the years with court processes.[32] This dissatisfaction stems from the cost to society of the duration of process; this has motivated the growth and use of ADR, and is now motivating the emergence of ODR in resolving international business disputes.[33] Our capacity as human beings to acquire, use and store

---

[28] Susan Summer Raines and Melissa Conley Tyler, "From eBay to Eternity: Advances in Online Dispute Resolution," (2006) Melbourne Law School: http://ssrn.com/abstract 955968. Accessed on 31.05.2011

[29] Ijeoma Ononogbu, "The growth and impact of ADR and the vanishing court trials", QMUL, 2011

[30] Simon Roberts & Michael Palmer, *Dispute processes: ADR and the primary forms of decision making,* 'Cambridge University Press (2002), p. 83.

[31] Lee Bygrave and Jon Bing, *Internet Governance: Infrastructure and institutions.* Oxford University Press (2009), p. 35.

[32] Simon Roberts & Michael Palmer, *Dispute processes: ADR and the primary forms of decision making.* Cambridge University Press (2005), p. 32.

[33] Ibid.

information is essential for our survival:[34] nothing is certain, but on a practical level, through the use of information disasters can be avoided, accidents prevented, and sustenance provided.[35]

IV. The Role of Africa in Implementing ODR

Online dispute resolution (ODR) is an excellent way of resolving disputes in Africa, with its relatively cheap cost, its speed, and most importantly, the privacy it accords to disputants. There are a number of international organisations concerned with commercial dispute resolution in Africa. However, the alternative dispute resolution service in West Africa provides services for countries within the region, which are developing and which, with time, will reach their full potential.[36] The growth of public and private sector power in Africa is increasing and becoming more clearly defined, as seen in areas such as the media. In Ghana, The National Media Commission (Complaints Settlement Procedure) Regulations, 1994 states, under the initiation of investigation by the Settlement Committee:

> Without prejudice to the other provisions of these Regulations, the Commission may where it considers it necessary for the discharge of its functions under the Act, refer to the Settlement Committee for formal investigation any publication, act or omission of any journalist, newspaper proprietor, publisher or any person in respect of any publication in the media and the relevant provisions of these Regulations shall apply to the investigation.[37]

The existence of such legislation increases the active participation by individuals and governmental bodies in what happens within society. One may attribute such advancement of transparency and accountability to globalization, and to an increase in the awareness of Africans. However, when government trust in the people is limited, such a situation gives rise to absolutism, which affects the relationship between the state and society, as well as within the government itself, after which it may reach a point

---

[34] Lee Bygrave & Jon Bing, *Internet Governance: Infrastructure and institutions.* Oxford University Press (2009), p. 35.

[35] Patrick Birkinshaw, *Freedom of Information: The Law, the Practice and the Idea.* Cambridge University Press (2010), p.18.

[36] Lee Bygrave & Jon Bing, *Internet Governance: Infrastructure and institutions,* Oxford University Press (2009), p. 36.

[37] Akoto Awpaw, "Legislation on Media, Speech and Expression in Ghana." Media Foundation for West Africa Accra, (2004), p. 1128.

that the community is no longer able to hold itself together.[38] Until recently, democracy has not been properly practiced in most African states, but today the reverse is the case, with most countries in Africa striving to be as democratic as possible; this has been a long road, but with the respect for rule of law and the independence of the Judiciary now established in most African states, undemocratic states could soon be a thing of the past.[39] Asserting this notion in his address in a conference session as the Chief Justice of Nigeria, the late Sir Adetokunbo Ademola categorically stated:

> It has been said that the rule of law is mainly an Anglo-American institution; that the concept of 'government under law' and such phrases as the 'supremacy of law' and 'the rule of law' are all purely Western inventions. The communist analysis maintained that everything is legal which is good for the State and the problem of adjusting the legitimate claims of the individual and his society has no place. The African, it was suggested, might find a third legal system which is neither 'the rule of law' nor the 'socialist legality' propounded by the Communist. But the rule of law is not a Western idea, nor is it linked up with any economic or social system. As soon as you accept that Man is governed by law and not by whims of men, it is the rule of law. It may be under different forms from country to country, but it is based on principles; it is not an abstract notion.[40]

Therefore, since man is governed by law, it is no surprise that with the evolution of the Internet, which is a global network of connections, there has been an increase in international contacts and contracts for consumers and businesses alike: thus, regulation by means of cyberspace law is not only important but essential.[41] The area of cyberspace disputes needs some form of ADR, as opposed to litigation.[42] Due to its obvious advantages—which include its voluntary nature, tailored to the dispute and to the disputants' needs, and its delocalization, which means the matter is taken away from the courts—it appears that cyberspace law is growing from

---

[38] Patrick Birkinshaw, *Freedom of Information: The Law, the Practice and the Ideal.* Cambridge University Press (2010), p. 23.

[39] T.O. Elias, "*Law* and Social Change in Nigeria"' Evans Brothers Limited Nigeria (1972), p.197-199.

[40] African Conference on the Rule of Law Lagos Nigeria (1961), p. 86.

[41] Commonwealth Secretariat. *"Law in Cyber space,"* Publications Unit Commonwealth Secretariat, October 2001, page 5.

[42] Commonwealth Secretariat. "*Law in Cyber space*," Publications Unit Commonwealth Secretariat, October 2001, page 25.

strength to strength.[43] Currently, cyberspace law, through which ODR gets its legitimacy, is usually used in the resolution of small claims disputes—which are, coincidently, the hallmark of African Society.[44] In South Africa, the use of the court is highly constrained by the rules issued under Section 25 of the Small Claims Court Act.[45] Fundamental to its role is the mandate on the court to ensure justice is made to be done, on the reasoning that the ideal should be sought, in order to be achieved. [46] The issue of jurisdiction in Africa continually crops up in litigation, as seen in Chapter 111 of the Small Claims Courts Act No 61 of 1984, South African Law, which states:

> **Area of Jurisdiction:** The area of jurisdiction of a court shall be the district for which it was established.[47]To give credit to the emergence of ODR and its potential growth and success in Africa, to the exponents of ADR or even the Pound Conference would be mistaken; rather the growth of ODR is envisaged in the well-established mechanism in most African systems. The African Union (AU) is not preoccupied with issues that confronted the Organisation of African Unity (OAU) such as the forces of colonialism, de-colonization and apartheid.[48]Instead different issues confront the (AU) such as interstate and intrastate conflict, HIV/AIDS, communicable diseases, poverty, illiteracy, systematic gender discrimination, general underdevelopment and the new monster globalization with its various multifarious impacts.[49]

As such, the AU seeks, above all, to achieve greater unity between African States and peoples, to accelerate socio-political and economic integration, and to encourage international cooperation and strict

---

[43] Commonwealth Secretariat. Law in Cyber space. Publications Unit Commonwealth Secretariat October 2001, page 25.

[44] Lee Bygrave & Jon Bing, *Internet Governance: Infrastructure and institutions,* Oxford University Press (2009) p. 8.

[45] IM Bredenkamp, *"The small claims court", Butterworth* Durban (1986), p. 78.

[46] Ibid.

[47] Section 12: "the area of jurisdiction of the Small Claims Court will be similar to that of the Magistrate's Court in which district it is situated. The question of jurisdiction becomes important when jurisdiction is claimed in terms of section 14(1) (d); in other words when the plaintiff alleges in his summons that the cause of action arose wholly within that area."

[48] Jeremy Levitt, *Africa; Selected Documents on Constitutive, Conflict and Security, Humanitarian, and Judicial Issues,* Transnational Publishers (2003), p. 36.

[49] Ibid.

conformity to the international rule of law.[50] This will invariably promote peace, security, stability, democratization and good governance, as well as protecting human rights and creating a good environment for sustainable development at all levels—such as interstate and regional economic integration,—full involvement in the global economy and, most importantly in today's world,[51] will promote research in all fields, particularly in science and technology for both men and women, regardless of social status.[52] With the way Africa is moving in general, as in Kenya for example, the importance of electable government has become a necessity which has given rise to accountability.[53] With the concept of democracy comes elections, and with elected people comes the need make the voices of the people heard, as well as the need for people to obey and respect the laws of the state. Quite simply, the growth of governmental power necessitates greater security against abuse.[54]

V. Interface between Legal Expert/ADR Practitioner and the Internet

Searching for information in legal databases is time-consuming, and there are lots of potential obstacles to be encountered in doing so. Even though there are challenges in legal research, lawyers (as well as ADR practitioners) have found the Internet to be a valuable tool in the search for answers and the proper handling of legal matters.[55] The Internet not only serves as a platform for information dispensation, it also serves as a medium for communication: this applies both to communication between parties, and to communication from one party to another. For the ADR practitioner, communication as a source of legal information is evaluated based on

---

[50] Ibid.

[51] Levitt, Jeremy, *Africa; Selected Documents on Constitutive, Conflict and Security, Humanitarian, and Judicial Issues,* Transnational Publishers (2003), p. 36.

[52] Levitt, Jeremy, *Africa; Selected Documents on Constitutive, Conflict and Security, Humanitarian, and Judicial Issues,* Transnational Publishers (2003) p. 36.

[53] Kuloba, Richard, *Judicial hints on Civil Procedure,* Law Africa Kenya (1984), p. 1-6.

[54] Birkinshaw, Patrick, *Freedom of Information: The Law, the Practice and the Ideal,* Cambridge University Press (2010), p. 23.

[55] Matthijssen, Luuk, "Interfacing between lawyers and Computers; An Architecture for Knowledge-based Interfaces to Legal Databases," Kluwer Law International (1999), p. 3.

legislation, judicial decisions and literature.[56] Legal experts' interest in ODR grew mainly because of the constant use of the Internet as a platform to obtain and access legal information. Society is constantly evolving, and human beings are sensitive to an environment where conflicts frequently occur; thus, legal experts are constantly exploring options for preventing conflicts and, where possible, to deal with existing disputes speedily, economically, and amicably. Cyberspace has become the new frontier, an active place where the number of transactions can only grow.[57]

Whether it is a human mediator or an e-mediator, intelligent assistance concerning the interaction between the recipient and the provider is fundamental. In ODR, the relevant sequence would be between the user and the database.[58] Naturally, with the effectiveness and efficiency of the use of ODR, certain challenges have been addressed: these include anonymity, the lack of face-to face interaction and the interception of electronic communications; these factors have caused ODR enthusiasts to look for ways of resolving these problems, in order to give ODR the legitimacy it deserves.[59]

VI. Challenges Facing Online Dispute Resolution as a Form of Alternative Dispute Resolution

Skeptics have raised concerns about data protection and access to information in the use of online dispute resolution (ODR) mechanism. These are well-founded reservation, although it has to be remembered that data protection involves restrictions on the use of personal data and access by the person who is the subject of the data, and supervision by an

[56] The legal information sources generally correspond to the sources of law stated in legal textbooks, statute law, judicial decisions and customs. Customs form an integral source of law in Africa that is too large and complex to be fully documented. Customs are considered under a residual category as a source of legal information. Lastly, the legal literature provides commentaries and explanations to these sources of law.

[57] Ethan Katsh and Janet Rifkin, *Online Dispute Resolution; Resolving Conflicts in Cyberspace,* Jossey-Bass 2001, p. 3.

[58] Matthijssen, Luuk, "Interfacing between lawyers and Computers; An Architecture for Knowledge-based Interfaces to Legal Databases," Kluwer Law International (1999), p. 52.

[59] Edward Cavazos & Gavino Morin, Cyberspace *and the Law; Your Rights and Duties in the Online World,* MIT Press (1995), p. 27.

independent adviser.[60] As with all perceived challenges facing the Internet, the fact cannot be disregarded. The Internet is a determinant in many spheres of our lives:

> There's no turning back. Once a novelty, the Internet is now transforming how people live, think, talk, and love; how we go to school, make money, see the doctor, and elect presidents. This isn't just about the future—it's about the here and now.'[61]

Different forms of online communication offer various ways of communicating via the world-wide web. The initial illusion that the Internet was "no-man's land" has now been transformed, arguably into a view that "it's every man's land."[62] However, the borderless nature of the Internet provides more interactions and transactions involving parties located in different jurisdictions, thereby intensifying international transactions and contacts at all levels.[63] The initial stakeholders in the running of the world were those with the highest number of weapons, or the richest, or those who owned the energy sources: this does not apply anymore—the tide has turned, and the greatest as well as the most powerful party is the one who has the information. In some cases, this could be classified information. A clear example is the WikiLeaks founder Julian Assange, who actually released classified information and sought to bring down governments and establishments. His action raised awareness, and people became interested in both the benefits and the demerits of the Internet. It became obvious that the Internet could be used for either good or bad. The recent notion is that the Internet is every man's land, giving every individual the same rights and privileges as any other. Unfortunately, people in developing countries are unable to lay claim to this notion in its entirety, because of their lack of financial strength. The challenges that may be encountered in the success of ODR include cyber-literacy, which requires gaining Internet consciousness, and concerns the issue of literacy in an electronic age. According to Kathleen Turner, literacy is about

---

[60] Birkinshaw, Patrick, *Government and Information: The Law relating to Access, Disclosure and their Regulation*, Tottel Publishing (2005), p. 324.
[61] Newsweek, 20th September, 1999, p. 39.
[62] Dan Jerker & B Svantesson, "Private International Law and the Internet", Kluwer Law International (2007), p. 2.
[63] Julia Hornle, *Cross-border Internet Dispute Resolution,* Cambridge University Press (2009), p.21.

higher levels of cognitive ability, as opposed to the earlier notion of the ability to read and write.[64]

VII. The Importance of ODR

The paramount importance of online dispute resolution as a form of resolving disputes lies in the emphasis its procedures place on the appointment and independence of neutrals.[65] The neutrals, who operate in cyber courts—sometimes regarded as virtual courts or even cyber tribunals—on reputation-ranking schemes that invariably build trust and help in the provision of efficient ODR mechanisms, have been tried and tested in countries such as Puerto Rico, Australia, the US and the UK.[66] However, what distinguishes ODR and other forms of dispute resolution, such as litigation and ADR, is the former's absence of jurisdiction. ODR is a simple procedure: it is helpful, convenient, and practical, and does not require the physical presence of the parties involved, thereby making jurisdiction inconsequential.[67] Interestingly, in ODR, parties can be in different countries and still have their dispute resolved amicably. The important issue is that the parties must have agreed to the ODR procedure electronically before the commencement of the procedure.[68] Similarly to the conventional methods of alternative dispute resolution, such as arbitration and mediation, online dispute resolution provides for arbitration and mediation, commonly referred to as e-arbitration and e-mediation. Presently, ODR can be carried out by a human being as the neutral, which is quite attractive to litigants, or through the use of a software database. Some ODR providers have no specific rules for the appointment of their e-mediators and e-arbitrators. The procedure is evolving as a means of dispute resolution, and quite a number of providers have now established guidelines and procedural process, as seen in the use of ODR by eBay. As a result of the swift growth and expansion of the global Internet market known as e-commerce—a term which has been referred to as the

---

[64] Gurak, Laura, *Cyberliteracy; Navigating the Internet with Awareness*, Yale University Press (2001) p. 12.

[65] Gabrielle Kaufmann-Kohler & Thomas Schultz, *Online Dispute Resolution; Challenges for Contemporary Justice*' Kluwer Law International (2004), p. 46.

[66] Wang, Faye Fangfei, Online *Dispute Resolution; Technology, Management and Legal Practice from an International Perspective*' Chandos Publishing (2009) p. 24.

[67] Ibid.

[68] Ibid.

buzzword of the new millennium—defaults and disputes have arisen in website/electronic contracts, with conflicts frequently occurring.

The undisputed fact that the Internet is the fastest growing commercial market in recent times, through the use of EBay, is remarkable.[69] According to Colin Rule of eBay,[70] the use of ODR by eBay accounts for the resolution of over 35 million disputes yearly.[71] It follows that an Internet forum in the form of ODR is imperative to the sustenance of this ever-growing area of dispute resolution.[72] The exemplary means eBay employs in the resolution of disputes cannot be ignored. Its use of e-trust strategy, whereby buyers and sellers feel comfortable doing business, and the parties are comfortable relaying grievances through the complaints procedure (or even the feedback process), is one which makes eBay's ODR process exceptional.[73] The use of ODR in certain fields has created consumer confidence and access to justice in the online business environment. However, in ODR (just as in ADR), jurisdictional challenges are overcome in cross-border disputes, and arguments are avoided between the parties concerning which state court is competent to hear a matter.[74] Moreover, in ODR, as seen in eBay, virtually all disputes concern objective technicalities, and thus the tensions and emotions which may arise in cases requiring strict confidentiality to be resolved (for instance, cases involving sexual harassment or trade secrets) are avoided.[75] The enforcement and acceptance of the outcome of online dispute resolution is

---

[69] Wang, Faye Fangfei, *Online Dispute Resolution; Technology, Management and Legal Practice from an International Perspective,* Chandos Publishing (2009), p. 24.

[70] Colin Rule has been Director Online Dispute Resolution in eBay and PayPal from 2003-2011. He is the CEO of Modria.com, an ODR provider based in Silicon Valley.

[71] Wang, Faye Fangfei, *Online Dispute Resolution; Technology, Management and Legal Practice from an International Perspective,* Chandos Publishing (2009), p. 24.

[72] Yee Fen Lim, *Cyberspace Law; Commentaries and Materials,* Oxford University Press (2002), p. 62.

[73] Wang, Faye Fangfei, *Online Dispute Resolution; Technology, Management and Legal Practice from an International Perspective,* Chandos Publishing (2009), p. 67.

[74] Hornle, Julia, *Cross-Border Internet Dispute Resolution,* Cambridge University Press (2009) p. 88.

[75] Fangfei Wang, Faye, *"Online Dispute Resolution; Technology, Management and Legal Practice from an International Perspective,"* Chandos Publishing (2009) p. 67.

one of the driving forces behind the success of the process. The ease of access to justice that ODR provides makes it a reality.[76]

VIII. Africa Perspective on Online Dispute Resolution (ODR)

A reality is what we make for ourselves; Africa can, and will have to, embrace ODR. According to the African Unity Charter, to which most African States are signatories, implementing its provisions is possible because of their practicality. Among the objectives of African Unity is to promote and defend African positions on issues of interest to the continent and its people.[77] The use of ODR would be of interest to the continent and its people, because Africans would like its speed, its privacy and its economical nature. The AU Charter categorically states that Member States shall settle all disputes by peaceful means.[78] Notably, the South African Law Commission, which undertakes research in the study and investigation of all aspects of law in order to make recommendations for the development, modernization and reform of the South Africa legal system, is willing to undertake reforms which would help in the growth of its legal process.[79]

Such measures of flexibility as seen in South Africa are needed by more African States, in order for ODR to be accepted and to grow. In most Africa settings, there is no such provision for dispute resolution as can be seen in developed countries as a form of dispute resolution—though it must be said that Africans have always resolved their disputes through consultation with elders and sometimes with traditional rulers. Africa is a patriarchal society with respect for its elders, a tradition that is embedded

---

[76] Gabrielle Kaufmann-Kohler & Thomas Schultz, *"Online Dispute Resolution; Challenges for Contemporary Justice,"* Kluwer Law International (2004) p. 54.

[77] The Charter and the African Union: http://charter-human-responsibilities.net Accessed 25.06. 2011.

[78] Article XIX of Commission of Mediation, Conciliation and Arbitration provides: "Member States pledge to settle all disputes among themselves by peaceful means and, to this end decide to establish a Commission of Mediation, Conciliation, and Arbitration, the composition of which and conditions of service shall be defined by a separate Protocol to be approved by the Assembly of Heads of State and Government. Said Protocol shall be regarded as forming an integral part of the present Charter."

[79] South Africa Law Commission `Community Dispute Resolution Structures Discussion Paper 87 Project 94' South Africa Law Commission 1999. http://restorativejustice.org/articlesdb/articles/5459. Accessed on 03.06.2011.

in its society; disputants have always found it easier to adhere to the decision of the elders, and for these reason elders became dispute resolution custodians. On the other hand, traditional rulers have become increasingly instrumental in the resolution of disputes, mostly because they are revered, and sometimes have the backing of the government. Elders and traditional rulers have been making use of ADR mechanisms in the form of negotiation and mediation, and although not legally trained, they have been seen to have carried out this duty well. Strictly speaking, Africa dispute processes are quite different from Western forms of dispute resolution, though recently Africa is seeking to model her dispute processes on Western ideologies, including the use of alternative dispute resolution mechanisms such as arbitration and mediation. Africa has always had mediators mediating in disputes, although these processes were not called mediation in earlier times; these activities involved mediation in its full and entire form. The culture was such that when young men and their elders had disputes, these were not resolved by violence or revolution; rather, disgruntled young men would either leave their communities to form new communities for themselves or, sometimes, would challenge the principles within the existing society.[80] The African society was such that some families were more successful than others, and over time, the successful families established themselves as permanent rulers, in the form of traditional rulers.[81] Inasmuch as the drive to model her dispute processes is based on Western models, it would be less productive if African dispute processes were classified in a manner based solely on the concept of consensual processes, as are the primary processes within ADR (negotiation, mediation, arbitration and other hybrid processes). This is because the terrain in Africa is different than it is in Western countries: Africa should only cherry-pick ideas and reforms from western countries when those ideas and reforms conform to its people, its history, its cultural heritage and its vision.

In most Africa settings, the process of the informal practice of dispute resolution has been in existence and is continually being explored as a procedure for social transformation and as a vehicle for growth and development, particularly in the area of governance.[82] This clearly illustrates the need for good governance in Africa, especially with democratic

[80] Walter Rodney, *How Europe Underdeveloped Africa,* Howard University Press (1972) Page 44-45.
[81] Ibid.
[82] Unisa Online, "*Dispute Resolution; towards a new vision,*" <http://unisa.ac.za> , accessed 20 June 2011.

reforms taking place globally. Africa, thankfully, has not been left behind, with countries such as Ghana, Kenya, and most recently Nigeria holding free and fair elections. The Federal Trade Commission in the United States of America observed that the "`number of direct, international business-to-consumer transactions involving electronic commerce is expected to increase significantly in the future", with Africa being the least responsive to the trend until consumers become confident about commercial activities carried out over global networks, and businesses are assured of a reliable, stable and predictable commercial environment.[83]It is therefore recommended that in response to the present challenge, in both the West and especially in developing countries, the encouragement and development of a global marketplace is needed, one that provides safety, transparency and legal certainty in the disputes resolved online. [84]

ODR may be a difficult case, on the other hand, since the multi-door court house which originally started in the United States of America has been successful in Africa. The Multi-door court house is a concept that arose out of the dissatisfaction with litigation, and with the notion that litigation was perhaps not the only means of resolving disputes amongst parties.[85] This concept, learnt from the United States of America, stems from the need to fill the void seen in litigation. It has been shown that this concept can be as successful anywhere as it is in the US, as seen in the Multi-Door court houses in Nigeria, notably in Lagos and, subsequently, in Abuja. It goes without saying that online dispute resolution can be equally successful.

IX. Future trends in the establishment of ODR as a form of ADR

Globalization has made it simpler and easier to move goods, capital and services across borders and around the world. This is also due to the era we live in, the technological age.[86] The Internet has been the catalyst for

[83] Ethan Katsh & Janet Rifkin, *Online Dispute Resolution; Resolving Conflicts in Cyberspace,* Jossey-Bass (2001), p. 58.

[84] Jeremy Levitt, *Africa; Selected Documents on Constitutive, Conflict and Security, Humanitarian, and Judicial Issues,* Transnational Publishers (2003), p. 36.

[85] Gabrielle Kaufmann-Kohler & Thomas Schultz, *Online Dispute Resolution; Challenges for Contemporary Justice,* Kluwer Law International, 2004, pp. 72-80.

[86] Jack Goldsmith and Tim Wu, *Who Controls the Internet? Illusions of a Borderless World.* Oxford University Press (2006), page 179.

contemporary globalization and the emergence of ODR. The United States of America, China and Europe have used their power to establish a presence on the Internet, as well as to establish different *modus operandi* of what the Internet ought to be. The main beneficiaries of ODR are governments, business organisations, consumer organisations and institutions of dispute resolution, many of whom have stated their views, as well as made recommendations on the implementation and use of ODR.[87] In the European Union, Article 17 of the e-Commerce Directive advocates the use of ODR. It states:

> [...] member states shall ensure that, in the event of disagreement between an information society service provider and the recipient of the service, their legislation does not hamper the use of out-of-court schemes, available under national law, for dispute settlement, including appropriate means. [88]

The U.S.A. also emphasizes the need to increase awareness of ODR, in its report on the ABA Task Force on Electronic Commerce and Alternative Dispute Resolution, and its importance regarding e-commerce.[89] It is not only the West which advocates the use of ODR: the East does too, notably China and Singapore.[90] ODR is all about cyber settle, which means that the mechanism or platform used must be in conformity with stipulated guidelines.[91] These guidelines could mean the training of facilitators or neutrals, and could result in the mechanism being accorded some legitimacy. With this in place, the parties to ODR must be aware that it is a contract by which they are bound.[92] A contract such as that undertaken in ODR is an agreement between two or more people, with rights and obligations which are enforceable legally, and who are entitled to any benefit that may accrue in the course of the agreement.[93] For this reason,

[87] Gabrielle Kaufmann-Kohler and Thomas Schultz, "*Online Dispute Resolution; Challenges for Contemporary Justice*", Kluwer Law International (2004) Page 83.
[88] Faye Fangfei Wang, Online *Dispute Resolution; Technology, Management and Legal Practice from an International Perspective,* Chandos Publishing (2009), p. 42.
[89] Ibid. p. 46.
[90] Faye Fangfei Wang, Online *Dispute Resolution; Technology, Management and Legal Practice from an International Perspective,* Chandos Publishing (2009), pp 50-51.
[91] Ibid. pp. 76-77.
[92] Ibid.
[93] Rachal Burnett & Paul Klinger, *Drafting and Negotiating Computer* Contracts, Tottel Publishing (2005), p. 53.

ODR practitioners are expected to meet some minimum level of education and professional knowledge, to ensure that ODR is built on a solid foundation of quality.[94] The general legal principles that apply to contracts also apply to IT contracts; therefore, a signatory to an ODR is bound by the terms of agreement.[95]

As a result of globalization, it is possible to set up a provision within the African Union Charter concerning a platform between AU and the EU on an Alternative Dispute Resolution mechanism focused on resolving cross-border disputes between the private and public sector, in the case of a potential misapplication of AU law. Unlike contentious litigation, the ADR system (and possibly ODR) provides the private sector with a non-contentious dispute resolution mechanism that is easy to use and free of charge. Online Dispute Resolution aims to resolve disputes quickly, and on-demand.

X. Recommendations for ODR as a Form of ADR in Africa

There is a significant rift within the elite; this should not be the case, because the educated elite must be pacesetters, as was observed in the standing source of tension within traditional African leadership, and in the contest between modernity and tradition.[96] Most importantly, Africa should embrace change, as it has done in some aspects of her society. Recommendations for the success of online dispute resolution (ODR) mechanisms in the Africa society include:

- The provision of Internet services in the form of Internet cafes by government, through revenue as well as assistance by private individuals —possibly the educated elite.
- Increasing the computer literacy levels of the population through mass education.
- Intervention by ADR practitioners, where necessary in the use of ODR mechanisms.

---

[94] Fangfei Wang, Faye, Online *Dispute Resolution; Technology, management and legal practice from an international perspective,* Chandos Publishing (2009), p. 77.

[95] Rachal Burnett & Paul Klinger, *Drafting and Negotiating Computer Contracts,* Tottel Publishing (2005), p. 53.

[96] Landauer, Carl, "Things fall together; the past and future Africans of T.O. Elias's Africa and the development of International law," LJIL 2008, 21 (2), 351-375.

- The essential use of mandatory ODR clauses in electronic contracts.
- The mandatory use of ODR in small claims.
- The enforceability of binding awards/judgments through ODR processes.
- The implementation of the OAU Charter in its entirety.
- The regulation of legal standards for ODR in the form of ADR in the OAU Directive.
- The inclusion of provisions requiring ODR providers to comply with minimum international legal standards.

Conclusion

With the growth and acceptance of ADR internationally, Africa shows sign of the adoption of ODR on the condition that all measures are put in place to ensure its successful implementation. The measures required are determined by the forces of demand and supply. These measures include the provision of the basic infrastructure in society, such as schools, computer training colleges, and the provision of Internet cafes in rural areas, as well as the creation of awareness within communities of the need to be computer literate. The provision can only be made feasible through a government elected by the people. Such provision will obviously create jobs and lessen the burden on the government through its courts, which are noted for invariably handling large number of cases annually. As a result, private individuals become providers of labour and distributors of wealth in the system.

Africa has seen remarkable expansion and growth recently, and continues to grow at great pace. However, along with growth there will be reforms and adaptations. E-commerce is having a significant effect on the way business is conducted and, in some aspects, the way lives are lived. The success of e-commerce is a result of the Internet; with the Internet has come an influx of transactions, which has evidently caused conflicts. These conflicts have given rise to the need to have such disputes resolved by similar means, which in this circumstance is online dispute resolution (ODR). The e-marketplace deals with parties from diverse jurisdictions and, as a result, there are various cross-border disputes on commercial issues. Since ODR cuts across jurisdictions it makes it an excellent means of the resolution of online disputes in commercial transactions, notably in e-commerce. The use of ODR both in the private and public sectors is becoming, to a large extent, a necessity. There is a need to highlight the adoption of ODR in Africa because of its fundamental characteristics, namely its convenience, trust and proven expertise: for these reasons, it cannot be underestimated. The West embraced ODR, as seen in the success of eBay, and is reaping the rewards. Africa can embrace it too, and although currently it is an evolving means of resolution of disputes open to ideas and initiatives, Africa can also streamline it, in accordance with and taking into consideration the continent's cultural and historical values.

CHAPTER SIX

AFRICAN WOMEN'S PARTICIPATION IN PEACE AND CONFLICT RESOLUTION: AN EVALUATION OF THE NIGERIAN AND BURUNDIAN WOMEN

CAROL IJEOMA NJOKU

Introduction

Throughout history, war and conflict have been a major cause of great suffering to many, and have subjected victims to extreme violence, losses, unrest and instability. Research data from the 20th century reveals that there have been more war-related deaths than in all previous centuries combined. Statistical reports by R.L. Sivard further replicate the harsh reality that between 1900 and 1990, about 107.8 million lives were lost as a result of warfare. Wars and conflicts in modern day society record more fatalities than ever. In modern warfare, missile attacks and bombings do not differentiate between soldiers on a warfront and women and children.[1] Civilians are more often the targets than soldiers. Rape, massacre, hunger, sexual assaults and evictions are employed as weapons of war. The consequences of these brutalities inflict physical, mental and psychological damage on the civilian population. The problems and consequences of armed conflict are not limited to physical injuries and fatalities, but often devastate human, moral, social, political, economic infrastructure and even natural resources. The family and social structures, which are the bedrock of human existence, often suffer gross debilitating consequences as a result of war.

Incidences of declared war may have declined gradually, but in most African states today, there are varying incidences of armed conflicts, most

---

[1] 1991: 20

of which lead to a vicious circle of violence that threatens the physical, political, economic and social lives of citizens, especially women and children. These ravaging cases of armed conflict often generate gender-specific consequences, such as rape and its related health consequences, the displacement of women and children, hunger, and all forms of crime and vandalism. For instance, within the last five years, research data has shown that the majority of the estimated 8.1 million refugees, displaced persons and post conflict returnees in Africa in 1997 were women and children. War and conflict have increased violence against women and worsened the social and economic conditions under which they live. In situations of conflict, refugee and displaced women and girls have often been sexually assaulted. Reports compiled by women's human rights groups indicate that in Mozambique, Liberia, Rwanda Sierra Leone, Burundi, and even some parts of Nigerian, women and girls face extreme violence, including rape and torture. Women living as refugees have been pushed into prostitution. The UN 1996 report to the UN General Assembly stipulates that women of all ages may be victims of violence in conflict, but adolescent girls are particularly at risk, for a range of reasons including body size.[2] These dreadful consequences have, over the years, compelled the United Nation's intervention on the Prevention of Conflict to implement some stringent measures: these have significantly improved the status of women victims in armed conflicts, especially in Africa.

The impact of armed conflict on children, especially girls, is atrocious, and reflects the overall slow progress in improving the status of African women in conflict situations. Programs to promote the health of African women through maternal and childcare services and family planning services have been undercut by the reduction of finances and other resources at various levels. A review of the existing data covering the last five years demonstrates that as the continent is faced with harsh social economic conditions, women have had to bear the brunt, especially in such war-ravaged countries as Burundi, Nigeria, Somalia and Libya. The conflict dynamics and their consequences on women and children have urged women to make drastic increases in their diverse activities and projects of conflict management peace-building. This chapter sets out to investigate these phenomenal interventions in gender roles, in the national and transnational conflicts of Nigeria and Burundi.

---

[2] *African Platform for Action, 1996*

Conflict and War in Burundi

The Burundian conflict, according to the United Nation's reports, started before 1970, and continues today.[3] Studies have shown that most conflicts and wars are inevitably political, or in most cases are precipitated by organized protest against inequity with regard to the management, control and distribution of powers and resources. The 1996 National report of Burundi referred to abuses committed by soldiers in the commune of Gasorwe which led to the death of 200 civilians, most of whom were women and children. Further reports in Burundi show that an estimated 70% of Burundian refugees are women and children. The United Nations' assessment identified discrimination and unequal access to scarce resources as major causes of violence in Burundi. The discrimination took place along ethnic lines, and the violence and counter violence became ethnic.[4] They also identified superimpositions of social cleavages, with fault lines in political power, economic wealth and ethnicity, which reinforced each other.[5]

Damilola Taiye Agbalajobi further identified the factors responsible for the Burundian conflict:

- Past discrimination: Since independence in 1962, Tutsi dominated regimes have discriminated against Hutus.
- Weight of a violent history: Burundi's post-independence history is strewn with recurrent coups or attempted coups and inter-communal violence. Clashes took place in 1965, 1966, 1972, 1987, 1988, 1989, 1991, 1993, and 1996. This sequence of massacres has created a culture of violence which is hard to dissolve.
- State monopoly of resources: The population is preponderantly rural, and engaged in subsistence agriculture. The country's small industrial sector is confined largely to local production or uncompetitive exports such as coffee and tea, produced until recently by state industries. Control of state power almost coincides with control of economic resources.

---

[3] United Nations, 2002: 89

[4] *African Platform for Action, 1996*: 16-23)

[5] Agbalajobi, D.T. "The Role of African Women in Peace Building and Conflict Resolution: The Case of
Burundi" 2011:5

- Divisive leadership: The leaders of the country's political camps have engaged in demagogic rhetoric, which has sometimes incited violence[6].

Conflicts Situations in Nigeria

Nigeria, like Burundi, has over the years experienced incessant conflicts and wars resulting from political squabbles, insurgence, crises of resource control and management, and religious and ethnic violence. Since the bloodbath of the civil war of 1967-1970, there have been recorded cases of crises in different regions of Nigeria. These have often manifested through violent rioting, human carnage and the destruction of property, leading to displacement. Examples of such crises include the Sharia crises, the Niger Delta crises, Kaduna, Jos crises and, recently, the most ravaging crises of Boko Haram, which has introduced a dimension of armed conflict into Nigeria.

The "hotspots" of the middle-belt, notably Kaduna and Plateau States, have for the past fifteen years witnessed intense riots in the cities, which have even extended to some of the old Hausa trading settlements, in places like Zangon Kataf and Yelwa, which are situated in mainly non-Muslim areas. But there has also been much communal violence outside the middle belt in most northern cities since the 1980s, including Kano, Zaria, Katsina, Maiduguri, Potiskum, Bauchi, and Gombe,[7] and ethnic conflicts in other parts of the country.[8]

Kaduna State in 1987 and 1992, and Bauchi State in 1991, experienced several episodes of violence. Consequently, there was some movement of people, especially Christians, from other northern states to Plateau. Since 2001, this situation has reversed; there has been intermittent violence for a decade in Plateau State,[9] and in Jos no resolution is in sight. People have moved out in large numbers—the scale of out-migration from the state has not been precisely estimated, but there are thousands of (mainly Fulani) people in resettlement communities in neighbouring Bauchi State alone. These probably amount to only a fraction of the total number who have left or been displaced from Plateau State to other parts of Nigeria. Across the north as a whole, with the important exception of Plateau, the level of Muslim-Christian violence, since the thousands killed in Kaduna in 2000

---

[6] Agbalajobi, 2011:11

[7] Falola, 1998; Boer, 2004a, 2004b in Adam Higazi, 2011

[8] Yakubu et al, 2005a, 2005b in Adam Higazi, 2011

[9] 2001-2010: 26

and 2002, appears to be less than it was in the 1980s and 1990s. It is clearly a delicate situation, but large-scale inter-religious violence in Kaduna, Kano and Bauchi—the worst affected areas in the 1990s—has dampened. As of October 2010, there has been no mass violence in Kaduna State, since the 'Miss World' riots of 2002, and none in Kano since 2004.

Within the Niger Delta areas, the crises government and the local communities lasted for almost two decades, until the early part of 2011, when an amnesty was introduced by means of negotiated settlement. The period of crises resulted in large death tolls, extra-judicial killings (like the Odi incidents), the destruction of properties, and the destabilization of peace and mutual co-existence. A more catastrophic kind of armed conflict has been persistently unleashed by the Boko Haram terrorist attacks, which have been taking place since 2009. The recurrent attacks of Boko Haram in different parts of Northern Nigeria have not only posed serious security challenges, but have threatened the social, political, and economic lives of the citizens. The frequency of these attacks on churches, markets, hospitals, police headquarters and other important public places, and the impunity of the insurgent group, resulted in the declaration of a state of emergency in the three affected states of Nigeria (Adamawa, Yobe and Borno) on Tuesday, May 14, 2013. Such persistent incidences of conflict in Nigeria call for an irreversible momentum towards peace and conflict resolution.

Peace building as Remedy to Conflict

The clarion call for conflict resolution and peace building requires collaborative action, involving a gender-balance strategy and synergy across countries and societies. Since women and girls suffer greater violence in times of crises and war, they ought to be part of the global vanguards for peace and conflict resolution. Nigeria and Burundi have recorded high levels of ethnic and religious crises in Africa. General Indar Jit Rktye, the former president of the International Peace Academy, defines peace keeping as "the prevention, limitation, moderation and cessation of hostilities between or within States due to the intervention of a third party, which is organized and directed at the international level and which calls upon military, police and civilian personnel to restore peace".[10] The "Peace building Initiative Strategic Framework" by the

[10] www.un.org/aboutun/charter/

Canadian International Development Agency (CIDA) further defines peace building as follows:

> Peace building is the effort to strengthen the prospects for internal peace and decrease the likelihood of violent conflict. The overarching goal of peace building is to enhance the indigenous capacity of a society to manage conflict without violence. Ultimately, peace building aims at building human security, a concept which includes democratic governance, human rights, rule of law, sustainable development, equitable access to resources, and environmental security [...] Peace building may involve conflict prevention, conflict resolution, as well as various kinds of post-conflict activities. It focuses on the political and socio-economic context or humanitarian aspects. It seeks to [...] institutionalize the peaceful resolution of conflicts.[11]

The latter forms the paradigm for the discourse of peace building in this chapter. Peace building and conflict resolution are therefore considered to constitute simultaneous and reinforcing sets of activities, with an intricate and organic relationship, much as human rights principles relate to broad development goals. It is an operational strategy by peace managers to address the root cause(s) of conflict and to prevent possible reoccurrence. This may involve long term developmental aspects, which include the restoration of human, physical, natural, moral and technological infrastructure. These seek to lay the foundation for peace and post-conflict resolution.[12] Considering the social hazards caused by war, peace training has become a serious project and a global concern. The ethics of peace and conflict management are therefore very vital orientations that ought to be imbibed as part of familial and social orientations. It is imperative, then, that women and mothers who are agents of transformation and major informal instructors ought to be empowered and supported adequately in the implementation of these quintessential roles, so as to maintain a peaceful society.

African Women and Conflict Resolution

The roles of African women in conflict resolution dates back to the traditional African society, where mothers were highly prized as special agents of socialization, cultural transmission, value orientation and character moulding. In both patriarchal and matriarchal Africa, mothers who are wives or daughters play significant roles in child-upbringing. The

---

[11] CIDA 2002: 2

[12] *The Role of African Women in Peace Building and Conflict Resolution,2011: 22*

children or younger siblings confide in them and take instructions from them. Thus, women have greater influences upon husbands, children and siblings at this level. As wives, they play leadership roles in collaboration with their husbands, and as daughters they are powerful mediators and arbiters in dispute resolution. These important traditional roles have remained very important areas for African women activists, and gender politicians ought to balance taking cognizance of the cultural variations of different regions. Often, gender activists or politicians create a biased or stereotyped picture of African women as mere victims of gender subjugation, thus denying their significant roles in peace and nation building. And the result is the prevailing opposition that often creates gender disparity and bias within the African milieu, which usually fails to reinforce the gender-complementarity of African traditional society: this reinforces prejudices and impedes the task of peace and nation building in contemporary African societies.

Traditional African women have always participated as great peace builders. Chinwe Nwoye, in a recent study, evaluated the roles of traditional women in peace-building, especially in some African countries like Cameroon, Central African Republic, Namibia, Somali, and Tanzania. The results clearly demonstrate an interesting collage of traditional conflict resolution and peace-building practices in Africa, south of the Sahara. Consequently, a thorough review of traditional Africa provides important insights into the relevance of traditional African women's agency in peace-building and conflict resolution practices: these are worthy of attention, in our current search for solutions to the peace problems bedeviling the life and opportunities of people in contemporary Africa.[13]

African traditional societies assigned to women the role of educator. Such education is the type that starts from the cradle and continues to adulthood, when a mother becomes a mediator in family and community dispute, such as daughter/son in-law conflicts and vice versa. In traditional African societies, women play portentous roles in the character and personality formation of youngsters. In traditional Nigerian society, for instance, children are closer to their mothers than to their fathers. The girls are specifically trained in their duties and responsibilities by their mothers and elderly sisters. From early childhood, children are exposed to a variety of songs, stories, proverbs and sayings, directed by the mother or the aunt and conveyed at the fireplace or after the evening meal. These shape their consciences and moral thoughts, and aim at reducing violence and vandalism. The songs, stories, proverbs and sayings contain simple but

[13] Nwoye, 2011:18

clear messages and moral teachings. Chinua Achebe's *Things Fall Apart* resonates with this pattern of moral education (within the homestead) in the relationship between Nwoye's mother and her children.[14] Most often, these children develop their career of creativity and even their philosophy of life on the basis of these stories. Achebe's recent publication, *There was a Country*, gives credence to this, as the author testifies to the effects of folk stories on his writing career.[15]

Further studies also shows that traditional African women as wives exercise considerable influence over their husbands, but often within the homestead, in order to protect the man's respect and integrity outside. The wife is discreet in public, but often remains the most influential adviser of her husband within the intimacy of the bedroom. Mathey et al., validate this aspect of feminine power in their study, while reviewing the traditional people of the Central African Republic:

> Apart from the meals shared with the whole family, the traditional wife in the communities of the Central African Republic reserved a small dish called the 'bed dish', which she gave to her husband at the bedtime. It was during that intimate meal that confidential conversations took place between husband and wife. The wife called her husband by the name of her first son or first daughter, and gave him advice on the facts of life. That advice would greatly influence the decisions, which the husband later took. Sometimes, the husband faced with a problem would postpone his decision until the following night so that he could first seek his wife's opinion[16].

A similar study by Mohammed Abdi Mohammed indicates the use of wit and poetic songs among Somalian women to instruct and propagate the culture of peace and mutual cohesion. One such song is rendered below:

> *We the women*
> *Have a complaint against men*
> *In the name of marriage, love and friendship*
> *We the women*
> *Demand peace in the country*
> *We demand security and prosperity*
> *The boys that we bring up*
> *We want them to grow up in peace.*[17]

---

[14] Chinua Achebe, 1958:102

[15] Achebe, C. 2012:9-14

[16] Mathey, M.J., Dejan, T., Deballe, M., Sopio, R., Koulaninga, A., & Moga, J, 2003, pp. 35-46.

[17] Mohamed A.M, 2003: 75-110.

Nigerian Women and Conflict Resolution

Nigerian women participate as agents of peace making both in their families and in wider society. Within the family, women function effectively as peace makers, by intervening in disputes between members of their immediate and extended families. They do this individually and collaboratively in their groups, either as daughters or wives. Women's ability to function effectively as arbiters in maintaining the peace and sustaining the structure of justice within their society projects the matrix of African motherhood as *Nneka,* mother is supreme. A mother thus becomes not only a carer or life-giver but a leader, spokesperson, and an instrument of peace and justice. Catherine Acholonu illustrates this significant aspect of an African mother:

> The woman in her capacity as a mother finds her status grows with age as her children increase and grows into responsible people in society. Motherhood places a woman into a position of immense and ever increasing strength. By and large, all the children born to a woman are required by tradition to hold their mother in high esteem…No matter how highly placed a man may be – a king, an elder, a warrior – he must respect and honour his mother. When she speaks, he must listen. Mother is supreme (*Motherism, 27).*

The traditional notions of women's influences on their husband, children and siblings are derived from African's respect and loyalty to goddesses. Among the Igbo Nigerians, for instance, the *ani (ala)* earth goddess is highly revered, and invoked in moments of peace and war. Its retributive justice meets with violators of justice. Okonkwo's doom in *Things Fall Apart* is partly attributed to this.

Outside the traditional setting, African women also play effective roles as peace makers in churches, their traditional groups and secular organizations. Nigerian women, for example, have in so many situations of crises embarked on mass protests to either stop obnoxious policies or to demonstrate their grievances in times of crises or armed conflicts. Thus, the mechanisms of mass protest and demonstrations are among the most visible means of women's intervention in crisis situations in Nigeria. Zulu Sofola, for instance, provides empirical evidence of Nigerian women who waged a series of wars and riots to defend their people's course and to achieve lasting peace. These include: the Igbo Women's War in 1929, which waged war against the British administration for initiation of taxation, Mrs. Fumilayo Rasome-Kuti, who mobilized the Market Women of Abeokuta in 1940s and successfully got the king of Egbaland to go into exile for some years until things cooled down, and Omu-Ako of Issele-Oligbo of Aniocha who, as the head of the Omu Women's Council, took over the traditional government, combined both male and female lines of power, and confronted both warring camps of Federal Nigeria and Biafra in defense of her citizens during the Nigerian Civil War (1967-70). Madam Okwuanaya Okwumabo (her paternal aunt), was, according to her, a member of the governing council of the Nigerian Civil War.[18] Other forms of female activism among Nigerian women include: the mass movement of Abeokuta women's Union (AWU) and demonstration against flat rate tax of the Egba women[19] and the overall participation of African women in struggles against colonial rule and oppressive feudal and military regimes, for example in South Africa, Namibia, Angola and Guinea Bissau.[20]

The contributions of women to peace building and conflict resolution in Nigeria have been quite enormous, especially within the local setting. In families, communities and larger society, Nigerian women have strong organizations, whose primary duties are to ensure peace, cohesion and order. Among the Igbo families, for instance, we have the association of daughters called the *umuada*, who often mediate in family and sometimes community dispute. The *umuada* is made up of the married, unmarried, widowed and divorced daughters of a lineage or village group. They act as political pressure groups in their natal villages in order to achieve desired objectives. They stop quarrels and mediate or prevent wars. Their reputation at this level is so powerful that their natal villages reckon with them and their possible reaction to every major reaction (Kameme in *Motherism*, 29). Catherine Acholonu further appraises the significant positions of women in the Igbo traditional:

> There are no areas of the life of patrilineage to which daughters of the village of the family may not stretch their power. They are the guardians of the patrilineage and the wives. Always their eyes and ears are open to seek out faults, mistakes and wrongdoings of their brothers and the latter's wives and punish accordingly, demand redress and appeasement of the mother ancestors of the lineage…It is pertinent to note that the *umuada*, the daughters of the lineage and their aged mothers are the main force behind the patrifocal system in the Igbo case. They are feared (respected) by the wives of the kindred and even by the men of the men within the patrilineage (*Motherism, 29).*

---

[18] 1998:60

[19] Mba, 1982

[20] Olabisi Aina, 1998:65

These women assume different nomenclatures depending on their traditional societies. For the Igbos, they are the *umuada/otu umunwanyi*, for the Hausas *olubieri,* and for the Yorubas *zumu-tamata*, and they embark on active roles of peace and conflict resolution within their traditional societies. Each of these groups is charged with religious and judicial authority for peace building and conflict management. The Yoruba womenfolk also enjoy enormous powers and judicial authorities like the *Lisa-Lobun, Jumo-Lobun,* and *Odunwo-Lobun* (to mention but three). The Igbos have similar institutions of power, like the *umuada*, who mediate between the living and the dead in funeral rites and other important events in society, and who also intervene in conflicts, and settle disputes in their community and of lineage. They exude great power and command the respect of the entire community. The *umuada* can also intercede in the town's male council of elders on behalf of any (male or female) member of their own lineage. The *otu umunwanyi* also wield judicial and political powers among fellow married women, and also check the excesses of stern husbands. They also perform mediation and peace-keeping roles within their communities. There are also groups of market women, Christian women and Moslem women. Their fundamental duties are to ensure a constantly peaceful co-existence among themselves and other members of society. In situations of turbulence, they organize themselves in order to change society by way of protest. Madam Tinubu was among the most powerful women activists in Yoruba history. Her powerful impact in Yoruba politics and commerce remains visible in the city of Lagos (which was then the capital of Nigeria). For instance, Tinubu square, the most popular plaza in the city of Lagos, is dedicated to the memory of this activist and commercial giant. History records other popular market Queens of the Yorubaland, who remained peace-builders and mediators within their social milieu. These women are seen to have played active roles in maintaining peace and justice within their local and larger societies.

During the Nigerian Civil war of 1967-70, the contributions of the Biafran women were enormous in Peace building locally, nationally, and internationally. Emma Okocha's *Blood on the Niger: the Untold Stories of the Nigerian Civil War* captures the massacre of the Asaba men and other ordeals of the war by Nigerian soldiers.[21] This satirical documentation of the events of the Nigerian Civil War provides insight into the palliative and resilient roles of women who worked as nurses, breadwinners, social and humanitarian workers. A further account of the Civil War by Egodi

[21] 1994:125

Uchendu reveals the involvement of Anioma Women in the Civil War and post-war challenges, which they faced with creativity, resilience, the improvisation of resources for their ravaged communities, and peaceful negotiations with the men combatants and militia women.[22] The novels of Flora Nwapa (*Wives at War*), Chukwuemeka Ike (*Sunset at Dawn*), Amadi (*Sunset in Biafra*), Ken Saro Wiwa (*Sozaboy*) and Chimamanda Adichie (*Half of a Yellow Sun*) convey the interplay between fiction and reality. These narratives bring to bear the impact of women in the management of the crises and the response to the turbulent outcome of the war through active negotiations, prayers, protest marches, seminars and workshops on conflict management, voluntary services and tremendous sacrifices of energy, talent and even life through risk-taking. In analyzing these fictional representations, Carol Njoku [23] maintained that the roles of women in the Nigerian Civil War novels brought a focal rebuttal to some erroneous views of western feminists, African critics and radical African feminists, who analyze womanhood from weak, unrealistic and mythical perspectives. Rather than perceiving women as "woe-man" or "*nwoke luchaa ogu nwannyi enwere akuko*" (a storyteller in the events of war), the visible roles of restoration, rehabilitation and regeneration championed by women in the explored narratives identify them as "Big House", *Nnejiuno* (the pillar that holds the house), *Nneka* (Mother is Supreme), *Nnebuchi* (Mother is God) and *Ezinne* (Precious Mother), on whose maternal bosom the present and future Igbo generation can be succoured.[24]

In war narratives such as *Half of a Yellow Sun, Sunset at Dawn* and *Sunset in Biafra*, and in non-fictional stories of war, the term "Motherhood" is projected as a vocation to selfless service to one's family and society. Mothers derive their joy and fulfillment from the diligent execution of the demands of their honourable vocation. In these narratives, the authors project women like Kainene, Fatima, Inatimi and Muokelu, who embrace nationalistic commitment as a way of contributing to peaceful cohesion. Motherhood assumed a broader status in the services rendered by the women militia in refugee camps, military camps, hospitals, homes, in check-points, and even in their improvised schools and rehabilitation centers. Patriotism attains a redefinition, as an earnest quest for soul-searching and a determination to expunge the genie that engenders social and national destruction. Women characters in these novels and civil war documentations make active contributions as family

---

[22] *Women and Conflict on the Nigerian Civil War, 2007*

[23] "Representation of Women in the Nigerian Civil War," unpublished Master's Dissertation, University of Nigeria, Nsukka, 2010.

[24] 2010, 102.

leaders, breadwinners, palliatives, and vehicles of re-habilitation in families, refugee camps and larger society.

Beyond the voluntary services rendered in the camps, the Biafran women hold forth at home and abroad. Fatima, for example, moves to Libreville to cater for the Biafran refugees and continues the work of promoting the cause for which her husband died. The maternal potentialities of these women are inexorably felt at all points and in many circumstances. For instance, in *Half of the Yellow Sun,* Mrs. Muokelu becomes the only visible member in her family. She not only becomes the breadwinner (as Dorah and Halima are in *Sunset in Biafra* and *Sunset at Dawn* respectively), but also courageously moves around teaching other women how to survive the hard times.[25] She teaches Olanna how to make soap. A replica of Mrs. Moukelu is the woman leader in Amadi's *Sunset in Biafra*, and she coordinates the affairs of the voluntary agencies in-charge of making weekly prayers for peace, and supplies food items to the soldiers. The discovery of the extent of resourcefulness inherent in women is an important lesson to be drawn from these war narratives.[26]

Ifi Amadiume seems to buttress this assertion in her statement that "women continued even more vigorously their roles as nurturers, cooking and caring for home and war front. Women continued as risk-takers, crossing through the territory in long distance trade known as 'afia attack' (attack trade) [...] women continued to be matriarchs, administering the towns and villages in the absence of men and their sons...gender politics became more intense during the war."[27] The concepts of *Nneka* and *Ezinne* (motherhood) receive broader meanings and implications as women embrace greater definitive roles.

In contemporary Nigerian society, ravaged with ethnic, religious and political crises, women (both Christian and Moslem) have always participated in the conflict resolution as market women. In the Jos crises of 2010, the recurrent maiming of children at homes and in schools and the rape and killing of women and young girls led the Jos women into a demonstration, dressed in mourning cloths and carrying green leaves in their hands, as they marched in great ululation into the National Assembly. Their action awoke the consciousness of both the government and media to negotiate for a lasting peaceful settlement in the protracted conflict. The outcome of their protest brought tranquility in Jos for a while. Further protest marches by the women of Plateau in 2010 and 2011 made the headlines in different Nigerian dailies. The first peaceful demonstration by

---

[25] Adichie, C.N. 2007: 238

[26] Ike, C. 1976:109

[27] 2000:152

Christian women in Jos was made to the Governor of Plateau State, to register their grievance over the massive killings of their children and husbands. A few months later, Moslem women did the same. The outcomes of these protests were tremendous in calming the ferocious crises in Jos. Also in Akure, in the same year, women mediated in the political marginalization and crises through their peace march, dressed half-naked to show their displeasure. In the case of kidnapping and killing in the Eastern part of Nigeria, the Christian women in Imo and Abia States organized themselves in mourning clothes to protest against the incessant killing and kidnapping of their children and husbands. Each of these protests yielded tremendous results and served as a presage to peaceful negotiation.

In the Nigerian Niger Delta crises, the exploitative activities of the Nigerian state and oil multinational companies have impacted more on women than any other group. They suffer gross exploitation, loss of viable farmlands, and water pollution. During the military occupation of communities, women suffer psychological, emotional and physical harm. They are also raped and maimed. They suffer as their sons get arrested and killed, and they feel it most when their brothers, husbands and lovers are tortured, maimed, and killed by the military and when armed police have brutalized and sacked whole communities, assaulting and beating them indiscriminately. The objective is to humiliate, intimidate and eliminate those who resist oil exploitation activities.[28] On several occasions, the Bonny and Ogoni women embarked on peaceful protests for negotiation with the Federal Government and the oil companies. These protests often ended in brutal killing and assault of these women. For instance, a report from Emene Okon shows the mayhem created by the protest march of the Bonny women. It seems there have been more protest actions undertaken by women in the Niger Delta because they are worse affected by environmental degradation and conflict than their male folks.

Outside the collective efforts by women, individuals and NGOs have also embarked on peace training process. These include: the Young Mediators Association of Nigeria; YONAMAN; the Human Rights Association of Peace and Conflict Resolution, founded in collaboration with some women academics in the South East of Nigeria and geared towards training young mediators and negotiators in schools, colleges and tertiary institutions in Nigeria in the effective approach to conflict resolution; the NGO working for Women's Peace and Security (an arm of the United Nations); the Christian Women for Peace Association, and the

---

[28] Emen Okon, 2007

Moslem Women Association. Unfortunately, these NGOs have been operating on personal levels, without government support or recognition. However, ECOWAS has recently set up a West African Women Training on Peace Mediation, which is an innovation in training women as formal participants in conflict resolution and peace building. [29]

It is important to note that these NGOs have been operating—with little or no support or recognition from the government—as major institutions in the maintenance of peace and order in society. Encouragement from government institutions will buttress the efficiency and productivity of these organizations in building a generation of peace and conflict management.

Burundi Women's Involvement in Conflict Resolution Process

The traditional Burundi women, like other African mothers, are perceived as peace educators. They function as both mothers and mentors in the early years of their children's upbringing and, throughout their lifetime as mothers. Their closeness to their children and other members of the family gives them the privilege of mentoring and influencing their actions and decisions. Mothers are often at the center of the family as a uniting factor. The recent findings of Ntahobari and Ndayiziga give credibility to the facts about the significant roles Burundi mothers play in moulding the structures of the home:

> It was primarily the mother that had responsibility for the upbringing of the children. Children, especially when very young, remained with their mother, who would look after both boys and girls until they reached a given age (for boys, until the time when their father took over the responsibility). There were strict rules to be complied with on how to dress, speak, eat and even walk and sit (especially for girls).[30]

Further insights are given into the roles of women as instruments of peace. The position of Burundian women as mothers or women, therefore involves certain expectations regarding their role in peace building. Ntahobari and Ndayiziga articulate some of these expectations on women within traditional Burundi society:

---

[29] *Daily Trust, 2011: 11*

[30] 2003:18

> Although the traditional Burundi society was organized and structured in ways that encouraged cohesiveness and peaceful coexistence, from time to time, like any other human society, it experienced conflict. Conflicts arose between individuals, within a family, between different, families or between the inhabitants of different territories. To manage such conflicts, traditional society had well-organized regulatory machinery in which women generally played a major part. Under this system a woman was recognized as having an advisory role, behind the scenes, mainly where her husband was concerned, and as playing an active part in strengthening solidarity and social harmony generally. Within this structure, women played the more unobtrusive yet leading substantial role, both in their families and within their own circle.[31]

The researchers reappraise the strong influence of women as secret advisers and mentors of both husbands and children. The effect or efficacy of their influence within the home and social structures cannot be stressed enough. Studies by Miriam Agatha Chinwe Nwoye further reevaluate the traditional roles of women in peace building. Her findings show that the Burundian early education of children is the preserve of women, and that it these women who play the greatest part in transmitting important traditional Burundian values to their young ones. The outcome of her research proved that women are key players in cultural and value propagation, transmission and consolidation, and are thus the custodians of peace and harmony within traditional African societies.[32]

Eloquent testimonies to the above claims are to be drawn in the impact of Burundi women during the era of Burundian conflict, which started in 1970. This conflict, like most of the Nigerian conflicts, garnered steam from ethnic discrimination to crises relating to resource control and distribution and other political and gender issues. Burundian women have played many remarkable roles, through intervening in certain critical situations and offering different peace proposals as solutions to their national and inter-ethnic conflicts. Their participation in Burundi's conflict resolution helped to integrate gender equality within democratic governance and the peace building framework. This was as a result of the quotas in the peace agreement and Burundi's new constitution. Pressure from women's organization contributed to a culture of negotiation for national peace. The participation of women was initially inconsistent, due to lack of political will from all sides, and in some cases strong resistance from political parties.[33]

[31] Ibid, 16
[32] 2011:6
[33] Damilola Taiye Agbalajobi, 2011:89

The Burundian women, through their peaceful protests and NGOs, have tried to maintain some status quo of tranquility in the midst of turbulence. The Arusha peace process began with 17 different political parties meeting for the first round of talks in July 1998. When no civic organizations were authorized to participate, Hutu and Tutsi women decided to join forces to protest against this exclusion and to call for a place at the peace table. Their initiative led to the creation of numerous women's NGOs, among them the Group of Associations and Feminine NGOs of Burundi, the Women's Network for Peace and Non-Violence, and the Women's Association for Peace. These groups organized a wide range of activities, including workshops on non-violent conflict resolution, a forum gathering women from different ethnic backgrounds and uniting women from the Diaspora and from the country, to discuss strategies for national reconstruction. The *Dushirahamwe* ("Let us reconcile") network succeeded in bringing together displaced and refugee women with the aim of identifying obstacles to peaceful cohabitation within the country.[34]

As Alice Ntwarante and Marie-Goretti Ndacayisaba rightly observe, the various activities carried out in the name of peace have slowly helped to reconstruct networks of committed women that were shattered during the conflict. They further remark that "The mobilization for peace has brought together women from all walks of life; intellectuals and farmers, young and old, rich and poor women. The relations between them improve thanks to the atmosphere of harmony and transparency that prevailed during the different meetings." [35]

Further findings show that a breakthrough was reached when UNIFEM and the Mwalimu Nyerere Foundation sponsored the All-Party Burundi's women peace conference, held on July 17-20, 2000 in Arusha, Tanzania. As requested, each of the 19 Burundi organizations represented at the peace negotiation sent two women delegates. More than 50 Burundi women and observers participated in the event. The women's proposals were presented at a meeting with former South African President Nelson Mandela, who was designated to replace the late Mwalimu Nyerere (one of the patriarchs of the national liberation movement) as the facilitator for the Burundi peace negotiations. Among the steps of action requested were the following:

- A women's charter to be included in the constitution and the elimination of all laws discriminatory to women;

---

[34] Ibid, 90

[35] Ibid, 2000: 9

- Special measures for women's security;
- Women's right to land and inheritance;
- Equal access to education for women and girls;
- An end to impunity for gender-based war crimes, including domestic violence.[36]

All the women's recommendations were accepted by the 19 parties, and were integrated into the final document of the peace accord— with the exception of a clause requesting a 30% quota to promote women's representation at all decision making levels.[37] It took almost four years of persistence for the Burundi women to get their voice heard as part of the peace process. In the first round of the negotiations, women were absent. Burundian women felt this should not be so, and found ways to join in the negotiations, angering the male delegates. Eventually, women were allowed in as observers but had no right to take part in the talks. Further, when the negotiation began, women were prevented from entering the negotiating room. Determined to make their voices heard, they had to adopt a different tactic, and decided to intercept representatives of the political parties in the corridors of government buildings after meetings, urging representatives to integrate women's perspectives into the peace process. Their efforts were finally acknowledged. The mobilization of women in the peace process led to the creation of structures that helped women to assert their rights and to come to terms with the consequences of the civil war. The war gave the Burundian women more exposure and greater opportunities to participate in the peace process and the negotiations than ever. However, the women of Burundi are still struggling to be integrated into the formal setting of the peace process, trapped in traditional roles that do not allow them to be visible in the public sphere.[38] Despite the mobilization of women, the country is still divided along ethnic lines, impeding any attempt to bring peace and reconciliation.

The United Nations documentation on the women's peace mission reports that in December 1997, a high level African Women's Peace Mission went to Burundi to facilitate the peace process in the country. This mission contributed to building the internal capacity of Burundi to solve its internal conflicts in a peaceful manner. Further records show that the African Women's Committee on Peace and Development (AWCPD)

---

[36] Ibid, 11

[37] UNIFEM, 2001

[38] Agbalajobi, D. T. "The Role of African Women in Peace Building and Conflict Resolution: The Case of Burundi," 2011:6.

was set up in April 1998, and officially launched on 11th November 1998 in Addis Ababa. The Committee is a joint initiative between the Organization for African Unity (OAU) and the United Nations Economic Commission for Africa (ECA). Among other things, the AWCPD is charged with advising the Secretary-General of the African Union (AU, formerly OAU) and the Executive Secretary of the ECA on issues of mainstreaming women's concerns and a gender perspective into peace and development initiatives in the continent. There are two main plans for this broad mandate of the AWCPD: the first is to facilitate the effective involvement of the women of Africa in advocacy for alternative options to war and violence; the other is to promote the increased participation of women in decision-making, particularly in relation to the prevention, management and resolution of conflicts and other matters of war and peace, thereby inculcating and nurturing a culture of peace and peace-building.[39] The Burundian women obviously took a great step towards gender emancipation and equality. Most paramount in their ground-breaking accomplishment is their role in peace building in Burundi, though it is not without challenges.

Challenges of Women in Conflict Resolution

Eighty five percent of the displaced population in Africa is made up of women and children. Statistics have shown that women and children are often the most vulnerable in war, crises or armed conflicts. These facts partly explain why in most cases women are usually the first to protest for peace and disarmament. But still, evidence has shown that in most cases the outcome or consequences of such protests endanger, jeopardized or even end the lives of some women. Research has shown evidence of female casualties in most places, as women victims struggle to de-escalate conflict and to restore peace. For instance, in the Niger Delta crises (Nigeria), the empirical findings of Emen Okon were based upon the tragedy of the Bonny women on March 29-30, 1986, during the shut-down of Shell's operation. The women blocked the helipad with their bodies in an effort to win the compensation that the communities demanded from Shell for destroying their environment and for eroding their livelihood structures. Soldiers of the Nigeria state came by air and by water and raided the Opia and Ikebiri communities in the Delta state. Women and children were killed. The soldiers were contracted by Chevron Nigeria

[39] Agbalajobi, D. T. "The Role of African Women in Peace Building and Conflict Resolution: The Case of Burundi," 2011:7-8.

Limited.[40] Such extra-judicial killings of unarmed women protesting against the destruction of economic resources and means of livelihood are common in the Niger Delta region of Nigeria.

Women are often the first to cry out to the Government or the disputing parties for peace, but in most cases they are excluded from the ideological or political framework that negotiates for peace. The actual round table negotiations in most African countries are not gender responsive, in the sense that in most cases at higher levels the views and interests of women are not properly represented, and this affects their participation in conflict resolution, especially at the national level. Furthermore, Agbalajobi reveals the following further setbacks to African women's participation in peace and conflict resolution:

- Lack of political and economic wherewithal affects the potentialities of women in their individual and collective move to effective national and transnational conflict resolution. Most of the time, women's groups lack the means to back up their actions. In some instances, they are unable to get information across to the media network to enhance their peace campaign, because they do not have the budget for multi-dimensional activities. Further, they are not part of the main fundraising channels and networks. They work on a voluntary basis at the grassroots level, pooling their own resources together to get an office, desk, and phone line. This may lead to their views and viable initiatives going unrecognized.
- Lack of experience, exposure and skills in negotiation, advocacy and lobbying techniques. These may be caused by a high percentage of illiteracy and religious/traditional, social or political restrictions. Women have always been kept apart from the political arena and sphere of decision-making, even in matters that affect their interest.
- Political exclusion: Africa's patriarchal structure has been identified as an impediment to women's activism and active participation in the peace building process.
- Lack of sustainability in political participation: Representation does not necessarily mean meaningful and recognized

[40] "What are the roles of women and youth in peace building and conflict resolution in Niger Delta Crisis": http://www.weegy.com/home.aspx?ConversationId=57627424 Retrieved on 05.01.2011

participation that has an impact on substantial inputs in peace agreement. In addition, once a peace process is over, women often return to more traditional activities, losing the gains they have fought for and their public presence. These losses make it very difficult for women to return to the public stage later when resolution begins.

- Lack of visibility: Women's conflict-resolution activities are confined to the informal sector, very often at the periphery of official peace negotiation. In addition, even if women contribute to the promotion of peace, they are not invited to participate in formal negotiations.[41]

Findings

The findings of this study have shown that women have had a tremendous impact as local mediators in family and community disputes. Their interventions have often been indispensable in quelling national crises. However, women's thresholds with regard to participation in national and international issues have not expanded significantly, and remain limited. The United Nation's report on Peace Building recently observed that despite the commitments made by African governments at the Fifth African Regional Conference and the Fourth World Conference on Women, there has not been a significant increase in the participation of women in national, sub-regional and regional mechanisms for conflict prevention and resolution.[42]

Conflict resolution and peace building can only flourish on the soil of such values as patience, tolerance, honesty, mutual respect for human dignity, communality and mutuality, equity, justice, gentleness, modesty, self-control, tolerance, caring, moderation, flexibility, and open-mindedness. Women, as promoters of these values ought to be encouraged, empowered, and involved in the project of peace building both at national and international level; their input is bound to bring sustainable peace in Africa and beyond.

Recommendations

- There is a need to overcome the obstacles that hinder women from participating in peace building and post-conflict resolution

---

[41] Damilola Taiye Agbalajobi, 2011:89

[42] www.un.org/millennium/sg/report/ Retrieved January 12, 2013.

processes. Women need to take advantage of the transformative experiences of war to break new ground in peace building and to destabilize the patriarchal order, bringing stronger female synergy for peace and social cohesion.

- Government, NGOs and women's groups should endeavour to encourage and educate other women about the societal expectations on them as effective peace builders, and thus harness the skills of conflict resolution. Continuous efforts should be made to breach the gap caused by gender disparity which affects women's active participation in peace building.
- African women in warring countries and beyond must endeavour to rise to the responsible demands of their time, by being effective models for peace building roles. They must organize themselves, strive for institutional, political and legal representation, and create solidarity and support through local, regional, and international networks.
- International bodies like the UN, ECOWAS, AU, etc., should also continue to facilitate the involvement of local women in peace negotiations. The community should also help to promote more gender awareness, and review: the content of laws that perpetuate discrimination against women; constitutional reforms; judicial reforms; election participation, as well as access to and control over economic resources, education, and training. This is because despite the ground breaking contributions made by women's groups, gender equity mechanisms created during peace negotiations still remain weak.

The United Nation's recommendations for African women are equally adopted as part of the recommendations in this study:

- an institutional framework is necessary for the promotion of women in decision making
- women's peace movements should be promoted amongst neighbouring countries, as regional peace and stability will enhance the likelihood of continued national peace
- women should integrate positive traditional conflict resolution mechanisms into peace initiatives
- recruitment of women into peace movements should include grassroots, rural, urban, and various religions, linguistic, social and political groups

- programmes to sustain peace through peace education in schools and the community must be initiated and strengthened
- after hostilities have ceased, women's continuing role in sustaining peace must be acknowledged and maintained. Women should not be relegated to the domestic arena
- Governments are called upon to ensure women's access to decision-making mechanisms, education and training and to national resources by undertaking the following:
- Ensuring greater access for women in the decision-making process by appointing more women to decision-making mechanisms at the national, sub-regional and international levels (including governments, parliaments and sub-regional, regional and international organizations). In this regard, the quota system should be preferred when it is to the advantage of women, while continuing to promote the principle of competition between men and women.
- Ensuring the effective representation of women in military institutions, appointing and encouraging more women to become officers at decision-making levels.
- Promulgating laws designed to give effect to the will of governments to involve women in decision making and, above all, to ensure that the laws are strictly applied CITE.

Conclusion

The findings presented in this chapter show that women have been key propagators of peace and value reorientation within the traditional settings which form a microcosm of larger society. The lack of political, economic and social mobilization have been a serious setback to women's effective participation in peace building within the larger society, as can be seen within Nigerian and Burundian society. In spite of the recent commendations of the United Nation's Educational, Scientific and Cultural Organization (UNESCO) on the noticeable developments in female participation in peace building and conflict resolution processes in Africa since the Beijing Global Conference, the fact clearly remains that the peace-building process within the official arena remains a male dominated arena in Africa. The enormous contributions of women notwithstanding, they have been denied strong national and international recognition in peace negotiations and decisions. The impact of women is felt more in local and traditional mediations. Despite their occasional interventions through mass protest and demonstration, their impact on the national and international arena is minimal due to inadequate support and insufficient motivation from the government and peace institutions. There is a need to empower and support women's peace operations in Africa, especially in regions with recurrent ethnic or political crises like Nigeria and Burundi. Finally, the untapped potential of women and their dynamic qualities for peace building and conflict management should be explored in order to maintain a stable society in Africa and beyond. The need to engage women in continuous peace negotiations and in a mentoring and capacity building is imminent, and would break new ground in conflict management. There is still much to be done to accelerate and enhance the involvement of women, including refugees and the internally displaced, in all the processes of conflict prevention, management and resolution. The input of women in terms of lobbying, peace missions, conferences, recommendations and creating forums and networks at all levels will certainly enhance the advancement of peace building in Africa. Governments, UN Agencies, NGOs and Inter-governmental Regional and Sub-regional organizations and National Peace networks are therefore urged to contribute their human and financial resources in encouraging women's giant's strides in implementing the culture of peace across the continent and beyond. Adequate attention should be drawn to the gender dichotomies or barriers affecting women's active participation in peace building, in order to provide and build a stronger synergy between the male and female actors for peace. Until the gender imbalance in the peace building process in Africa is reviewed, the peace project in Africa (particularly in Nigeria and Burundi) will obviously remain inchoate.

Works Cited

Achebe, C. *Things Fall Apart. London*: Heinemann Educational Publishers, 1958.
—. *There was a Country.* New York: Penguin Press, 2012.
Acholonu, Catherine. *Motherism: The Afrocentric Alternative to Feminism.* Owerri: Afa Publications, 1995.
Adichie, Chimamanda. *Half of the Yellow Sun.* London: Harper Perennial, 2007.
African Matriarchal Foundations. London: Karnak House, 1987.
Aina, Olabisi. "African Women at the Grassroots: The Silent Partners of the Women's Movement" in *Sisterhood, Feminism & Power.* New Jersey: Africa World Press, 1998.
Amadi, Elechi. *Sunset in Biafra.* London: Heinemann Educational Books Ltd, 1973.

Bop, C. Women in Conflicts, their Gains and their Losses. In S. Meintjes, A. Pillay, & A. Tinshen (Eds.), *The Aftermath: Women in Post-conflict Transformation*. London: Zed 2002, pp. 19-34.

Emen J. Okon *Rural Women Under Siege* Port Harcourt: Liberty Press, 2007

Higazi, Adams. Jos Crises: A Recurrent Nigerian Tragedy. Abuja: Fredrich Ebert Stiftung, 2010.

Ifi Amadiume. "The Politics of Memory: Biafra and Intellectual Responsibility." in Ifi Amadiume and Abdullahi An-Na'im, eds., *The Politics of Memory: Truth, Healing and Social Justice.* New York: Zed Books, 2000.

Ike, Chukwuemeka. *Sunset at Dawn.* Glasgow: William Collins, 1976.

Joeng, Ho-won. *Peace and Conflict Studies: An Introduction.* Burlington: Ashgate Publishing Company, 2000.

Karamé, K.H. Military women in peace operations: Experiences of the Norwegian Battalion (in UNIFIL 1978-98 In L. Olsson & T.L. Tryggestad) Eds. *Women and International Peacekeeping*. London: Frank Cass & Co. 2001, (pp. 85-96)

Mathey, M.J., Dejan, T., Deballe, M., Sopio, R., Koulaninga, A., & Moga, J. The Role Played by Women of the Central African Republic in the Prevention and Resolutions of Conflicts. In UNESCO, *Women and Peace in Africa*. Paris: UNESCO Workshop, 2003, pp. 35-46.

Mitchell, C., & Banks, M. *Handbook of conflict resolution: The analytical problem-solving approach*. London: Pinter, 1999.

Mohamed A.M. "The Role of Somali Women in the Search for Peace." In UNESCO, *War and Peace in Africa*. Paris: UNESCO Workshops, 2003, pp. 75-110.

Ntwarante, A., & Ndacayisaba, M.-G. Expérience des femmes dans la résolution des conflits au Burundi [Women's experiences in conflict resolution in Burundi]. In *Report on the workshop on conflict transformation in Africa: African women's perspectives*. Dakar, Senegal: Gorée Institute, May 23-26, 2000, pp. 9 -28.

Nwapa, Flora. *Wives at War* .Enugu: Nwanife Publishers, 1975.

Okocha, Emma. *Blood on the Niger: The Untold Story of the Nigeria Civil War*. Port Harcourt: Sunray, 1994.

Sivard, R.L. *World Military and Social Expenditure.* Washington: World Priorities, 13th Edition, 1991.

Sofola, Zulu. "Feminism and African Womanhood" in *Sisterhood, Feminism & Power.* New Jersey: Africa World Press, 1998.

Uchendu, Egodi. *Women and Conflict on the Nigerian Civil War.* New Jersey: African World Press, 2007.

CEDAW (Convention on the Elimination of All Forms of Discrimination against Women). *Women, Culture,* and *`Traditional Practices', Women and Armed Conflict, Legal Status and Legal Reality.* UNICEF and UNIFEM. Federal Republic of Nigeria. *National Medium Term Action for the Implementation of the Beijing Platform for Action.* Federal Ministry of Women Affairs and Social Development, Abuja, 1997.

International Women's Rights Action Watch (March 1997). *The Women's Watch Vol. 10. No. 3.*

International Women's Rights Action Watch (December 1996). *The Women's Watch Vol. 10. No. 2.*

UNESCO. *Women and Peace in Africa: Case Studies on traditional Conflict Resolutions practices.* Paris: UNESCO Workshops, 2003.

UNITED NATIONS and OAU (Organisation of the African Unity) (1996). *African Platform for Action: African Common Position for the Advancement of Women.* Adopted at the Fifth African Regional Conference on Women: Dakar Senegal 16-23 November 1994

USAID (2000). Intrastate conflict and gender, *Information Bulletin* No. 9, December 2000. Office of Women in

Development, U.S. Agency for International Development, pp. 1-4.

Websites

www.un.org/millennium/sg/report/

www.un.org/aboutun/charter/) *"Motherism: The Afrocentric Alternative."*

Ishmael Reed's Konch Magazine. Online: http://www.ishmaelreedpub.com/CatherineAcholonu.html. (March–April 2002).

UNDP (August 1999) *UNDP Women 2000: Gender Equality, Development and Peace for the 21st Century. Beijing +5 Bulletin Issue #2.* UNDP Website: www.undp.org/gender/gb/bjbullet2.html.

http.//www.run.edu.ng.colleges/AgbalajobiDamilolaTaiye. The Role of African Women in Peace Building and Conflict Resolution, 17th July, 2011.

http://c.women and conflict resolution.htm, Miriam Agatha Nwoye, 18th July, 2011.

www.nigeriandailysun.portal, July, 2010.

CHAPTER SEVEN

CIVIL SOCIETY AND CONFLICT RESOLUTION IN THE NIGER DELTA OF NIGERIA

ROBERT DIBIE

Introduction

Tackling the immense and multidimensional challenges of environmental pollution in Nigeria requires extraordinary ingenuity and cooperation. Whenever collaboration and ingenuity do not take place, conflicts tend to arise. The conflict in the Niger Delta is between three groups: (1) citizens living in the region, (2) the federal Government of Nigeria, and (3) multinational oil companies that drill for petroleum and pollute the rivers and farmlands.[1]

Further, man-made and natural disasters are two factors that have contributed to the conflict in the political and sustainable development process in Nigeria (Dibie, 2007). According to Robert Dibie (2010), man-made disasters include: (1) the deliberate policy of exploiting the land and oil resources in the Niger Delta area, to the dismay of the people; (2) the problem of not addressing the high rate of unemployment for displaced farmers and fishermen; (3) the lack of environmentally responsible development to promote the value of community sustainability all over Nigeria; (4) the lack of appropriate environmental policies; (5) inadequate implementation of the few environmental policies there are; finally, (6) the lack of respect for human rights. On the other hand, natural disasters in the Niger Delta region include ocean tides, flood, excessive rainfall, hurricanes, and so on (Dibie, 2008). In most cases, man cannot do anything to prevent natural disasters.

---

[1] An earlier version of the paper was presented in honor of Professor Ernest Uwazie's 50th birthday program, December 11, 2010, at California State University, Sacramento.

Most current efforts to address environmental problems in the Niger Delta area tend to benefit well-connected elites, to the dismay of the majority of the citizens in the region. Rather than protecting the citizens in the region from the environmental harm that is been created by multinational oil companies, the government of Nigeria tends to do the opposite. Conflict in the Niger Delta region of Nigeria, due to the scramble for oil revenue and the demand for the implementation of better environmental policies, has resulted in the death of several citizens living in the region in the past three decades (Idemudia and Ite 2006). From the early 1990s to 2010, conflict over the equitable allocation of oil revenue resulted in over three hundred deaths in the region (Dibie, 2008). During the same period, conflict resulted in over six million people being displaced from their homes (Adunbi, 2010). Worse still is the fact that the unemployment rate has increased fivefold due to oil spillages on farmland and rivers as well as other fishing waters in the region. Fishermen and their families are suffering from malnutrition due to inadequate income and food (Bassey 1999; Mbendi 2002).

The history of the Niger Delta region of Nigeria reveals that the people living in the area were originally farmers. The majority of the people living in the coastal or riverine areas are also fishermen. Further, Nigeria is frequently categorized as a deeply divided society (Dibie, 2008). The nation is divided both by religion (a predominantly Muslim north and predominantly Christian south) and by ethnicity (experts estimate that Nigeria contains between 250 and 400 distinct ethnic groups, which include three major players: the Yoruba, Hausa, and Igbo). Minority issues have become the greatest socio-economic and political problem in the country. One sub-national minority group that forms the major residence of the Niger Delta region is the Jaw people. The Niger Delta region is the store of Nigeria's crude oil, which accounts for approximately ninety percent of Nigeria's revenue. Crude oil provides more than ninety percent of Nigeria's total exports (Central Bank of Nigeria 1981).

Given its position as the foundation of the Nigerian economy, the Niger Delta region has always been a source of concern to the government of Nigeria. Demands for local autonomy and resource control by the locals have occupied the center-stage of Nigerian politics over the past two decades. Such demands became more pronounced during 1999, when Nigeria made a landmark transition to democratic governance. With the laying of this democratic foundation came the promise to grant a degree of local autonomy and true federalism, which implied local benefits from local resources. The prospects for local autonomy and resource control greatly increased competition for political control of such areas as the

Niger Delta region and the economic benefits they promise. Echefu and Akpofure (2000) observed that in the Niger Delta area, the economic competition brought about by the potential for political control over economic resources has fractured society along three lines. First, it has pitted local political interests over the derivation formula—how much of the oil profit falls into local government coffers, as compared with the profit taken by the national government. Second, it has pitted local political interests against each other, creating conflict over which local government controls the oil resources and therefore over who has a right to any revenue that the federal government allows them to keep. Third, there is a violent schism between the oil producers (multinational corporations and their Nigerian workers and security personnel) and the local inhabitants, who feel that they own the land but yet are given no claim to the oil profits. These grievances have set the stage for activism, struggles, restiveness and violence.

This paper examines the nature of the conflict in the Niger Delta region which has arisen due to oil drilling and the pollution of the environment. It contends that Nigeria will continue to bear the brunt of the effects of environmental pollution even as the country strives to overcome poverty and advance economic growth. It analyses how for those in the region oil and land are a symbol of impending wealth, and how the mythic quality of such forms of wealth drives the basis for the claims of the indigenous populations. It explores the ways in which opportunity may be the key influence upon and source of conflict. In contrast, the paper also examines the nature of governance, so as to clearly delineate power structures that encompass cooperation, collaboration, confrontation, and consultation. It also identifies opposition among different actors—transnational and national NGOs, multinational corporations, the state and 'insurgency' movements. The paper proposes that these groups are interconnected, intertwined, and interrelated in their methods and scope, in creating new spaces of power and governance in the Niger Delta region of Nigeria. Some recommendations are provided in the concluding section of the paper.

Conflict Due to Human Competition

Conflict generally occurs when an individual's values differ from those of others in a work and social environment. Opportunity is a key influence and source of conflict (Greenberg, 2010). According to Ernest Uwazie (2010), conflict is the sense or perception by one entity/person—whether real or imagined—that his or her primary interests or basic needs are being threatened by another entity/person. Uwazie et al., (2008) contend that conflict may be due to human competition over interest satisfaction. Any successful resolution depends on whether the conflict is ripe: that is, on if and when the parties are motivated to resolve the issues and the appropriate process is available.

The concept of sustainable development stipulates that our present development must meet the needs of the present without comprising the ability of future generations to meet their own needs. The argument presented by the sustainable development concept contends that the Nigerian government must revamp its development policies by taking into consideration environmental protection as well as capital, labor, raw materials, and energy cost. According to Robert Dibie (2009), the distribution of the nation's wealth and environmental resources must be made equitable for both the Niger Delta people and the rest of the nation. Ernest Uwazie (2008) contends that conflict is a process in which one party perceives that another party has taken or will take actions that are incompatible with one's own interests. Jerald Greenberg (2010) and Ernest Uwazie (2010) identify the causes of conflicts as including: (1) perceptual distortion; (2) grudges; (3) distrust; (4) competition over scarce resources, and (5) destructive criticism. If conflict arises due to a perceived threat to one's interests, peace is the state of satisfaction of one's interest and the experience of justice (though not necessarily the absence of conflict or violence). Upreti (2003) contends that democratic control of crime emphasizes not only the power of the government but also the dignity of all individuals, even those who commit crime. Figure 1 shows the positive and negative impacts of conflict.

Numerous scholars have noted geographical patterns in the frequency and intensity of violence and warfare. Some of these studies focus attention on particular geographic regions (Miller (1999; Jain 1977; Haughton 1998; Rogers and Hall 2003) while others focus attention on the effect of climatic variables, such as temperature (Kosoy and Corbera 2010; Maxwell 2009; Wunder 2003) and rainfall and humidity (Aaron, 2003). Omolade Adunbi's (2010) analysis of the relation between ecological variables and the frequency of political violence found the highest levels of violence in countries with the most rainfall, the highest humidity, and moderately warm temperatures. Medndi (2002) and Wunder (2003) investigated the relation between climate and violence. They contended that people are generally more active in temperate weather and are therefore naturally more likely to engage in violent activities in such conditions. Wunder (2003) argued that the "long, hot summer" makes people irritable and therefore more aggressive in uncomfortably hot weather.

Figure 1: Positive and Negative Impacts of Conflicts

Positive	*Negative*
▪ Conflict may improve the quality of organizational decisions. ▪ Conflict may bring out into the open problems that have been previously ignored. ▪ Conflict may motivate people to appreciate each other's positions more fully. ▪ Conflict may encourage people to consider new ideas, thereby facilitating change.	▪ Conflict yields strong negative emotions. ▪ Conflict may divert people's attention from the task at hand. ▪ Communication between individuals or teams may be so adversely affected that any coordination of effort between them is compromised. ▪ Lowered coordination tends to lead to decrements in organizational functioning.

Source: Greenberg, Jerald. *Behavior in Organizations.* Upper Saddle River, N.J.: Prentice Hall (2010).

A number of scholars have specifically addressed the question of civil war in Africa. Goran Hyden (2006) and Vincent Khapoya (1998) found that Africa fits into a global pattern of behavior, with its poor economic performance leaving it prone to civil war. Likewise, Ellsworth (2000) found that the high frequency of civil war in Africa results from its high levels of poverty. Goran Hyden's (2006) findings agree with respect to civil war. He argued that Africa's low economic performance and high levels of poverty are the result of the severity of infectious disease stress. In addition, Uwazie (2010) contends that intrastate armed conflict in Africa and elsewhere is a direct result of infectious disease stress and its evocation of xenophobic and ethnocentric cultural values.

The climate of much of Sub-Saharan Africa is particularly conducive to infectious diseases that lead to the development of collectivist values and thus to widespread poverty. Additionally, as Africa is the place of origin of the human species (Nwilo and Bajdejo 2008; McCauley 2006), the pathogens endemic to Africa have had a particularly long period of antagonistic coevolution with humans. As a result, the diversity of parasites and the associated intensity of human infectious disease in Africa may be even greater than in other similarly tropical regions. The ancient ancestors of the modern residents of those regions (e.g., south-east Asia, tropical South America) may have escaped some of their most virulent parasites when they migrated through more temperate regions that do not support high parasite richness (McNeely 2007).

While the sustainable food production model could be implemented in Nigeria to some extent, the millennium ecosystem model presents a very interesting possibility. The model suggests that organic agriculture can contribute substantially to a more sustainable system of food production (Easton, 2012). On one hand, if properly implemented in the nation, organic agriculture could produce much of Nigeria's food. On the other hand, the model is associated with several challenges. These challenges include social problems of an agro-economical, educational, and economic nature. Large scale research institutions dedicated to agro-ecological methods of fertility and pest management, strong extension systems and pragmatic public policy systems are not available in most African countries (Badgley et al 2012). Dibie (2000) observed that since the government of Nigeria had not been effective in implementing its environmental policies, it would require a more drastic step for the nation to be transformed into one which was dedicated to adopting comprehensive agro-ecological methods of fertility.

It is important to note that appropriate production methods are but one component of a sustainable food system. Nigeria's viability of farming methods, land tenure for farmers, market accessibility, availability of water, trends in food consumption, and alleviation of poverty are essential to the assessment and promotion of sustainable food production systems in the country (Badgley et al., 2012; Easton 2012). Robert Dibie et al. (2011) contend that population growth, poverty, and pollution are closely connected to environmental health. Thus, the Nigerian government and its environmental regulatory agencies would need to determine a way of holding multinational and domestic companies accountable to the same standards as those upheld in other nations in which they operate, such as some western industrialize countries. Nigerians can no longer dump trash in their neighbor's yard, farmland or rivers, or assume that such acts will not affect the nation's social and economic lifestyles and values.

According to Stephen Polasky (2012), putting a monetary value on ecosystem services will improve decision making by clearly illustrating the consequences of alternative choice. "The Polasky Concept" tends to serve the purpose of highlighting the relationship between ecosystem degradation and sustainability. The monetizing ecosystem approach brings with it the idea that if monetary values could be placed on ecosystem functions, concrete incentives could be designed to promote sustainable use of ecosystems. Opponents of placing a monetary value on ecosystems present the argument that the exclusive use of the monetization of ecosystem services may only favor short-term consumption of goods and services (McCauley, 2006). Opponents argue that such a short-term view of nature could be catastrophic, and this has been seen in practice with the collapse of fisheries. Kosoy and Corbera (2010) contend that an attempt to value any one component will never be able to capture the true overall value of the system as a whole. A very important point to note is that ecosystems are interrelated, and that as a result any disruption in one ecosystem could have negative effects on other ecosystems in Nigeria. Thus, any disruption of the ecosystem in Nigeria may destabilize the biodiversity of the entire affected region. The frequent oil spillages in the Niger Delta region and their subsequent impact on fishing and farming help to explain the interrelationship between ecosystem degradation and sustainability. However, some scholars contend that unless some economic incentives can be presented for nature conservation, most people in Nigeria will opt to take the cheaper route, which often results in the degradation of nature (Goldman 2010; Polasky 2008; McNeely 2007).

The Mertonian perspective of illegitimate means can be applied to environmental crime in the Niger Delta of Nigeria. Nigerian public administrators, political leaders and officers of multi-national corporations are likely to abandon morality to achieve economic prosperity (Clifford and Edwards, 2012). The abandonment of ethical environmental values includes the failure to regulate multinational corporations' exploration activities in Nigeria, the failure to effectively implement environmental policies in the country, and the failure to protect citizens from oil pollution. Abandonment may include the failure to provide treatment to citizens infected by diseases due to air, water, and hazardous pollution. Possible forms of unethical behavior also involve indulging in corrupt practices that may save money but create environmental harm to the citizens in Nigeria.

The "Self-Control Theory" by Gottfredson and Hirschis (1990) contends that individuals who have been subjected to poor or inconsistent parenting practices are likely to have low level of self-control. Those with low self-control in government, multi-national corporations, and civil society organizations are more likely to engage in unfriendly environmental behavior that may harm both the ecosystem and citizens. The Self-Control Theory could be used to explain environmental crime in the Niger Delta region of Nigeria. Individuals with low self-control may not care about anyone or the environment, and may therefore engage in environmental crime due to their self-interested (selfish) nature. Further individuals with low interest may perform physical harm to the environment because they are attracted to certain forms of physical behavior (Pratt and Cullen, 2000). Piquero et al. (2010) argued that environmentally criminal behavior may be simple and easy to perform because of differential association, imitation, reinforcement and greed.

According to Rogers and Hall (2003), poor governance leads to increased political and social risk, institutional failure and rigidity, and a deterioration in the capacity to cope with shared problems. Some analysts have shown that there is a strong causal relationship between better governance and better development outcomes, such as higher per capita incomes, lower infant mortality, and higher literacy (Kaufmann et.al., 1999). Effective governance is thus essential to poverty reduction, as it can help the poor to help themselves. Poor governance is a barrier to development, and hurts the poor through both economic and non-economic channels, making them more vulnerable and less able to adapt to change.

To conceive of a just society is to conceive of two key principles, namely need and equality (Dibie 2008; Enahoro and Ehi-Ebewele 2007). The need question borders on that of basic and inexcusable human needs (UNDP, 2006; UN, 1977). The principles of equality demand that people must be treated as equals in a political community and in their position as citizens, and that they must have equal political, legal and social rights. The equality principle is mostly entrenched in constitutional provisions, and it is very important if the minority question is to be effectively addressed in development and resource allocation (Ebeku 2003; Miller 1999, 250). Thus, sustainable development is more than the passage from poor to rich or from a traditional rural economy to a sophisticated urban one. Development includes distributional issues and carries with it not only the idea of economic betterment, but also of greater human dignity, security, justice, and equity, in the Niger Delta region of Nigeria.

Civil Society, Conflict, and Oil Resources Exploration

Apart from the Nigerian civil war (1967-1970), some of the worst violence in the nation occurred in the Niger Delta region, which produces most of the oil that is the mainstay of Nigeria's economy. Around the oil town of

Warri, the area's three main ethnic groups (Ijaws, Itsekiri and Urhobo) battled, as each lay claims to ownership of land that would accrue more benefits and influence from oil operations to their communities (Guardian, November 30, 2002). Since 1999, a militia group called the Bayelsa boys in Bayelsa State, and the Area Boys of Delta State of Nigeria, have been confronting multinational corporations' staff drilling petroleum from their land. The battle between MOSSOP, the Bayelsa Boys, the Delta Area Boys and the Nigerian government has been an on-going conflict over reparations from the petroleum bounty derived from their land. The negative effects of the conflict have invariably overshadowed the efforts of civil society organizations, such as MOSSOP, the Bayelsa Boys, the delta area boys and other Ogoni community-based organizations, to work towards a better quality of life.

As a result of these conflicts, most of the worst crimes against humanity have been committed in the name of the fight to protect the environment of the Niger Delta. The difference between a police state and a democracy appears most clearly in the way the Nigerian government has administered justice since 1999, when it became a democratic country. The Nigerian government's response to the violence of civil society groups has been nonchalant at times, and has not been in line with the above democratic principles. In November 1999, when a militant civil society group (the Bayelsa boys) in Bayelsa State in the Niger Delta killed 12 policemen, the government responded with military force. The troops sent by the government razed the town of Odi, where the policemen had been killed, destroying every building except a bank and a church (Guardian, November 30, 2007). At the end of the operation, the soldiers left hundreds of people dead, including children and women (Igwara, 2007).

The Federal Government of Nigeria announced in May 2009 that the country was losing over $8.7 billion (USD) daily due to the instability in the Niger Delta region, and as a result of militant activities that included killing oil corporation workers, burning down drilling terminals, and holding officers of multinational corporations to ransom (Newswatch, 2009). Members of the Movement for the Emancipation of the Niger Delta (MEND) constitute the majority of the militant groups in the Niger Delta region. Before the amnesty and the implementation of a policy program by the federal government of Nigeria, the activities of the militants had forced down production of crude oil for export by half of the country's 3.2 million barrels per day (Nigerian Tribune June 3, 2009). In early 2009, attempts to dislodge the militants cost the nation many lives and a lot of property. Within the first few months of 2009, more than 900 persons (many of whom were women, children, and non-militants) were reported killed (Nigerian Tribune, June 3, 2009). Members of the National Assembly of Nigeria were reported to have blamed the conflict in the Niger Delta region on the multi-national oil corporations operating in the region. The National Assembly contended that the multinational oil companies seemed to show no concern for the well-being of the people in Niger Delta, thus neglecting their social responsibility (Adunbi 2010). The National Assembly contended that they would probe the activities of Shell Petroleum, as well as Chevron, Agip, and Exxon-Mobile, among others. Another major problem in the Niger Delta region is the international oil bunkering of fuel. International merchants buy stolen crude and exchange it, supplying arms and ammunition to the militants (Newswatch 2009, 8-9 & 53).

The area referred to as the Niger Delta region was limited to the geopolitical zone occupied mainly by the minorities of Southern Nigeria, which currently comprises the six states of Akwa Ibom, Bayelsa, Cross River, Delta, Edo and Rivers. In recent years, the Niger Delta region has been redefined and enlarged to include all nine contiguous oil-producing states. The new states of Abia, Imo and Ondo were therefore added to the original six. Today, the Niger Delta people form the largest group amongst the ethnic minorities spread over the South-South geographical zone of Nigeria. It has a population of over 7 million people, distributed across over 1600 communities.

The region has some unique characteristics, which tend to make development difficult. It is, for instance, one of the largest wetlands in the world. It covers an area of 70,000 square kilometers and is noted for its sandy coastal ridge barriers, brackish or saline mangrove, fresh water and permanent and seasonal swamp forests, as well as low land rainforest (Nwilo and Bajdejo, 2008). The whole area is traversed and crisscrossed by a large number of rivers, rivulets, streams, canals and creeks. The coastline is buffeted throughout the year by the tides of the Atlantic Ocean, while the mainland is subjected to floods by the various rivers, particularly the River Niger. The Niger Delta region is the second largest Delta in the world and the largest wetland in Africa (Akpan and Akpabio 2003). The Delta is home to an extraordinary variety of people, mostly fishermen and farmers with a history and a cultural heritage.

In transforming the subject population into a new form of citizenship, non-governmental organizations (NGOs), considered to be "experts", are relying on particular sets of knowledge-production that set them apart from the local networks and project them into transnational networks and alliances (Annelise Riles 2000). These networks are inscribed with the notion that change is possible through the acquisition of a particular form of knowledge that can be transmitted in particular ways through connections to the transnational. Many of the NGOs operating in the Niger Delta region of Nigeria tend to have acquired certain proficiencies that connect them to transnational systems of circulation and exchange of information. These NGOs are engaged in producing new forms of citizenship for multinational corporations and the Nigerian state, through the deployment of their "expertise" and mastery of transnational human and environmental rights rhetoric. Thus, development has become a form of political institution that constitutes rural populations as a field of intervention and planning (Bornstein 2005). This is because development helps to justify the colonial and post-colonial realm of knowledge that continues to produce and reproduce itself.

Therefore, multinational corporations such as Shell and Chevron are engaged in practices that are not conducive to the environment or to the people of the Niger Delta: these practices are transnational in outlook but destructive to the local land and rivers. Aiding these practices are nongovernmental organizations engaged by multinational corporations because of their proficiency in human and environmental rhetoric of governance. It is this form of proficiency that is producing and transforming subject populations into oil citizens, in ways that are normalized and internalized. This form of transformation arguably produces different outcomes for the oil companies that are not mutually exclusive. First, it gives a semblance of minimization of conflict in resource enclaves, because its purports to redefine the ownership structure and to confer some level of "ownership" of resources on oil citizens. Second, it helps the subject population to make claims of' ownership of land and resources in ways that stimulate the production of new forms of citizenship. These induce the creation of sites of power for multinational corporations, in ways that are evocative of colonialism in the post-colony.

Chevron Nigeria Limited, an arm of ChevronTexaco, with headquarters in San Francisco, California, is one of the major oil corporations in the Niger Delta region. Its Nigerian corporate headquarters is located on the Lekki Peninsula, an upscale area on the outskirts of Lagos. Lekki is known for its exclusivity, and is an area widely known to be inhabited by the Nigerian ruling elite and business leaders, as well as other members of the upper class. It is an area that overlooks the Atlantic Ocean, close to Victoria Island, another upscale neighborhood, and is home to many beautiful beaches. Public transportation in the area is erratic, because the transport system exists primarily for casual workers who do cleaning work for the "big and rich boss", artisans who repair the "big boss's" car, or restaurant workers in the fast growing eatery industries in the area. However, commuting is made easy for the upper-class core employees of Chevron, who are also situated in Lekki and have homes at a comfortable distance from their Chevron workplace.

The Niger Delta region is also the main center of oil producing activity in Nigeria, and is therefore the center of Nigeria's economy, accounting for more than 90% of Nigeria's foreign exchange earnings and more than 80% of government revenue (CBN, 1981). Petroleum was discovered by Shell-BP in 1956, following half a century of exploration. Oil production became important in the 1960s, but the Biafra conflict and the civil war of 1967-1970 delayed further expansion. The main reservoirs are located in and around the Niger Delta, in both on-shore mangroves and shallow off-shore basins. Since 1990, exploration has increasingly moved to deep, offshore areas. Unclear boundary demarcations in the Niger Delta have caused disputes relating to several strategic areas. Wunder (2003) observed that Cameroon and Nigeria both claim zones on and off the Bakassi Peninsula, and ownership of the Zafiro oil field is disputed with Equatorial Guinea. Shell continues to be the largest company, but has been joined by a series of other multinationals corporations over the years.

Despite being the richest geopolitical region in terms of natural resource endowment, Akpan and Akpabio (2003) observed that the Niger Delta's potential for sustainable development remains unfulfilled and is now threatened by environmental devastation and worsening economic conditions. The inhabitants of this region depend heavily on the environment for their livelihoods, mostly in the form of fishing, farming and gathering. Consequently, oil exploration and exploitation have had a far-reaching negative environmental, social and economic impact on the host communities (Akpan and Akpabio 2003).

Many of the oil production and exploration areas are located in 700,000 hectares of delta mangroves (Wunder, 2003). These represent the remaining forested biomass in Nigeria and about two-thirds of all the mangroves left in Africa. The area constitutes an essential ecosystem, both for local people and for fisheries off West Africa's coast. Wunder (2003) observed that no deforestation estimates are available, but that operations and infrastructural development in the mangroves have been quite intense: 349 drilling sites, 700 km flow-lines, 400 km pipelines, 22 pumping stations and one terminal (Bassey, 1999). There are a great many cases of oil spillage, some of which have not been accounted for. According to Rowell (1995), cited in Bassey, (1999), Shell alone has spilt 1.6 million gallons of oil in twenty-seven incidents between 1982 and 1992, which accounts for no less than 40 percent of Shell's global oil spills. Equally important are the extensive ecosystem changes from water flow disruptions, including involuntary damming, tidal changes and the exchange of fresh and salt water, which are caused by road construction, dredging and the use of heavy machinery. Other direct effects include pollution from drilling mud and the effects of explosives. Indirect effects are also present, such as accommodating 6,000 temporary workers for the gas plant, who practice hunting and other forms of forest extraction (Bassey 1999). Gas flaring is higher than anywhere else in the world (Wunder 2003). According to Mbendi (2002), current and ongoing efforts aim to eliminate the current levels of 75% flaring, while 12% is being reinjected. In addition, Wunder (2003) observed that the oil companies' environmental practices in such a sensitive ecosystem have been deficient; direct and indirect deforestation effects have been limited but forest degradation has been serious.

Environmental hazards spawned by oil spillages now define the daily lives of the Ilaje people in many of their communities. The fishing business has become a nightmare. This is because of environmental pollution, while cash crops are no longer as abundant as they once were before the advent of oil exploration in the region. There are no good roads, hospitals, or schools.

Most houses are constructed with raffia palms, in most cases on top of the river that connects to the Atlantic Ocean. Toilet facilities are constructed with raffia palms on top of the river. When the toilet facilities are used, waste falls into the river and flows away. The river is also used for cooking, bathing and drinking, as well as being a means of livelihood for the fishermen and women who paddle their canoes daily. When asked if using the river to dispose of human waste constituted a health hazard for members of the community, many of my informants told me how the part of the river used for toilet facilities flowed in a different direction from the part used for other purposes.

The oil modernity that has projected Nigeria into the world capitalist system is most noticeable in Lagos and Abuja, with its skyscrapers and nicely paved roads, which are completely absent in the Niger Delta region. Strikingly, one can still see some youths and adults enjoying an Internet connection that operates with an electric generator. The absence of social amenities does not in any way deter the people, especially the youth, from enjoying the trappings of national wealth.

The very idea that he who controls the power controls the wealth and resources means a lot in the context of the oil producing Niger Delta region, and the numerous communal conflicts arising due to pollution of lands, rivers and the result high unemployment rate. Competition for power has both a national and a local dimension. Ajagu (2000), cited in Ameh (2001), observed that: "in recent years, there have been the perceived feelings by some ethnic groups that key institutions have been dramatically restructured in such a way as to create imbalances in favor of some ethnic nationalities."

The major oil companies operating in the Niger Delta are summarised in Table 1.

Table-1) Major Oil Companies Involved in the Exploration and Marketing of Oil in Nigeria

Consortium	Shareholders	Joint Venture Operator	Productio n barrels/ Day (2003 estimate)	Prod-uction (%)
Shell Petroleum Development Company of Nigeria Ltd	NNPC (Nigeria, 55%) Shell (Dutch/British, 30%) Elf (France, 10%) Agip (Italy, 5%)	Shell	950 000	42.2%
Mobil Producing Nigeria Ltd	NNPC (Nigeria, 58%) Mobil (USA, 42%)	Mobil	500 000	21.2%
Chevron Nigeria Ltd	NNPC (Nigeria, 58%) Chevron (USA, 42%)	Chevron	485 000	18.6%
Nigeria Agip Oil Company	NNPC (Nigeria, 60%) Agip (Italy, 20%) Philips (USA, 20%)	Agip	150 000	7.5%
Elf Petroleum Ltd	NNPC (Nigeria, 60%) Elf (France, 40%)	Elf	145 000	6.1%
Texaco Overseas (Nigeria) Petroleum Company	NNPC (Nigeria, 60%) Texaco (Nigeria, 20%) Chevron (USA, 20%)	Texaco	55 000	2.7%

Other Producers	Ashland (USA) Deminex (Germany) Pan Ocean (Switzerland) British Gas (British) Sun Oil (USA) Conoco (USA) BP (British) Statoil (Norway) Conoil (Nigeria) Dubri Oil (Nigeria)	Various	35 000	1.7%
Total		2320 000	100%	

Source: Idemudia, U. and U. Ite (2006). Corporate-Community Relations in Nigeria's Oil Industry: Challenges and Imperatives. *Corporate Social Responsible Environmental Management* 13,194-204.

There is an argument that the position that confers the power of recruitment and the power to control the nation's resources is now being controlled by a section of the country. These gross imbalances are the reasons for the rise of ethnic militia and agitation for a sovereign National Conference and a restructuring of the Federation. At the national level, key and self-interested political elites decide remotely—as far away as Abuja—who controls the key institutions of government and the development agencies in the Niger Delta. For instance, during local and state elections, the questions of who contests and who wins are determined by a few political elites, while the affected people do not have any say (Adunbi 2010; Idemudia and Ite, 2006). In the appointment of key officers of governments, the rules are not followed, while merit is discarded, leaving room for political patronage, even when such appointments are not acceptable to the people.

What this implies is that the struggle and competition for power often sets communities against communities, and communities against individuals and governments. It is even more pronounced when the leaders use political means to decide upon the distribution of infrastructures and oil wealth. During every election period, there is always a high incidence of political assassination and massive rigging and fighting among people as political tools to achieve persistent control over the resources of the region. Communities often react by way of conflict and violence. Reactions can take many forms, such as conflict directed against political leaders, community against community, or community against government.

It is common knowledge that any time there is an outbreak of conflict in communities in the Niger Delta, the Federal government of Nigeria responds swiftly with direct military action, without proper consultation with stakeholders or community leaders. This has always escalated the problem, and has led to more harm and to more problems. The case of the Odi direct military action is a good pointer. With an interactive conflict management approach, community stakeholders and leaders can be brought to a round table, and this has been proven to be very useful in resolving conflicts in many situations (Uwazie, 2010). From the testimonies of the people in the area, it is clear that the frequent incidence of high handedness and disregard for their views in matters affecting them only helps to worsen conflict situations.

Conflict Due to Revenue Sharing

According to Clarke (2009), the global circulation of justice implies that human and environmental rights discourses have become tools for the mobilization of a new form of membership. Thus, civil society groups, in the form of social movement and grassroots organizations, are now trying to fill the vacuum created by the distance between citizens, their representatives, and the crisis of legitimacy. In the Niger Delta region, lack of government has given privileges to the transnational oil companies in creating spaces of governance in resource enclaves. Uwazie (2010) contends that we should view human and environmental rights networks as not only antagonistic to the state and multinational corporations, but also as in cooperation, collaboration, and competition with them. This is due to the instituting of shared governance structures in resource enclaves of the Niger Delta.

The peculiarities of the Niger Delta problem attracted the developmental attention of governments, from the colonial periods to the period of independence. In the colonial days, the Queen of England's Government set up the Sir Henry Willink's Commission to recommend the best strategies for the development of the region, which has the most difficult terrain in the country (Aaron, 2003). When the commission submitted its report in 1958, it specifically recommended that the Niger Delta region deserved special developmental attention and that it should therefore be made a special area to be developed directly by the Federal Government.

This was before crude oil became the mainstay of the Nigerian economy. The advent of crude oil found in the region led to the use of the idea of derivation as a revenue allocation formula. According to Aaron (2003), the derivation formula witnessed a progressive decline.

Table-2) Rate of Decline in Derivation Formula 1953-1999

Year	Percentage	Leadership
1953 to 1959	100%	British Colonial Government
1960-1967	50%	Alahaji Tafawa Balewa
1967-1975	45%	General Gowon
1976-1979	20%	General Murtula/Obasanjo
1979-1983	2%	Alahaji Shehu Shgari
1984-1985	1.5%	General Buhari
1985-1999	3%	General Babangida/ Salami
1999-2010	13%	President Obasanjo/ Shehu Ya- redua

Source: Enahoro, John E. & Ehi-Ebewele (2007), "Effect of the Oil Industry on the Environment: Shift in Paradigm on Financial Reporting Disclosure for Sustainable Environmental Development." Paper presented at the International Conference on the Nigeria State, the Oil Industry, on October 22-27 2007 at Niger Delta University, Bayelsa State Nigeria. Adunbi Omolade. (2010). Belong to the Soil: Multi-national Oil Corporation, NGOs and Community Conflict in Post-Colonial Nigeria. Ph.D. Dissertation of Yale University, USA.

According to Table 2, oil revenue allocation by the federal government of Nigeria to the oil producing states declined from 100% in 1953 to 50% in 1960 and from 50% to 45% under Gowon in 1970. Further, oil revenue dropped from 45% in 1970 to 20% under Murtala and Obasanjo in 1975 (Idemudia and Ite 2006). It also declined from 20% in 1975 to 2% in 1979 to 1982 under Shagari. Further oil allocation declined from 2% in 1982 to 1.5% under Buhari in 1989. The rate, however, increased from 1.5% to 3% under Babangida (Enahoro and Ehi-Ebewele 2007). In 1999-2010 the 13% constitutional provision was implemented by the Obasanjo administration (Adunbi, 2010). Even so, there is a widespread allegation that through the application of the offshore/onshore dichotomy, the presidency pays 7.5% and not the 13% constitutional provision. Table 2 shows the rate of decline in the derivation formula in Nigeria.

Apart from the disagreements this revenue sharing formula has frequently generated between the oil region and the Federal Government of Nigeria (FGN), the oil communities themselves are perpetually locked in clashes and conflicts as to who should have the highest share of oil revenue according to the derivation principle. While the FGN has explicit criteria on sharing oil revenue among oil producing states in the Niger Delta, the oil producing states in the region do not have any clear revenue sharing criteria to reflect the concerns of the oil communities. This boils down to the lack of autonomy of local government councils in the region, and Nigeria in general, leaving their state governments in a much stronger position to control all that accrues to government as revenue from oil. The nature of inter-communal struggle is founded on the idea of which community belongs to the core oil community and which does not. Between 1999 and 2003, the frequency of such fights was high and, in most cases, went unreported in the media.

During my field research trip to the Nigeria Delta region in 2009 and 2010, some of the local people that I interviewed in the Eket and Ibeno communities in Akwa Ibom State indicated that because of oil, these two communities had not had a cordial relationship over the years. While Ibeno people believe they are the core community from which oil is derived, the Eket, whose home is less than four kilometers away, say they are also affected by the activities of oil exploration. Consequently, the Ibeno expect that they should receive a larger share of oil revenue and benefits than other communities (Dibie, 2009). They expect to have the largest share of employment benefits, notwithstanding merits. Between 2002 and 2003, such fights culminated in most non-indigent staff of Exxon Mobil being chased out of their operational headquarters. Between 2008 and 2009, the Ijaw community did not share a good relationship with the Ibibio groups, particularly when the FGN appointed one of the Ibibio indigenes as the Minister of the newly created Niger Delta Ministry (Newswatch, 2009: 8-9 & 53). They believed that an Ijaw indigene should have been appointed as the pioneer Minister of the newly created ministry. In the distribution of federal and state infrastructures to the region, major disagreements arise concerning in which community a given infrastructure should be located. In most cases, those communities who classify themselves as the "core" oil communities would prefer to see major infrastructures located in their communities, even in the absence of any other reason for such a location. These are a few examples of the nature of such conflicts which play out, not only between communities in the oil region but between communities in the oil region and those in the non-oil region. When this happens, The FGN and the oil multinationals always capitalize by promoting "divide and rule" as a way of sustaining the marginalization agenda.

Appropriate Approach to Address Conflict Resolution

According to Ernest Uwazie (2008), conflict or dispute is inevitable in any societal or human relationship; the challenge is in its management or resolution. Finding a solution that is acceptable to all the parties involved is a process known as bargaining (or negotiation). This involves a process whereby two or more parties in dispute with one another exchange offers, counteroffers and concessions in an attempt to find a mutually acceptable agreement. Conflicts will not go away by making believe that they don't exist. Doing so will make them worse. However, standard practice constitutes a prescribed procedure for carrying out business in a given situation. The success or otherwise of oil exploration activities in the Niger Delta depends to a great extent on the availability of baseline standards of operation. The government can play an important role in setting up a minimum operational factor for the oil multinationals and the affected communities. Such a role may either be in terms of helping to shape an institutional environment that fosters sustainable economic growth, the pursuit of an active distributional and social policy, or the provision of motivation for ecological appropriate behavior (Idemudia and Ite, 2006).

The government of Nigeria could adopt a set of procedures such as mediation and arbitration, in which disputing parties work together with a neutral party who helps them settle their disagreements out of court.

The procedures could include:

1. **Mediation:** The process in which a neutral party (known as a *mediator*) works together with two or more parties to reach a settlement to their conflict.
2. **Arbitration:** A process in which a third party (known as an *arbitrator*) has the power to impose, or at least to recommend, the terms of an agreement between two or more conflicting parties.
3. **Binding Arbitration:** The two sides agree in advance to accept the terms set by the arbitrator, whatever they may be.
4. **Voluntary Arbitration:** The two sides retain the freedom to reject the recommended agreement.
5. **Conventional Arbitration:** The arbitrator can offer any package of terms he or she wishes.

6. **Final-Offer Arbitration:** The arbitrator chooses between final offers made by the disputing parties themselves (Greenberg 2010).
7. **Win-Win Solutions:** Resolutions to conflicts in which both parties get what they want.

   Suggestions for finding win-win solutions:
   a. Avoid making unreasonable offers;
   b. Seek the common ground;
   c. Uncover the "real" issues
   d. Broaden the scope of the issues considered.

8. **Integrative Agreement:** A type of solution to a conflict situation in which the parties consider joint benefits that go beyond a simple compromise (Greenberg 2010; Uwazie 2008).

Granting amnesty to the militia group is another policy that the Nigerian government could explore. However, such amnesty policies should include training or retaining programs of the unemployed Bayelsa boys or militants. The policy option also calls for the creation of jobs in the Niger Delta area. An interesting point that should be noted is that if the Nigerian Federal Government had spent half the oil revenue obtained from the Niger Delta region in the State rather than using it all to build Abuja (the national capital) there would have been fewer crises. This lack of foresight and injustice by the government to the people of Niger Delta region is what has constituted a major social and economic problem in the region. In the future, government policies should be based on honesty, fairness, truthfulness, integrity, transparency and accountability.

The bone of contention, however, cannot be limited to the weak environmental policies in Nigeria, which choose to utilize the benefits and risks of oil spillage in the Niger Delta region or the constant exposure to fossil fuel all over the country. There is a shared global impact, which could cause longer-term damage to ecosystems in West Africa and around the world. According to Nancy Maxwell (2009), the ecological footprint of the earth's surface provides resources for absorbing waste and pollution. Forest areas in the southern part of Nigeria, which are needed to absorb carbon dioxide produced by burning fossil fuels, are diminishing as the demand for lumber increases in Nigeria. Unless these natural resources are replaced at a rate equal to or greater than the rate of reduction, the nation's environment and sustainable development problems will continue to escalate.

Absence of standard practice has implications for the operations of oil companies and the communities of operation. Robert Dibie (2008) also observed that poor regulation and a dearth of incentives for "Corporate Social Responsibility" initiatives within Nigeria means that oil companies are left to set their own standards. Being purely profit driven in their operations, it is difficult to imagine oil multinationals evolving acceptable operational standards within their areas of operation unless compelled to do so, either through community action or government regulations. For instance, the Conflict Expert Group Baseline Report (2003) observed that there is a "flexible" interpretation of Shell Company in Nigeria (SCIN) policies, a low level of standardization, and continuing unethical practice. The Report further noted:

> [...] poor consequence management undermines policy compliance. Audit experts report that in cases where they had clear evidence of violation of business principles, the superiors of guilty staff failed to take action. This sends a message of impunity to the rest of the organization (p.25).

Idemudia and Ite (2006) similarly observed that the absence of a minimum control mechanism means that oil companies face a high temptation to break the law, with little or no associated risk for doing so.

According to the Conflict Expert Group Baseline Report (2003), about 70% of the conflicts that lead to work interruptions relate to contractor issues, and there are currently no guidelines or policies in contractors' contracts that determine their behavior in dealing with communities. For instance, Shell's contracting policy states that contractors are responsible for their own community relations, which means that each contractor adopts their own approach. For communities, who see every activity as an oil company's activity in its area of operation, this implies much confusion in identifying who should be held accountable for actions in the area, as over 99% of oil companies contractors count themselves "unaffected" by community demands or environmental policies. It is also important to note that in dealing with oil companies, some communities wield more power than others. Some have signed a Memorandum of Understanding (MOU) while others have not; some communities have high leadership command and elite groups that could facilitate dealing with oil companies, while others may not; again, some communities are very aggressive or militant (e.g., the Ijaw communities) in their dealings with oil company operators, while others may not be. The tendency is that more powerful communities are able to extract more (in terms of money, goods, opportunities and infrastructures) than others. This generates a perception of favoritism (as some communities watch their neighbors very closely in terms of the benefits they obtain from oil companies) and creates an atmosphere of animosity and tension. For instance, the 2009 violence that led to the death of over 25 persons in Rivers State was partly a culmination of such animosity between communities over oil benefits (Newswatch, 2009).

Setting guidelines for standard practice should be the role of the Federal Government of Nigeria. The absence of weak regulatory guidelines undermines "best practices" by oil companies and contractors in their areas of operation. The truth about Nigeria today remains that corruption is deeply rooted, and always undermines any effort at promoting effective Corporate Social Responsibility or Community Relations of the oil companies.

Conclusion

This paper has examined the conflict in the Niger Delta region in Nigeria. It contends that the Nigerian government, the civil society groups in the Niger Delta region and multinational corporations drilling petroleum in the region are the major disputants. Pollution of the environment, perceptual distortion, grudges, distrust, competition over scarce resources, and destructive criticism of the government are causes of the conflict. The paper begs to ask the question: why is the Nigerian government not protecting the citizens of the Niger Delta region from environmental pollution?

The paper also presented an argument that the rise in communal conflicts between the years 1999-2010 during the democratic government in Nigeria could be related to the problem of inappropriate revenue allocation and infrastructure for the Niger Delta people. This paper also noted that the high rate of conflict in the Niger Delta during the current democratic government is not a mere coincidence of events; it has a governance connection. From 1999 (when the present democratic experiment took off) until today, communal violence and conflicts in the Niger Delta are rising with alarming rapidity.

Due to significant economic, political, and social inequalities among the various ethnic groups in the region, challenges to the dominant social order periodically arise. In addition, cultural and religious differences among the ethnic groups may continue to galvanize ethnic conflict in the region. By combating socio-economic insecurity, which arises from scarcity and inequality, Nigeria will move towards becoming either an equalitarian pluralism state or a corporate pluralistic nation. Pragmatic and appropriate policies associated with regional autonomy, assimilation, pluralism and power-sharing have the potential to accommodate the essential interests of the most disadvantaged and politically active ethnic groups. Such policies include the following: (1) Ensure that all areas in the nation receive services and basic infrastructure whether or not they support the ruling party; (2) Equal distribution of capital programs and projects around the nation; (3) All states in Nigeria should be allowed some level of economic freedom or resource control; (4) Education and degree programs in conflict resolutions; (5) Introduce conciliation committees and forums; (6) Equitable redistribution of national wealth; (7) Introduce pragmatic law-enforcement policies that will promote the values of a government that respects the law and the constitution, not individuals; (8) Introduce the carrot and stick strategies or the use of threat and coercion without human rights abuses, and (9) Introduce a justice policy in which nobody is allowed to be above the law.

In reshaping and reconfiguring notions of citizenship and belonging, subject populations of various communities in the Niger Delta are being molded into new sets of practices, where spaces of the "conduct of conduct" are being structured into governance spaces within the communities. Using the examples of the establishment of Regional Development Councils (e.g., the Ilaje Regional Development Council, sponsored by Chevron) and Cluster Development Boards (sponsored by Shell), this paper explored how political power could be decentered within these communities in order to produce a shared governance system.

The paper has highlighted some of the major sources and causes of communal conflicts in the Niger Delta, including the problem of revenue and oil benefit sharing among resource communities, the absence of standard practice, and competition for political power, among many others. Competition for political power has been a very common phenomenon since the advent of democratic governance. This probably has to do with the high economic benefits associated with political power, given the huge oil revenues incidental to its exploitation. The previous state and local government elections in Nigeria attracted a high incidence of communal conflict and the consequent killings associated with it. This was partly because of the persistent attempts by the federal authorities and oil multinationals to corruptly influence the election of their candidates of choice in order to protect their interest.

With regards to the negative impact that communal conflicts tend to generate in the region, the following recommendations can be made: There is a need for inclusive and accountable governance at all levels of Nigerian society, as a prelude to efficient, effective, equitable and realistic benefit sharing of oil wealth. From oral accounts, it is very clear that the "dividends of democracy" is not accessible to the people on whose land oil is mined. Because of intense and high competition for political power, there is concomitant competition and consequent benefit capture among stakeholders. This deprives the real people from having access to oil resource benefits. Generally, the Niger Delta region is known for its lack of basic physical and social infrastructures. Inclusive and accountable governance demands that the proceeds of oil wealth should be used to provide an accessible and good road network, a constant power supply (the abundant gas in the region could be harnessed for this purpose instead of flaring) and affordable health care facilities, among others. The people should be allowed to be partners in this process of development. If this were the case, the implementation of projects through contractor/ government machinery who inflate prices, underpay labor or discriminate in labor recruitment matters should be discarded, in preference for the grassroots and community consultation in "development delivery." These recommended policies are positive steps in capacity building and poverty alleviation. When the people are gainfully engaged, they are able to provide for themselves, and thus idleness is checked. These are clear routes to good community relations.

There is the need to manage conflicts through the Interactive Conflict Management (ICM) approach (Upreti, 2003) as opposed to the persistent militarization model of government. ICM is a community-focused, learning-based and action-orientated methodological approach to the resolution of conflict at a local level. It is less expensive and moves beyond the structurally designed and compartmentalized blue print approach of conflict resolution. It focuses on the continuous interaction between people and their position in the broader socio-cultural setting, with governments and other social agents acting as facilitators. ICM acknowledges the knowledge, skills and experiences of the community in helping to manage conflict. It is a pragmatic approach, and the diversity embedded in the local community can be mobilized to resolve and manage conflict. The amnesty granted to the militant groups in the Niger Delta by the Federal Government of Nigeria is a good policy; however, the government needs to do more in order to alleviate poverty in the region. In order to foster poverty alleviation and environmental sustainability, all stakeholders in Nigeria must act now, act differently, and act together.

References

Aaron, K. K. Human Rights Violations and Petroleum Pipelines Vandalization in the Niger Delta Region of Nigeria. *The Nigerian*

Social Scientist. A Bieaanual Publication of the Social Science Academy of Nigeria: (2003), Vol 6, No. 2. pp 14-20.

Abdallah, J. Hussaina, "Religious Revivalism, Human Rights Activism and the Straggle for Women's Rights in Nigeria" In Mahmood Mamdani (ed.) *Beyond Rights Talk and Culture Talk: Comparative Essays on the Politics of Rights and Culture,* St. Martin's Press, New York: (2000).

Adelekan Ibidun, "The Nigerian Press and Environmental Information for Sustainable Development." *Local Environment*, Vol. 14, No. 4, pp. 297-312: (2009).

Ade-Ajayi, Joseph F., *Milestones in Nigerian History.* Ibadan, Nigeria: Ibadan University Press: (1962).

Ade-Ajayi, Joseph F. and E. J. Alagoa. "Nigeria before 1800: Aspects of Economic Development and Inter Group Relations." In Ikime: (1980b), 224-235.

Ade-Ajayi, Joseph F. and Michael Crowther. (1985). *History of West Africa*, Longman Publishers, (1980).

Ade-Ajayi, Joseph F., and Robert Smith. *Yoruba Warfare in the Nineteenth Century*, Ibadan University Press: (1971).

Adejumobi, Said and Abubakar Momoh. "The Nigerian Military and the Crisis of Democratic Transition: A study in the Monopoly of Power, Civil Liberties Organization," Lagos: (1999).

Ademoyega, Adewale, *Why We Struck: The Story of the First Nigerian Coup.* Ibadan, Nigeria: Evans Brothers (1981).

Adunbi Omolade, Belong to the Soil: Multi-national Oil Corporation, NGOs and Community Conflict in Post-Colonial Nigeria. Ph.D. Dissertation of Yale University, USA: (2010).

Afigbo, Adiele, "The Consolidation of British Imperial Administration in Nigeria: 1900-1918." In *Nigerian History, Politics and Affairs: The Collected Essays of Adiele Afigbo.* Ed. Toyin Falola. Trenton, NJ: Africa World Press: (2005), pp. 213-36.

Ahmad, Ehtisham, and Raju Singh, "Political Economy of Oil-Revenue Sharing in a Developing Country: Illustrations from Nigeria." IMF Working Paper. WP/03/16. Washington, DC: International Monetary Fund: (2003).

Agamben, Giorgio, *Homo Sacer: Sovereign Power and Bare Life.* Trans. Daniel Heller-Roazen. Stanford, CA. Stanford University Press: (1998).

Ake, Claude, *Democracy and Development in Africa.* Washington, DC: Brookings Institution: (1996).

Akindele, R. A., (1988), "The Domestic Structure and Natural Resources Profile of Nigeria's External Trade." In R. A. Akindele and Bassey E. Ate, eds., *Nigeria's Economic Relations with the Major Developed Market Economy Countries, 1960-1985.* Lagos: Nigerian Institute of International Affairs/ Nelson Publishers: (1988).

Akinjogbin, I. A. and E. A. Ayandele, (1980) "Yorubaland up to 1800,"In Ikime (1980b): 121-143.

Alayande, Babatunde, "Decomposition of Inequality Reconsidered: Some Evidence from Nigeria." Paper submitted to the UNU-WIDER conference on Inequality, Poverty, and Human Well-being, Helsinki, Finland: (May 30-1 2003).

Agim, C., *Understanding Community Relations in Nigeria's Oil Industry. Nigerian Petroleum Business: a Handbook*, Eremosele V. E. (ed). Advert Communications. Lagos: (1997), 129-139.

Amadi, Ako, (2010) "Environment Focus: Biodiversity in Niger Delta." July 14, 2010 02:42AMT.

Anago, Ifeany, Environmental Assessment as a Tool for Sustainable Development: TheNigerianExperience. www.jepplaw.net/pageBuildermage/Pages/Environmental2010 Legislation changes (2001). Accessed12/03/2010.

Ajagu (2000). Interview. Cited in Ameh, B. G. (2001*). Ethnic Conflicts and the Nigeria Police: the Way Forward.* Kan Education Books, Uyo. 25-37.

Akpan, N. S. and E. M. Akpabio (2003). Youth Restiveness and Violence in the Niger Delta Region of Nigeria: Implications and Suggested Solutions, *International Journal of Development Issues*, Vol. 2, No. 2, CSAS. Sydney Australia, pp 37-58.

Ameh, B. G., *Ethnic Conflicts and the Nigeria Police: the Way Forward.* Kan Education Books, Uyo. (2001), 25-37.

Asford Nicolas. "An Innovation-based Strategy for Sustainable Environment" in Jens Hemmelskamp, Klaus Rennings & Fabio Leone (ed.), *Innovation–Oriented Environmental Regulation: Theoretical Approaches and Empirical Analysis.* Zew Economic Studies, Heidelberg, Germany (2000).

Badgley Catherine et al (2012). "Can Organic Farming Feed the World?" in Taking Sides on Environmental Issues, Thomas Easton edited, New York, N.Y.: Mcgraw Hill.

Bassey, N. (1999). The Mangroves in the Niger River Delta. In Oil Watch:The Oil Flows, the Forest Bleeds. www.oilwatch.org.ec.

Bullard, R. (1993). Anatomy of Environmental Racism and theEnvironmental Justice Movement. In Confronting Environmental

Racism: Voices from the Grassroots. In Bullard R. (Ed). South End Press, Boston, MA. P15-39. Haughton, G. (1998). Geographical Equity and Regional Resource Management: Water Management in Southern California. *Environmental Planning B: Planning and Design* 1998, Vol 25: 279-298.

CBN (1981) Annual Reports, Central Bank of Nigeria.

Clark, William and Levin, Simon. (2009). "Towards a Science of Sustainability," Princeton Environmental Institute, Princeton, New Jersey, pp. 21-23.Clark, William and Levin, Simon. (2009). "Towards a Science of Sustainability," Princeton Environmental Institute, Princeton, New Jersey, pp. 21-23.

Clifford Mary and Terry Edwards (2012), *Environmental Crime*, Burlington, M.A: Jones & Bartlett Press, pp. 31-51.

Committee for the Defense of Human Rights: 2001: Annual Report on the Situation of Human Rights in Nigeria, Lagos.

Comaroff, John L., and Jean Comaroff. 1999. "Introduction," in Comaroff and Comaroff, eds., *Civil Society and the Political Imagination in Africa: Critical Perspectives.* Chicago: University of Chicago Press, 1—43.

Conflict Expert Group Baseline Report (2003). Shell Contractor Memorandum of Understanding, pp. 1-5.

Curran, G. ,(1997). Contesting Consent: Contemporary Democracy and Ecological Crisis. *Policy, Organisation and Society* 13: 149-166.

Dibie, Robert,. (2008). *Civil Society: Compaerative Perspective*. Laham, Maryland: Lexington Books, pp. 127-163.

Dibie, Robert, (2008). *NGOs and Sustainable Development in Sub-Saharan Africa*. Laham, Maryland: Lexington Books, pp. 51-70.

Ebeku, K. (2003) Judicial Attitudes to Redress for Oil Related Damages in Nigeria, RECIEL 12(2) 199–208.

Echefu, Nerry, and Akpofure (2000) Environmental Impact Assessment in Nigeria: Regulatory Background and Procedural Framework: www.iaia.org.public/ documents/EIA/casestudies. Retrieved 12/03/2010.

Enahoro, John E. and Ehi-Ebewele (2007) Effect of the Oil Industry on the Environment: Shift in Paradigm on Financial Reporting Disclosure for Sustainable Environmental Development. Paper presented at the International Conference on the Nigeria State, the Oil Industry and Niger Delta on October 22-27 2007 at Niger Delta University, Bayelsa State Nigeria.

Engeset, A M,. (2007) *Justice in Basic Water Distribution*. Masteroppgave i Statsvitenskap. Institutt for Statsvitenskap. STV-3900.

Ellsworth, K. H., (2000) Identities' Conflicts: Wedding Nigeria's Sub-national and International Identities and the conflicts they enable. Draft paper presented at the 2000 Conference of the International Studies Association, March 16.

Goldman, R., (2010). "Ecosystem Services: How People Benefit from Nature." *Environment*, pp.15-23.

Gottfredson, M. and Hirschi, T. (1990). A General Theory of Crime, Stanford, C.A.., Stanford University Press.

Greenberg, Jerald, (2010). *Behavior in Organizations. Upper Saddle River*, N.J.: Prentice Hall.

Guardian, Newspaper November 30, (2002). "Niger Delta Crisis." Lagos, Nigeria: Guardian, Press.

Haughton, G. (1998). Geographical Equity and Regional Resource

Management: Water Management in Southern California. *Environmental Planning B: Planning and Design* 1998, Vol 25: 279-298.

Hyden, Goran, (2006). African Politics in Comparative Perspective. New York, N.Y.: Cambridge University Press.

Idemudia, U. and U. Ite (2006). Corporate-Community Relations in Nigeria's Oil Industry: Challenges and Imperatives. *Corporate Social Responsible Environmental Management* 13,194-206.

Jain, R.K et al (1977) *Environmental Impact Analysis: A New Dimension in Decision Making*. New York: Nostrand.

Kaufmann, D., A. Kraay and P. Zoido-Lobaton, (1999). *Governance Matters. Policy Papers* 2196, World Bank Institute. October.

Kyapoya, Vincent. (1998). The African Experience. Upper Saddle River, N.J.: Prentice Hall.

Kooiman, J. (ed) (1993). *Modern Governance. New Government-Society Interactions.* Sage Publications.

Kosoy, N. and Corbera E., (2010). Payments for Ecosystem Services as Commodity Fetishism. *Ecological Economics*, Vol. 69, pp. 1228-1236.

Maduka, W.O., (1998) Evolving Vibrant Communities for Development Proceedings in International Seminar on Petroleum Industry, Abuja, Pp. 907-925. Maxwell, Nancy, (2009). Understanding Environmental Health. How We Live in the World. Boston, M. A.: Jones & Barlett Press, 39-51.

Mbendi, (2002). Cited in Wunder, S. (2003). *Oil Wealth and the Fate of the Forest: A Comparative Study of Eight Tropical Countries.* Routledge, London. Pp. 303-305.

McCauley, D.J., (2006). Selling Out on Nature. *Nature,* Vol. 444, pp. 27-28.

McNeely, J.A. (2007). A Zoological Perspective on Payments for Ecosystem Services. Integrative Zoology, Vol. 2, pp. 68-78.

Miller, D. (1999). *Principles of Social Justice*. Havard University Press, Cambridge. Massachusetts.

Newswatch Magazine, (2009). "Niger Delta and Oil Revenue in Nigeria" Lagos, Nigeria: Newswatch Press, pp. 8-9 & 53.

NDDC (2001). NDDC Profile, Niger Delta Development Commission, Port Harcourt, Nigeria.

Nigerian Tribune, June 3rd, (2009). "Genocide in the Delta" Ibadan, Nigeria: Tribune Press. P.14.

Nwilo, P.C and Badejo, T.O., (2008) Impact and Management of Oil Spill in Nigeria Coastal Environment. A paper presented at the International Conference on the Nigeria State, the Oil Industry and the Niger Delta, at The Department. Of Political Science, Niger-Delta University, Bayelsa State, Nigeria, March 11-13, 2008.

Polasky Stephen, (2012). What's Nature done for you lately: Measuring the Value of Ecosystem?" in *Taking Sides: Clashing Views in Sustainability*, Robert Taylor edited, New York, N.Y.: McGraw Hill, 228-238.

Rogers, P. & Hall, A. (2003). Effective Water Governance. Global Water Partnership, *TEC Background Papers*, No. 7.

Taylor, Robert. (2012). *Taking Sides: Clashing Views in Sustainability*. New York, N.Y.: McGraw Hill.

UNDP (2006). *Nigerian Human Development Report*. United Nations Development Programme. Lagos.

UN (1977). *Report of the United Nations Water Conference*. United Nations, Mar del Plata.

UN- WWAP (2003). *Water for People, Water for Life*. UNESCO Publishing.

Uwazie Ernest. (2010) "The Role of Higher Education in Conflict Resolution and Peace Education: Challenges and Prospects for African Universities." *Journal of International Politics and Development*, Vol. 8, No. 1, pp. 47-59.

Uwazie, Ernest, Daniel Yamshron and Patricia Malberg, (2008). *A Conflict Resolution Training Manual*. California State University, Sacramento. Center for African Peace and Conflict Resolution Publication.

Uwazie, Ernest (2003). *Conflict Resolution and peace Education in Africa*. Lanham, Maryland: Lexington Press.

WCED (1987). *Our Common Future*. World Commission on Environment and Development. Oxford University Press, Oxford.

Upreti, B. R., (2003). Interactive Conflict Management: An Interactive Methodology to Address Social Conflict at a Local Level. *International Journal of Development Issues*. Vol. 2, No. 2, CSAS, Sydney. Australia, pp. 77-90.

Wunder, S., (2003). *Oil Wealth and the Fate of the Forest: A Comparative Study of Eight Tropical Countries*. Routledge, London. Pp. 303-305.

CHAPTER EIGHT

INSTITUTIONALIZING DISPUTE RESOLUTION TRAINING AND PRACTICE: THE WAY FORWARD FROM EDUCATIONAL AND REGULATORY PERSPECTIVES

SAEED MUSAH-KHALEEPHA

Introduction

Since ADR has been introduced in Ghana, an institution that runs accredited training programmes to train ADR practitioners has yet to be established. The establishment of such an institution is important if the issue of mainstreaming ADR into the justice system is to be taken seriously. With general recognition for legal pluralism in almost every legal jurisdiction, the development of alternative justice systems—state or non-state—poses increasing challenges regarding the quality of practitioners and the satisfaction of users. Michael L. Moffit posits that "most mediators operate without significant influence from any ... quality-assurance mechanisms" (Moffit, 2008, p. 36). Most importantly, he writes:

> [I]n order for ... mechanisms to play a stronger role in the assurance of mediator quality, we would probably have to see a truly creative, almost impossibly bad set of facts emerge from at least one mediation gone awry. We would not, however, necessarily need to see such facts frequently. Even one case could have significant effects on mediators' practices. (Moffit, 2008, p. 34)

However, such a situation can be avoided mechanisms were pre-emptively put in place to safeguard both the practitioner and the consumer of ADR services from the many professional and ethical issues that may arise.

The sustainability of the ADR campaign and practice hinges on the availability of human resources, and the capacity of those resources to respond adequately to the demands of the public and/or users of ADR services. But the need for any user of ADR services to be assured that the person handling his/her case is sufficiently trained, competent, and professional enough to discharge such tasks is even more important.

The level of confidence that parties have in the practitioner is not only a matter of respect, but also important in terms of the level of regard and confidence in the process that produces the practitioner, and the structures that are in place to ensure that the practitioner conducts himself within acceptable limits and standards.

This paper therefore takes a look at how such expectations can be met by institutionalizing the practice of ADR as a profession at critical levels of business, state governance, and the community. It does so by employing various theories of education such as "Bloom's Taxonomy of Educational Objectives" (Bloom et al., 1956; Bloom et al., 1964. etc.), as well as theories of curriculum development (Ann Chapman 2007) which directly address the issue of the credibility and validity of any form of education and training. There will be a brief examination of possible training contents.

The paper will also take a look at the regulatory framework governing professional bodies in Ghana, and suggest some steps Ghana can take to institutionalize Alternative Dispute Resolution—or, more broadly, Dispute Resolution/Conflict management and Resolution—as a profession.

Perspectives on Streamlining the Practice of Dispute Resolution

Dispute resolution practices, especially those mechanisms that have largely being recognized as falling under the Alternative Dispute Resolution (ADR) Mechanism, are undergoing a great transformation. This is due to an increase in the awareness of their potential and to the increase in their usage. As a result not only of the name theme—"Alternative"—but also as a result of the general worldview of a rights-based idea of life, ADR has often received a cold reception and been treated with skepticism in some circles.

Though the non-litigious aspects of the dispute resolution continuum are yet to receive the attention needed to precipitate their use, training, and regulation, it behooves practitioners to turn their minds to this task, rather than to proceed in the shadow of already established professions such as teachers, lawyers, business professionals, accountants and so on.

Different programmes organized by different institutions tend to have varying views on what constitutes mediation. In Ghana, the most widely utilized ADR training programmes are usually franchised programmes from the US and Canada, which subscribe to the facilitative approach to mediation and appear deeply rooted in counseling psychology and workplace dispute resolution. In itself, this is not a bad thing. However, we ought to broaden the practice areas and knowledge base of the field beyond these existing franchised courses. According to Christopher Honeyman, there are five element of Mediation:

1. **Investigation:** effectiveness in identifying and seeking out relevant information that is pertinent to the case
2. **Demonstrations of Empathy:** conscious appreciation and consideration of the needs of others
3. **Invention:** inventiveness and problem-solving—pursuit of collaborative solutions
4. **Persuasion:** presentation skills—verbal expression, gesture and body language
5. **Distraction:** effectiveness in reducing tensions at appropriate times by temporarily diverting parties' attention, and a possible sixth knowledge of the subject matter (Honeyman, April 1988).

To ensure that these elements are translated into skill sets that a mediator can acquire, objective standards of measurement are required. As the field of ADR grows and as it becomes applicable in many sectors and at critical levels of business, national governance and community life, users of ADR services may begin to demand assurances of professionalism. In particular, this may be the case when they experience unprofessional conduct from some practitioners. They may begin to question the training credentials of the practitioners and ask whether they are adhering to a professional code of conduct. The public—both current users and potential users of ADR services—would like to know what remedial measures are in place if a practitioner is found guilty of misconduct. Honeyman writes:

> Almost no one greets the prospect of being evaluated with unalloyed joy—and the psychological pressures work both ways, so that the evaluator, too, has sound reasons to avoid the enterprise. The consequence of this general air of scepticism, I believe, is that programs are often unable to develop their mediators' skills to the utmost or to make sufficiently well-informed judgments as to whom to assign to particularly difficult cases. The potential for staff improvement and "program control" is thus rarely realized. In addition, "there is a significant public interest in the evaluation of those individuals who are in a position to exercise influence in public disputes. At present, mediators tend to be poorly evaluated or even, in

> effect, not evaluated at all (Honeyman, On Evaluating Mediators, January 1990, Emphasis mine).

So, it is no wonder that Honeyman opined:

> [...] if a mediator's performance cannot be evaluated according to intellectually respectable standards, we have no dependable way to select those who are best suited to do this work. Furthermore, it becomes difficult to explain what a given mediator could do to improve effectiveness, and a mediator's own claims of unfairness become impossible either to advance or to defend on logical grounds. As the practice of mediation becomes more widespread, and as more people come in contact with it, our inability to define standards of quality may well result in increasing numbers of people who are adversely affected by mediation and who consequently become opponents of the practice. Such opposition could ultimately prevent the adoption of mediation as a dispute resolution mechanism on the scale, for instance, of the litigation system. (Honeyman, On Evaluating Mediators, January 1990)

Aside from the above, there are ample reasons why there ought to be a painstaking review of training programmes, coupled with the need to establish an objective evaluation system and a highly regarded code of professional conduct. Otherwise, the gains made in promoting ADR as the best means of resolving disputes, especially civil disputes, may be corroded.

Methods of Assessing Mediators

Honeyman (1990) notes that conventional practice tends to identify three criteria by which a mediator's performance can be judged: rate of settlement of disputes, the opinion of the parties involved, and the mediator's general reputation among his/her peers. However, all these criteria have their flaws.

First, relying on the settlement rates of one mediator as compared to those of another in a similar situation immediately raises the objection that since no two cases are the same, the mediators cannot be compared fairly—mediating "more" cases does not mean mediating cases "better", and this emphasizes the quantity/quality dichotomy. Secondly, considering the parties' opinions brings some problems to the fore. While parties may develop strong opinions about particular mediators, they but are often unfamiliar with what may properly be expected of a mediator, and their opinions are just as firm after a single, abnormal case as they would be after twenty years of daily exposure to the mediator. Finally, a sterling reputation remains a kind of Holy Grail, much sought after by all mediation practitioners and equally difficult to attain. It takes a long time, and many cases, to arrive at a professional reputation of any consequence in this line of work, in which the "product" simply isn't as clear or as public as, say, an architect's product (Honeyman, 1990).

It is obvious that Honeyman recognises the need for specific factors or criteria in the assessment of the performance of mediators. In Honeyman (1988), reference was made to five elements of mediation, as discussed above. However, in Honeyman (1990) two further elements are added, *Managing the Interaction* and *Substantive Knowledge*. He explained that though these elements seem to be related, they are more useful to experienced mediators as opposed to those undergoing training.

In Honeyman's view, these two tools of evaluation are useful to experienced mediators as opposed to those in training; however, they will no doubt be useful to trainees of an advanced level if appropriate levels of certification are established. As mentioned earlier, it is apparent that Honeyman is referring to evaluating mediators while they are performing the task of mediating, not necessarily to the evaluation of trainee mediators.

Honeyman also advocated the use of what I will term "qualitative tools of evaluating mediators." Using a scale of 1-3, a mediator's observable performance in any of the five elements listed is marked as 1, 2 or 3, where 1 represents weak performance, 2 represents average performance and 3 represents good performance (Honeyman, 1990). With growing interest in mediation and the dispute resolution industry generally, and the growing popularity of international and commercial arbitrations, it would be somewhat anachronistic to pursue only such a trajectory when assessing mediators and dispute resolution practitioners.

So, it is no wonder that more than a decade after Honeyman's work, Ellen Waldman mentioned the three forms of credentialing approaches (Waldman, Vol. 8, No. 1, Fall 2001). She listed these as Degree-Based Approaches, Training and Experience-Based Approaches, and Skills-Based Approaches.

Waldman stated that some organisations place a person's level of education in high regard, and thereby assume that a degree holder is most capable of serving as a mediator. She notes that both theorists and practitioners have rejected this view.

With respect to the Training-and-Experience-Based Approach, Waldman writes that it is the most commonly used approach in court-annexed programmes, private mediation providers and trade organisations. She adds that this is not surprising, since using training and experience as a basis for credentialing mediators is both administratively simple and intuitively attractive. It is adminstratively simple because it requires only a simple review of the application submitted, and is intuitively attractive because it makes sense to assume that mediators who have received didactic training and who have refined their skills in the mediation trenches would, at least, be minimally competent. However, Waldman thinks this may be misleading (Waldman, Vol. 8, No. 1, Fall 2001).

Furthermore, Waldman referred to the Skills-Based Approach as the "cutting-edge approach that marries training and experience requirements with skills-based evaluation." She stated that although it being [sic] used by a "small minority" of private providers, trade organisations and state courts some of which are the San Diego Mediation Center (SDMC), the Maryland Council for Dispute Resolution (MCDR), and Family Mediation Canada (FMC) all of which offer voluntary certification programs. The Department of the Navy strongly encourages its use; and the Massachusetts Office of Dispute Resolution (MODR) and the District and Circuit Courts of Virginia require their mediators to obtain certification in order to participate in their programs." (Waldman, Vol. 8, No. 1, Fall 2001). She observes that:

> [B]asic questions regarding mediation's goals and methods still inspire spirited disagreement: Should mediators aspire to generate settlement, relationship repair, or psychological transformation? Does the mediator have responsibility for the fairness of any agreement reached, for its conformity with social norms? Is evaluation appropriate? If so, sometimes, always, never? Consensus remains elusive. The fact that no consensus yet exists on these rather foundational questions complicates any effort to establish performance-based certification standards. If the field holds within it multiple visions of what mediation is, then efforts to distill the essential qualities and skills of a mediator will remain problematic. Performance-based criteria for certification will likely be adopted only by organizations with a clear and cohesive definition of what mediation does or does not entail. Larger groups and constituencies, like state judicial councils or federal agencies, may avoid performance-based assessments if they are unable to settle upon a core set of mediation principles or methodologies. Adopting broader, more general, degree or education requirements is far simpler and skirts definitional quandaries. (Waldman, Vol. 8, No. 1, Fall 2001)

Waldman therefore makes her preference for skills-based testing very clear, although she favours a somewhat modified form of testing, as compared to the approaches initially proposed by Honeyman. It is important to note that following the views of both Honeyman and

Waldman requires the study and/or observation of the mediator on the job or in a role-play, by a mentor, a reviewer, or a review panel. Rather than use this as a sole means of assessing mediators, I believe that the method can be incorporated within an integrated approach to training. I agree to an extent with Waldman (2001) that "performance-based testing, if done correctly, promises an accurate and effective mechanism for ensuring competent and effective mediation." However, skills-based testing, also referred to as performance-based testing by both Honeyman and Waldman, requires that the person being tested should already possess a set of knowledges, skills, abilities, and other attributes (KSAOs). See Honeyman (June 1995, pp. 18).

However, these KSAOs cannot be acquired in unless the candidate has already been exposed to some form of education and/or training in the subject area. It is therefore curious to note the silence of both Honeyman and Waldman on what ought to be studied, or what orientation the candidate ought to have, before the skills test is administered.

Educational Perspectives

According to educational theorists, any form of education and training ought to pursue a set of objectives and measurable outcomes. Such theorists often refer to the process of putting together courses of study for adult education and/or professional education as programme planning, which is contrasted with curriculum development. Programme planning is much more involved than curriculum development/design (Chapman, 2007, p. 147). It entails questions about how to design the curriculum and how to articulate the rationale for the programme, and has a focus on cost, enrolments and marketing. Therefore, curriculum design/development is just one component of the broader notion of programme planning (Chapman, 2007). Thus, to implement Dispute Resolution programmes/courses successfully, programme managers ought to pay attention not only to the content of the training, but also to the cost of the training, enrolments and how to market the programme.

It is important to note that the name "Alternative Dispute Resolution" presupposes that ADR is not the dominant means of resolving disputes. Method of teaching such courses should be crafted in ways that challenges some of the learners' most fundamental assumptions, especially in programmes like Mediation Advocacy, which is geared towards lawyers. Chapman (2007) refers to Tisdell's work (Tisdell, 2001) as alluding to the fact that "to teach for social change generally means trying to alter the power relations of the dominant culture by calling attention to the politics of positionality, which for higher education, means looking at curriculum analysis and pedagogy. She calls for a greater inclusion of people from outside the dominant culture, to have representatives of people of ... other marginalized groups, and to conduct classes in a way that accounts for a diversity of ways" (Chapman, 2007, p. 150).

While acknowledging the fact that aspects of programme design could be handled in a less technical way, I shall here seek to briefly address the issue of curriculum design. Two curricularists, Tyler and Bloom, have influenced the method of curriculum design over a long period of time. Tyler's Rationale and Bloom's Taxonomy of Educational Objectives (also known as Bloom's Taxonomy of Learning Domains) have been widely used and applied in educational settings. According to the Tyler Rationale, there are four questions that the curriculum designer must answer:

> 1. What educational purposes should the institution seek to attain?
> 2. What educational experiences can be provided which are likely to attain these purposes?
> 3. How can these educational experiences be effectively organized?
> 4. How can we determine whether these purposes are being attained? (Tyler, 1949, p. 1)

These questions set the tone for Tyler's Rationale. In answering the above questions, the educator was to follow the following steps:

1. Select and define learning objectives
2. Select and create appropriate learning experiences
3. Organize learning experiences to achieve maximum cumulative effect
4. Evaluate the curriculum. (Chapman, 2007, p. 9).

The Tyler Rationale is based upon an epistemological assumption that the scientific way of prescribing learning (i.e. through a linear cause/effect process) is unquestionable. It assumes that the planner is objective, and that he or she scientifically plans the means necessary to produce the desired learning outcomes. This leads to the assumption that decisions on such issues as instructional method and content are technical, value-free and appropriate for a technical expert to make (Chapman, 2007, p. 121). For these reasons, Chapman (2007) does not subscribe to the rationale.

In contrast, Benjamin Bloom's Taxonomy of educational objectives seems to be more focused on application to a specific subject matter. He notes that the educational experiences for any learner should cover three domains: the cognitive domain, the affective domain, and the psycho-motor domain. The cognitive domain deals with relevant knowledge of the subject matter, mental skills (or simply 'knowledge'). The affective domain deals with the need for the learner to appreciate or see the importance of the knowledge and develop a growth in feelings and emotional attachment to the subject matter (or simply "attitude"). Finally, the psycho-motor domain deals with the ability of the learner to apply the knowledge through practice and to develop manual or physical skills (or simply 'skills'). (Isaacs, 1996).

It is acceptable for programme managers/planners in ADR to adopt and use both the Tyler Rationale and Bloom's Taxonomy in the design and implementation of their programmes and course contents. However, Chapman (2007) proposes a new approach to designing and implementing adult professional education which dispenses with the linear means-to-end module of curriculum design proposed by Tyler. Instead, Chapman integrates Mezirow's transformative learning theory and Schwab's deliberative curriculum theory:

> In my experience in higher education, I have often been on governance committees that provided oversight for the creation of new academic programs. It is not unusual to see individual academic chairpersons come forward with proposals that indicate lists of courses for students to take, and sometimes a list of core knowledge and skills they need to be successful. The proposers are operating on the assumption that a list of courses focusing on knowledge and skills will produce graduates who are professionals. This is contrary to both Mezirow's theory (Mezirow, 1997) and Schwab's theory (1978/1971a). An integration of these two theories will provide a richer context for understanding the experience of curriculum work. It will take faculty deeper into how students can experience transformation and how they can intentionally plan for it. (Chapman, 2007, p. 250)

According to Chapman, in developing a curriculum it is necessary to factor in four commonplaces: the teacher, the student, the educational milieu, and the subject matter (Chapman, 2007, p. 181). These commonplaces ought to be a constant presence in programme planning. This view partly coincides with Waldman's (2001) view on testing instruments:

> [T]he testing instrument adopted should be the product of collaborative effort, with input sought from experienced mediators and mediation consumers alike. [...] The main focus of professional education is to "help students become authentic professionals—those who answer the call to serve the public good. (Chapman, 2007, p. 336)

Chapman summarizes the idea of being professional as follows:

> In sum, to become a professional means more than to acquire knowledge and skills. It is artistry, and it is vocation or a calling to service, to the public good, and to a professional community. Being professional means more than having a career or being competent. It means seeking to serve others rather than self and becoming proficient and expert rather than merely competent. Developing expertise requires wisdom and the ability to make sound judgments in the face of uncertainty and ambiguity. Having one's own assumptions, beliefs, and values examined is part of transforming into a professional who thinks autonomously, more openly and critically. (Chapman, 2007, p. 180)

Chapman suggests a curriculum caucus guide for professional education (See Chapman 2007, pp. 326-347). This guide, based on the integration of Mezirow's Transformative-Learning Theory and Schwab's Deliberative Curriculum Theory, will no doubt be useful in the development of dispute resolution training modules.

Training Contents

Honeyman and Waldman have shown that there are several competencies (or KSAOs) that a person has to develop in order to become a good dispute resolution practitioner. Honeyman (1988) lists five elements of mediation, namely investigation, demonstrations of empathy, invention, persuasion and distraction; he adds a further two in his later work, namely knowledge of the subject matter and managing the interaction. He admits that "Landsberger (1956) used somewhat similar terms to describe the skills involved in mediation, and referred to a "halo effect" in which unusual ability in one aspect of mediation would carry the mediator over relatively low ability in another respect." (Honeyman, Five Elements of Mediation, April 1988). Much later, he adds "Ethical Behaviour" to the list (See Honeyman, June 1995, p. 27).

It was mentioned earlier that these elements relate to "being a mediator" and not necessarily "becoming a mediator." There are more concerned with "what to do as a mediator" than with "what to study to become a mediator." On the basis of the existing literature (including Honeyman and Waldman) one can see that it has been taken for granted that the candidate knows something about mediation, and that assessment is based on the existing skills and competencies of the mediator.

In what follows, I mention some of the subject matter areas that programme planners could consider including or incorporating in a programme design. The list is not exhaustive, and will certainly change over time, when new areas of practice are identified and certain competencies are emphasized over others. The list will, however, be useful for those training as mediators, arbitrators and negotiators:

- ✓ Theory and practice of conflict management and conflict resolution
- ✓ Theory and practice of Negotiation
- ✓ Theory and practice of Mediation
- ✓ Theory and practice of Arbitration
- ✓ Psychological perspectives of persons in dispute and applications of psychology to dispute resolution
- ✓ Sociological analyses and implications of types of disputes and disputing modes
- ✓ Communication skills in dispute resolution
- ✓ Introductory Law with emphasis on rules of natural justice and evidence procedures
- ✓ Collaborative Law
- ✓ Perspectives on the work of Ombudsman
- ✓ Review of statutes related to the practice of dispute resolution
- ✓ Case Management
- ✓ Pupilage—possibly a pro-bono service after training pending admission into the professional body (to be evaluated by a supervisor).

Specializations

- ➢ business disputes resolutions;
- ➢ international disputes resolutions;
- ➢ religious/congregational dispute resolutions;
- ➢ property dispute resolutions;
- ➢ family dispute resolutions;
- ➢ sports dispute resolutions;
- ➢ intellectual property and entertainment dispute resolutions;
- ➢ construction dispute resolutions;
- ➢ extractive industries disputes resolutions;
- ➢ governance/political dispute resolutions;
- ➢ environment and natural resources disputes resolutions;
- ➢ health and medical care disputes resolutions;

- finance, insurance and debt dispute resolutions;
- employment dispute resolutions, and
- educational dispute resolutions (for managers of educational institutions, teachers, and leaders of student government).

As previously mentioned, the list is not exhaustive, and is intended to serve only as a guide to programme planners. Programme planners need to settle upon one style of mediation, for the purposes of consistency. However, any educational exercise has a duty to the students to introduce them to the many different methods available, and then to emphasize the style that the programme in question has chosen to adopt. As Waldman writes:

> [E]valuators must be well trained to implement the instruments provided. And, perhaps most important, the leadership in any skills-based credentialing effort must decide either to adopt an instrument that explicitly tests for one particular mediation style, or to adopt an instrument whose criteria are sufficiently broad and general to allow for multiple styles. The lack of consensus that currently exists in the mediation field generally need not impede particular programs in their quest to identify mediators who are able to provide the kind of service each program requires. The particular nature of that service may differ from program to program. What matters is that program leadership knows what it is looking for and that mediation consumers know what they are being provided. (Waldman, Vol. 8, No. 1, Fall 2001).

Regulatory Framework for Professional Bodies

In Ghana, professional bodies are regulated by the Professional Bodies Decree, or Act (N.R.C.D. 143). The law makes provisions for registration and formations of professional bodies and their autonomy to self-regulate their professional practice. Section 6, subsection 2 of the Act, provides that a body that applies to be registered must be a society, institution or group of persons (*by whatever name called*), the members of which are:

(a) Trained and qualified in a profession recognized as such, and

(b) United in a common interest for the purposes of pursuing research and other activities concerned with the progress of knowledge in any such profession and for maintaining and advancing a code of ethics and conduct among its members, and in the general maintenance of the highest ideals of the profession concerned (Ghana, 1973).

I wish to mention in passing that through my association with the Ghana Association of Certified Mediators and Arbitrators (GHACMA), I became aware that the association was initially registered as the Ghana Association of Chartered Mediators and Arbitrators (GHACMA). However, it was suggested that the association needed a presidential charter in order to use the word "chartered." Although the word "chartered" is not edited out of the registration documents, it is absent from the letterhead and other documents of the association, and has been replaced by the word "certified." As this anecdote shows, the law is not very specific about what a prospective professional body must be called, considering the provision in Section 6 (2) "by whatever name called". Secondly, the body that registers all organisations in Ghana, the Registrar General's Department, is the same body charged by this law to register professional bodies. As experience has shown in dealing with the Registrar General's Department, a choice of name that is inconsistent with Ghana's laws is automatically rejected. By not rejecting the name "Ghana Association of Chartered Mediators and Arbitrators", the Registrar General's Department found nothing wrong with it. It should therefore be possible for GHACMA to revert to the use of "chartered" in its name instead of "certified": (To the claim that I appear to have digressed from the crucial aspects of this paper here, I would reply that a name is important in successfully marketing of the profession and its members).

Section 7 of N.R.C.D. 143 provides for the registration procedure of professional bodies. It requires only the following:

a. Constitution
b. List of members of that body, as at the date of the application, together with their qualifications
c. A statement of the activities of that body, within the past 12 months
d. Such other particulars as the Registrar may reasonably require (Ghana, 1973)
e. Section 7 subsection 2 requires the constitution of a professional body to include the following: the objects of that body; rules regulating discipline of members of the profession in question and the manner of enforcing such rules. (Ghana, 1973, p. 3).

Section 8 subsection 1 provides that the Registrar shall, subject to the other provisions of this Decree, register anybody applying for registration, if he is satisfied that:

a. The body has complied with the requirements of Section 7 of this Decree;
b. There is such a body, as described in subsection (2) of section 6 of this Decree;
c. The body represents not less than 75% of persons trained and qualified in the profession in respect of which that body desires to be registered. (Ghana, 1973, p. 3).

Following from the provision of section 6 subsection 2 (b), section 14 gives disciplinary authorities of professional bodies powers to enforce the attendance of witnesses, examine such witnesses (14 (1)(a) and compel the production of documents (14 (1)b). (Ghana, 1973, p. 5). Section 14(2) further provides for corrective measures for breach of the directives of disciplinary boards of professional bodies. Section 15 allows professional bodies to make rules governing the admission and code of ethics of its members compatible with its traditions including rules and regulations, providing for the ceasing of a person to be a member of the profession. It is obvious that the whole outlook of the Professional Bodies Decree (NRCD 143) coincides with Freidson's definition of professionalism:

> […] professionalism may be said to exist when an organized occupation gains the power to determine who is qualified to perform a defined set of tasks, to prevent all others from performing that work, and to control the criteria by which to evaluate the performance…The organized occupation creates the circumstances under which its members are free of control by those who employ them. (Freidson, E. (2001). *Professionalism: The third logic*. Cambridge, UK: Polity Press 2001, p. 12 quoted in Chapman (2007) p. 160).

It must be stated that by advocating for the professionalization of dispute resolution, one is not seeking to make dispute resolution (or, if you like, ADR) practice complex, cumbersome and difficult to access. What is proposed is essentially a mechanism to tidy up the practice and to make it attractive to those who need it and give assurance to those who use it that the practitioners are sufficiently trained and that there are mechanisms of self-correction for misconduct. Finally, what is proposed is intended to allow the individual practitioner gain a sense of worth, through belonging to a "profession" or being "professional" and, most importantly, to avoid possible cases of negligence, misconduct and malpractice.

Since the work entails a lot of confidentiality, it is important to establish such mechanisms that will serve to assure both practitioners and users that their interests are being adequately catered for. Such mechanisms may not be necessary at the community level, where the prime objective of the alternative justice system is to increase access for the indigent, and where very little training is required. However, in cases where the stakes are high, proponents of ADR cannot afford to have a single bad case, because this will trigger discontent that may influence users, such as government agencies, multinational corporations and international NGOs, who may then stop patronising the system.

The need for mediator quality is now being increasingly recognized, especially in the United States, where the term *Alternative Dispute* Resolution (ADR) is being considered a misnomer, since fewer than 5% of cases go through trial, while 95% of cases are resolved through mediation and allied mechanisms.[1] Michael Moffit (2008), for instance, mentions four ways of assuring mediator quality: public front-end mechanisms, public back-end mechanisms, private front-end mechanisms and private back-end mechanisms. He goes on to say why none of these work (Moffit, 2008). Yet, even Moffit admits that:

> [...] most mediators operate without significant influence from any of these quality-assurance mechanisms. But something will change. No significant practice or profession operates so thoroughly outside of all four of these quality-assurance mechanisms as mediation currently does" (Moffit, 2008, p. 36).

> [T]he fact that mediation operates without any of these mechanisms, and therefore, the fact that something will change with respect to mediation, is no indictment of mediation. I certainly do not intend to suggest that mediators operate as a band of rogues, committing malpractice with indifference. Many mediators are outstanding. Still more are at least well-intentioned. Mediation is merely undergoing a process of speciation and maturation at this moment in time. That developmental process is occurring under the influence of complex market forces, periodic government attention, and the self-interested attentions of many different established professions and practices. It is no wonder that something is going to change. In fact, many aspects of mediation are likely to change in the coming years. (Moffit, 2008, p. 37).

It is therefore no wonder that Waldman proclaims:

> [...] as the mediation field matures, it is likely that more mediation providers will continue to offer voluntary certification programs. Further, state and federal courts will likely continue, in increasing numbers, to

[1] See http://www.answers.com/topic/alternative-dispute-resolution.

> require mediators to clear certain hurdles before being able to join the court-referred rosters. (Waldman, Vol. 8, No. 1, Fall 2001).

She concludes that:

> [...] wheather these initiatives will include performance-based testing remains unclear. The future of such testing will hinge largely on how well the mediation community reconciles and assimilates competing visions of its craft, and how well a field committed to managing power among disputing parties can balance power within itself." (Waldman, Vol. 8, No. 1, Fall 2001).

The Way Forward

It seems fair to say that GHACMA can take a bold step in institutionalising dispute resolution training and practice. The important factors to take into account in institutionalising dispute resolution training and practice are:

- To develop a well-structured programme with international appeal
- To promulgate a constitution in the light of some of the provisions of NRCD 143
- To set ethical standards. (Here the International Mediation Institute (IMI) Code of ethics is a good point of reference).
- To apply to be registered as a professional body under N.R.C.D. 143.

These processes may appear straightforward, but having served on the committee charged with drafting the constitution of GHACMA, I can attest to how long it has taken for GHACMA to promulgate a constitution. In fact, if these processes are set up correctly, professionalising dispute resolution will almost automatically become a marketing tool for the profession itself. Finally, Moffit (2008) refers to the "self-interested attentions of many different established professions and practices." At the risk of being criticized, one can think here of lawyers and counselling psychologists (or simply counsellors). Then again, we can be guided by how public relations weaned itself away from journalism. In the past, at least in Ghana, journalists were engaged as public relations practitioners. It took some time to appreciate the unique role of the PR professional, as distinct from a journalist. Through new terms, such as communications, corporate affairs and public affairs, PR has come to assert its importance, although a few institutions still engage journalists to perform the work of public relations officers.

Some jurisdictions have already institutionalised or professionalised dispute resolution. The American Arbitration Association (AAA) in the US and the Chartered Institute of Arbitrators (CIArb) in the UK are two such examples.

References

Chapman, S. A. (2007). *Transformative-Deliberative Curriculum Theory.* Available at http://etd.ohiolink.edu/send-pdf.cgi/Chapman%20Shelley %20Ann.pdf?antioch1173793131.

Ghana, R. o. (1973). *Professional Bodies Decree (N.R.C.D. 143).* Accra: Ghana Publishing Corporation.

Mensah-Bonsu, H.J.A.N and Effah, Paul (2003). Conflict Management and Resolution Skills for Managers of Tertiary Education Institutions (A Training Manual). National Council for Tertiary Education.

Honeyman, C. (June 1995). *Performance-Based Assessment: A Methodology, for use in selecting, training and evaluating mediators.* Madison, USA: National Institute for Dispute Resolution, The Test Design Project.

—. (April 1988). Five Elements of Mediation. *Negotiation Journal* .

—. (January 1990). On Evaluating Mediators. *Negotiation Journal* .

Isaacs, G. (1996). *Teaching and Educational Development Institute; Bllom's Taxonomy of Edcational Objectives.* Retrieved August 2011, from The University of Queensland, Ausralia: http://www.tedi.uq.edu.au/downloads/Bloom.pdf.

Moffit, M. L. (2008). The Four Ways to Assure Mediator Quality (And Why None of them Work). ExpressO. Available at http://works.bepress.com/michael_moffitt/1/

Waldman, E. (Vol. 8, No. 1, Fall 2001). Credentialing Approaches: The slow movement toward skills-based testing continues. *Dispute Resolution Magazine, American Bar Association*

Websites Visited

Civil Justice Training: http://www.ADRcenter.com/international/cms/?page_id=65 Accessed in August 2011.

Rethinking teaching http://www.convenor.com/madison/rethink.htm Accessed in August 2011.

Qualifying Assessment Programme (QAP) www.imimediation.org

Accessed in May 2011.
About ADR http://www.answers.com/topic/alternative-dispute-resolution Accessed in August 2011.
Musah-Khaleepha, S (2010) Dispute Resolution as a Profession: The Ghanaian Experience http://ghacma.org/DISPUTE%20RESOLUTION%20AS%20A%20PROFESSION.pdf.

CHAPTER NINE

A COMPARATIVE ANALYSIS OF ADR LEGISLATION IN AFRICA: GHANA AND UGANDA

ERNEST UWAZIE AND DANIEL YAMSHON

Introduction

Over the last 15 years or so, several African countries have enacted varying forms and levels of legislation towards the institutionalization, national standardization, and professionalization of Alternative Dispute Resolution (ADR), specifying and expanding ADR methods beyond judicial or customary arbitration. The main purpose of this chapter is to analyze key elements of selected forms of legislation from two countries that may represent experiences or influences in East and West Africa, with a comparative focus on their similarities and differences.

The unit of comparison and analyses will be on the provisions of the select legislations for ADR options, the role of the court, the qualifications of or criteria for selection of neutrals, timelines and quality control, the enforceability of agreements or awards, confidentiality, the disclosure of conflict of interests, institutional structure and oversight.

The mediation provisions of the Ghana Alternative Dispute Resolution Act and the Uganda Arbitration and Conciliation Act are similar, but are distinguished in terms of rhetoric and levels of detail. The Uganda Act is a model of legislative brevity, while Ghana's Act is broader, more inclusive of varying situations and somewhat more precise. Uganda's Act uses the term "conciliation" and Ghana's Act uses "mediation." [1] Both Acts

[1] While many neutrals understand mediation and conciliation to be different, with conciliators using highly proactive approaches and mediators more facilitative approaches; reality may show that most mediators in the private commercial sector use a hybrid process. Webster's dictionary defines mediation as "intervention

provide for third party neutrals to convene parties to facilitate or expedite settlement negotiations, and both Acts define the role of the neutrals rather abstractly.[2] Ghana's Alternative Dispute Resolution Act implies a difference between conciliation and mediation without defining the distinction. [3] The actual distinctions, if any, are rather *pro forma.*

Submission to the Processes

Both the Uganda and the Ghana Acts provide that any party may invite other parties to mediation, but there are important differences. Uganda's Arbitration and Conciliation Act requires a party to send an invitation in writing,[4] and does not provide for other methods of invitation. How that written invitation is to be communicated, however, is not defined. Ghana's Act, on the other hand, specifically allows for almost any conceivable communication method for submissions to mediate.[5] The Act is somewhat

between conflicting parties to promote reconciliation, settlement, or compromise." (http://www.merriam webster.com/dictionary/mediation) Conciliation is defined as: "to make compatible, reconcile, appease."
(http://www.merriamwebster.com/dictionary/conciliation).
In linguistic terms, the difference between mediation and conciliation amounts to a distinction without a difference, although a number of neutrals would disagree.

[2] The Uganda Act does not define conciliator or conciliation, rather sets out the conciliator's roles (Section 53) and defines what the conciliator is not. (Section 65, Role of the Conciliator in Other Proceedings.) Similarly, Ghana's Act defines the powers of the mediator as in an enabling Act, but does not define mediation. (Section 74)

[3] Section 30 reads: "Conciliation conference.... The appointing authority [appointing the arbitrator(s)] or any institution or individual may, with the consent of the parties, at any time during the arbitration process, arrange a conciliation conference to facilitate the resolution of the dispute, except that an arbitrator in the dispute shall not be a conciliator." Thus, the function of the conciliator is the same as that generally thought of as being the function of a mediator; they share the qualities of being voluntary and, most worthy of note, *facilitative.* Section 30 also prohibits med-Arb., as an arbitrator in the dispute cannot be a conciliator as well.

[4] Section 49 (1): "The party initiating conciliation shall send to the other party a written invitation to conciliate under this Part, briefly identifying the subject of the dispute." (Uganda).

[5] Section 63 (2): "A submission to mediation may be made by writing, telephone, or other form of verbal communication, fax, telex, e-mail or any other electronic mode of communication and shall briefly state the nature of the dispute." (Ghana).

ambiguous, distinguishing a stipulated submission to mediation and extending an invitation to mediate.[6]

The breadth of the enumerated invitation methods in Ghana's Alternative Dispute Resolution Act, particularly the language allowing submission (invitation) by "any other electronic mode of communication", would seem to allow a party to invite others to mediate by social media such as Facebook, instant communication devices such as Twitter, IM,[7] or cell phone text messaging. Unlike Uganda's Arbitration and Conciliation Act, Ghana's Alternative Dispute Resolution Act allows oral submissions, as long as these are later confirmed in writing and unless the parties agree otherwise.[8] Allowing the parties to agree not to use written confirmations may be cumbersome, if there are later disputes about the nature of the submission, but this does recognize the importance and validity of a culture with a rich oral tradition. Indeed, in any event, in spite of the Act's ostensible requirement that acceptances of oral invitations to mediate must be confirmed in writing, failure to do so does not invalidate the proceedings. [9] Allowable methods of acceptance are as broad as those for invitations. [10]

Both the Ghana Alternative Dispute Resolution Act and the Uganda Arbitration and Conciliation Act anticipate that some invitations to mediation/conciliation will generate no response. Under the Ugandan Act, if a response is not received within twenty-one days (or another period of time specified by the inviting party), the inviting party may consider the

---

[6] For example, section 63, sub-paragraphs 1-3 use the word "submission, but sub-paragraphs 5-7 address "acceptance of an invitation to mediate." "Submission" in the context of this portion of the act may be read as interchangeable with "invitation." In the authors' opinion, that would be a logical interpretation, and indeed the most sensible one.

[7] Instant Messaging, allowing parties to send messages in real time to others who are on line without having the message go to e mail. IM's pop up on whatever screen people are using when they are sent.

[8] Section 63 (3): "A submission to mediation through telephone, or any other verbal mode of communication shall, unless the parties agree otherwise, be confirmed in writing and shall state the names, addresses including e mail addresses and telephone numbers of the parties and in brief the nature of the dispute."

[9] Section 63 (6): "An acceptance by telephone or any other verbal means shall be confirmed in writing but a failure to confirm an acceptance in wring shall not invalidate the proceedings."

[10] Section 63 (5) reads: "An acceptance of an invitation for mediation may be by letter, telephone or other form of verbal communication, fax, telex, or e-mail or other mode of electronic communications."

invitation rejected, and if so must notify the other party in writing. The period under the Ghanaian Act is fourteen days and the rejection is self-executing, not requiring notice.[11] This represents a major distinction between the two Acts; the Uganda Act does not provide direction if an invitation receives no response but the inviting party does not elect to send a written rejection notice.

Court Referrals

The Arbitration and Conciliation Act of Uganda does not provide for judicial reference to conciliation. This would not prevent a judge from encouraging or even pressuring parties to seek conciliation. The Ghana Alternative Dispute Resolution Act, however, presumes a great deal of court involvement in both arbitration and mediation; it provides a complete court reference scheme.[12]

Under the Alternative Dispute Resolution Act, the court has complete discretion to refer cases to mediation if it believes mediation will help resolve the dispute or part of the dispute.[13] Likewise, parties may apply, by stipulation and with notice, to have the matter referred to mediation at any point before the final judgment.[14] Thus, it is conceivable that an application to refer a case to mediation can be made after a trial has been completed, as long as the court has not rendered a judgment. It is difficult to foresee how often this might happen, but the authors observe that in many countries it is not unheard of for cases to be settled after all the evidence has been presented and counsel have a different perspective on the case.

The reference to mediation itself serves as a stay of the court proceeding under Ghana's Alternative Dispute Resolution Act.[15] Uganda's Arbitration and Conciliation Act is silent on the issue of court stays when Conciliation is pending, but does provide that arbitration or court proceedings may not be commenced while conciliation is pending.[16] A settlement resulting from court-referred mediation is recorded as a

[11] Uganda: Section 49 (4) Ghana: Section 63 (7).
[12] Section 64 (Ghana ADR Act)
[13] Section 64 (1) (Ghana ADR Act)
[14] Section 64 (2) Note that Section 64 (3) describes the documentary requirements once the referral is made either by application of the parties or by the courts' own exercise of discretion. (Ghana ADR Act)
[15] Section 64 (4) (Ghana ADR Act)
[16] Arbitration And Conciliation Act Section 62 (Uganda)

judgment, and is enforced by the courts as such.[17] Contrast this with Uganda's provision, in which the requirement for a written agreement appears to be within the discretion of the parties, [18] and rather than being enforced as a court judgment, is treated as an arbitration award [19] that may need to be filed in court anyway.

Number and Selection of Neutrals

Both Acts call for one mediator or conciliator unless the parties agree otherwise; Uganda allows two or three, whereas Ghana does not limit the number[20] but practicality would. Both acts require the neutrals, when there is more than one, to act jointly.[21]

While there are some similarities in the appointment process, there are significant differences between how neutrals are appointed under the Ghana Alternative Dispute Resolution Act and the Uganda Arbitration and Conciliation Act. In both Acts, the parties may agree to appoint a neutral, with Ghana allowing the parties to appoint an institution as their neutral.[22] Under the Uganda Act, if there are two conciliators, each party may appoint one, and if there are three, each party may appoint one and may agree on the third conciliator.[23] The process for the selection of three conciliators is somewhat similar to arbitrator appointment in many international arbitration rules such as UNCITRAL, the International Court of Arbitration and many others, with the difference being that the "typical" rule would provide for each party to appoint an arbitrator with the two party appointed arbitrators then selecting a third arbitrator.[24]

---

[17] Section 64 (5)(a)(b)(c) (Ghana ADR Act)

[18] Arbitration and Conciliation Act Section 58 (3) (Uganda).

[19] Section 59 (Uganda A & C Act)

[20] Section 50 (1) (Uganda A & C Act) Section 65 (1) (Ghana ADR Act)

[21] Section 50 (2) (Uganda A & C Act) Section 65 (Ghana ADR Act)

[22] Section 51 (1) (a) (Uganda A & C Act) Section 66 (1) (Ghana ADR Act).

[23] Section 51 (b), (c)

[24] While under international rules the party appointed arbitrators are expected to be neutral, in some countries such as the United States, party appointed arbitrators are not legally required to be neutral. This has and continues to cause many problems. See "Do Party Arbitrators Have Ethical Duties of Neutrality?" Daniel Yamshon, Dispute *Resolution Magazine*, Vol. 17 No. 4, summer, 2011 p. 28. (American Bar Association, ADR Section, pub.)

Both Acts allow the parties to seek the assistance of an appointing authority, such as an ADR Center or other suitable institution or person, in finding and selecting a neutral mediator or conciliator(s).[25]

Disclosure and Conflicts of Interest

The Uganda Arbitration and Conciliation Act is silent on this issue, whereas the Ghana Alternative Dispute Resolution Act contains extensive disclosure requirements. A mediator, prior to accepting appointment, shall disclose any circumstance that may create a likelihood of bias or affect the conduct of the mediation.[26] The duty of disclosure continues throughout the mediation; if information emerges that could affect the mediator's impartiality or affect the conduct of the mediation, it must be disclosed.[27] Disclosure allows the parties to replace the mediator if the disclosures are made prior to the commencement of mediation.[28]

In keeping with the need for impartial neutrals, the Ghana Act requires an appointing authority or person to take into account the mediator's background and independence, and prohibits mediators from having a financial or personal interest in the outcome of the dispute.[29] The Uganda Arbitration and Conciliation Act does not contain these particulars, but requires only an appointing authority to take into consideration the independence and impartiality of the conciliator, and in cases using a third or sole conciliator, should consider appointing a neutral of a nationality other than that of the parties.[30]

Delay and Vacancy

The Uganda Act has no provisions for dealing with delay or the conciliator operating beyond the ground rules of the conciliation. The Ghana Act, however, allows parties to replace a mediator who fails to start work within the time limits agreed to by the parties or who fails to follow the

[25] Section 51 (2), (3) (Uganda A & C Act) Section 66, (Ghana ADR Act.)
[26] Section 68 (1) (a), (b).
[27] Section 68 (2).
[28] Section 68 (3).
[29] Section 67.
[30] Section 51 (3).

ground rules.[31] The parties may then appoint another mediator, or any mediator who is incapable of performing the functions of a mediator.[32]

Representation, Place and Time

Uganda's Act is silent on this topic, whereas Ghana's allows a party to choose his/her own representative without restriction.[33] A represented party must provide written notice to the parties and the mediator within seven days of the representative's appointment. The notice needs to include the name and address of the representative, and the extent of their authority.[34] Similarly, the Uganda Act does not mention scheduling the conciliation. Ghana's Act allows the mediator to determine the date and time of the mediation in consultation with the parties,[35] using a similar process to determine the location of the mediation meeting.[36]

Statements and Pre-Mediation Documentation

Both the Uganda Arbitration and Conciliation and the Ghana Alternative Dispute Resolution Acts provide for written statements to be submitted prior to the commencement of conciliation or mediation. Under the Uganda Act, it is discretionary; the conciliator may request statements.[37] Under Ghana's Act, each party shall provide the other parties and the mediator with a position paper no longer than eight days before the first mediation session, unless the parties agree otherwise.[38] Uganda's Act also requires the statements to be sent to the other parties.[39]

Both Acts empower the neutral to request further information. The Ghana ADR act allows the mediator to request the facts and grounds a party is relying on to support his/her positions, request documents, evidence[40] and the mediator can make such requests throughout the

[31] Section 69.
[32] Section 70
[33] Section 71 (1)
[34] Section 71 (2)
[35] Section 72 (1)
[36] Section 72 (2)
[37] Section 52 (1) (Uganda A & C Act)
[38] Section 73 (1) (Ghana ADR Act)
[39] Section 52 (2) (Uganda A & C Act)
[40] Section 73 (2) (Ghana ADR Act)

process.[41] Uganda's Act gives the conciliator wide discretion to request additional information from the parties at any time during the process.[42]

Role and Powers

Some of the language used by the two Acts is remarkably similar. Both Acts call for the neutral to be independent and impartial in helping the parties reach an amicable or satisfactory resolution of their dispute.[43] Both Acts require the neutral to be objective, fair and just, while giving consideration to the rights and obligations of the parties, trade usage, the circumstances surrounding the case, and the previous business practices of the parties.[44] Ghana's Act specifically allows the mediator to obtain the advice of an expert if the parties agree to pay the expenses; the request may be made by the mediator or a party with the consent of the other parties.[45] The ability to hire an expert is implied in the Uganda Act, as it is among the final duties of the conciliator to fix the cost of the conciliation,[46] including the fees of witnesses requested by the conciliator with the permission of the parties,[47] and "any expert advice requested by the conciliator with the consent of the parties[.]"[48]

Ghana's Act is particularly interesting, as it divides off termination of the mediation when the mediator believes continuing the process will not help to resolve the dispute,[49] placing this particular mediator function under Section 74 (mediator's powers), then repeats this power again in section 80, defining when mediation ends. Reflecting the generally understood higher proactive nature of conciliation, the Uganda Act specifically empowers the conciliator to make proposals for settlement.[50] The proposals may be oral or written, and the conciliator does not have to provide reasons for the settlement proposals.[51] The Ghana statute's

---

[41] Section 73 (3) (Ghana ADR Act)
[42] Section 52 (5) (Uganda A & C Act)
[43] Section 53 (1) (Uganda A & C Act) Section 74 (1) (Ghana ADR act)
[44] Both acts are almost word-for-word identical in this regard. Section 53 (2) (Uganda A & C Act) Section 74 (5) (Ghana ADR Act)
[45] Section 74 (3) (4) (Ghana ADR Act)
[46] Section 63 (Uganda A & E Act)
[47] Section 63 (2) (a) Uganda A & E Act)
[48] Section 63 (2) (b) Uganda A & E Act)
[49] Section 74 (7) (Ghana ADR Act)
[50] Section 53 (4) (Uganda A & E Act)
[51] Section 53 (5) (Uganda A & E Act)

provisions for mediator developed settlement proposals appear in Section 81, which addresses agreements.[52]

Communication and Attendance

Although the statutory language is organized slightly differently, the provisions of both Ghana's Alternative Dispute Resolution Act and Uganda's Arbitration and Conciliation Act regarding communication are to all intents and purposes identical. Both Acts give discretion to the neutral to meet or to communicate orally or in writing, and both allow both plenary and separate communication.[53]

The Ghana Act prohibits non-parties from attending mediation sessions unless the parties and the mediator agree.[54] Uganda's Arbitration and Conciliation Act contains no prohibition against non-party attendance at conciliation meetings.

Confidentiality

The Ugandan Arbitration and Conciliation Act and the Ghanaian Alternative Dispute Resolution Act are very interesting in that they distinguish internal confidentiality during the conduct of the process and overall confidentiality arising from the global conciliation or mediation process. In the Uganda Act, when a party provides factual information regarding the dispute from one of the parties, the statute provides that "the substance" of the information shall be disclosed to the other parties in order that the other party may have the opportunity to present an appropriate explanation.[55] The Act does provide an exception to the rule; if a party specifically informs the conciliator that the information is confidential, then the information stays confidential in the context of the mediation.[56] Ghana's Alternative Dispute Resolution Act has the same provisions.[57]

As regards overall mediation confidentiality, the two Acts are not dissimilar, but confidentiality in the Uganda statute appears to be stronger. In the Ghana legislation, records, reports, the settlement agreement and

---

[52] Section 81 (1) (Ghana ADR Act)
[53] Section 76 (Ghana ADR Act), Section 54 (1), (2) (Uganda A & E Act)
[54] Section 77 (Ghana ADR Act)
[55] Section 55 (Uganda A & C Act)
[56] Ibid.
[57] Section 78 (Ghana ADR Act)

other documents are confidential and may not be used as evidence or subject to discovery in a court proceeding. The exception to this is where disclosure is necessary for the purpose of implementation and enforcement of the agreement. [58] Mediators may not disclose information received by the mediator during the course of the mediation without the permission of all the parties.[59]

Ghana's Act further prohibits a party from relying on a record of the mediation, statements made at the mediation, or information obtained during the mediation as evidence in court proceedings.[60]

Contrast Ghana's Mediation Confidentiality Provisions with Uganda's "Confidentiality"

> (1) Notwithstanding anything in any other law for the time being in force, the conciliator and the parties shall keep confidential all matters relating to the conciliation proceedings.
>
> (2) Confidentiality shall extend also to the settlement agreement, except where its disclosure is necessary for purposes of implementation and enforcement." (Uganda, Arbitration and Conciliation Act)

Uganda's Act, on its face, does not permit the use of records, reports and other documents, even for implementation of the agreement. While Ghana's Act does prohibit records, statements and information obtained during the mediation from being used in evidence, Uganda requires confidentiality in "all matters relating to the conciliation proceedings."

End of the Processes

The ending of mediation or the termination of conciliation is similar in both Acts, with one exception in the Ghanaian Act. Both processes terminate with the signing or execution of a written settlement agreement.[61] Uganda requires a written declaration from the conciliator, after consultations by the parties that further efforts at conciliation are not justified,[62] while Ghana allows a mediator's declaration after consultation

---

[58] Section 79 (1) (Ghana ADR Act)
[59] Section 79 (2) (Ghana ADR Act0
[60] Section 79 (3) (a), (b), (c)
[61] Section 61 (a) (Uganda A & C Act) Section 80 (1) (a) (Ghana ADR Act)
[62] Section 61 (b) (Uganda A & C Act)

with the parties, but does not require a written declaration.[63] Both Acts allow the parties to address a written declaration to the neutral indicating that the proceedings are terminated.[64] Any party can terminate the proceedings by declaring to the neutral and the other parties that the proceedings are terminated; however, Uganda's Act requires the declaration to be in writing.[65] If mediation is terminated pursuant to an oral declaration, the mediator is required to record the declaration.[66] Ghana also allows a mediator to terminate the process for non-payment of an advance deposit of funds for mediation expenses.[67]

Relationship of Mediation and Conciliation to Other Processes

Both Acts prohibit the neutral conciliator or mediator from appearing as counsel in other processes as regards the dispute, prohibit the neutral from acting as an arbitrator, and prohibit parties from calling the neutral as a witness.[68]

Conclusion

It is apparent that the Ghana Alternative Dispute Resolution Act and the Uganda Arbitration and Conciliation Act are quite similar, and provide related processes. There are some differences, but they are relatively *de minimus*; the major difference between the two Acts is in their organization, and in the exclusion of environmental cases from the Ghana Act. Both conciliation in Uganda and mediation in Ghana should provide satisfactory processes, relieve court congestion and provide timely and effective individual justice for disputants in both countries. Operationalization of the Uganda and Ghana Acts will, over time, provide useful lessons for similar attempts in other countries, including opportunities for review and reform; the challenge remains to avoid the same or

[63] Section 80 (c) (Ghana ADR Act)
[64] Section 61(c) (Uganda A & C Act) Section 80 (1) (d) (Ghana ADR Act)
[65] Section 61 (d) (Uganda A & C Act) Section 80 (1) (e) (Ghana ADR Act)
[66] Section 80 (2) (Ghana ADR Act)
[67] Section 80 (1) (b) Ghana ADR Act
[68] Section 66 (Uganda A & C Act) Section 84 (a) (b) (Ghana ADR Act.
Source: Etuk, C., Report of the Lagos Multi-Door Courthouse (LMDC) to the Governing Council of the LMDC, April, 2011.

equivalent pitfalls that led to the development of an alternative to the formal justice system.

As the use of ADR has grown in Africa, its legitimacy as an alternative justice system has become almost universally recognized. Some legislatures have modified the regulatory schemes governing the use of ADR. While the laws of the two countries in question have great similarities in certain areas, given their common law origins and prominence of indigenous justice, the fact that they have undergone independent evolutions has created substantial differences and instructive lessons among them as well. Understanding the similarities and differences between the laws governing ADR in Ghana and Uganda is of vital importance to other national attempts (in Africa) at creating access to justice, promoting judicial reform, and stimulating international investment.

CHAPTER TEN

TOWARDS SUSTAINABLE PEACE: A STRUCTURAL ASSESSMENT OF THE GHANA NATIONAL PEACE COUNCIL ACT, 2011 (ACT 818)

ISAAC OLAWALE ALBERT

Introduction

The post-Cold War years in world history has been characterized by different forms of violent conflicts and crises from which no particular region is excluded. The causes and effects of these problems are both local and global, thus making the search for solutions to them a universal responsibility. Until recently, when the impact of international terrorism is becoming more widespread and the war against the phenomenon more intense, most of the literature on global crisis focused on Africa. It was as if in a world of peace, the devil had chosen the continent as its permanent abode. However, the global conflict environment is now diffuse, and the world has never been this traumatized by both criminal and political violence. For example, the present-day Middle East is in disarray, not necessarily because of the much-advertised Arab/Israeli conflict but, more importantly, because of the capacity of the region to export or play host to different forms of angry international conflict actors. The problem in the region is further compounded by the ongoing "Spring Revolution", as a result of which the old regimes in Tunisia, Egypt and Libya have crumbled and the political stability of the region has become suspect. Even in Europe and America, people now openly protest against economic inequities in manners never before witnessed. The situation in Africa is also worrisome, with elections now becoming the leading cause of bloody conflicts (Albert 2011).

The sub-region with the highest cases of violent conflict in post-Cold War Africa is West Africa. The armed conflicts in the sub-region since the late 1980s include those in Liberia, Sierra Leone, Guinea Bissau, and Cote d'Ivoire (Adebajo 2002; Draman and Carment 2001; Olonisakin 2000 and 2008). In "peaceful" states such as Nigeria, Ghana, Mali, Senegal, and Niger, there are different forms of small scale insurgencies that overtax the security systems. To manage existing conflicts and prevent the occurrence of future ones, the Economic Community of West African States (ECOWAS) has developed one of the most respected peace architectures in the world. Yet, the West African sub-region remains precariously fragile and susceptible to relapses into violence and reversals in the democratization processes. To assess the nature of this problem in the context of the interventions undertaken so far, the ECOWAS Commission, in partnership with the Government of Liberia, and with the cooperation of the African Union, the United Nations and the Danish Government, organized an International Conference on the theme of 'Two Decades of Peace Processes in West Africa: Achievements, Failures, Lessons," in Monrovia, from 22-26 March 2010. The main objective of the conference was to consolidate the gains made in conflict prevention, management, resolution, and peace-building in West Africa, by evaluating the interventions carried out in the last twenty years with a view to learning lessons and building on existing achievements in the effort to further strengthen the evolving regional peace and security architecture. The conference came up with the following findings:

i. The challenges that plagued the initial ECOWAS interventions in the region, some of which persist today, include:
  a. Grossly inadequate and inappropriate logistical backup;
  b. Lack of clear and robust mandates;
  c. Language-barriers among troops which adversely affected smooth coordination on the field;
  d. Insufficient synergy and complementarity between military and diplomatic efforts;
  e. Weak police and civilian components of the intervention standby arrangement, and insufficient political will among leaders and senior officials of Member States to take decisive steps towards tackling the security challenges in Member States in accordance with extant ECOWAS *Protocols and Decisions;*
  f. Inadequate capacity to address the structural causes of conflicts and instability;
  g. The absence of a regional normative and structural framework for post-conflict peace-building, especially in areas relating to

transitional justice, DDR and the rebuilding of governance infrastructure;

h. The absence of a regional capability to deal with natural disasters and humanitarian issues;
i. The threat to democratic consolidation in the region through the manipulation of Constitutions and electoral laws, and the consequent resurgence of military coups;
j. The threat of entrenching a culture of impunity and institutionalized corruption;
k. The impacts of emerging illegal trades, including drug trafficking and other forms of transnational organized crime, and
l. Weak preventive diplomacy architecture (ECOWAS Commission 2010:5).

Several of the challenges mentioned above have more to do with individual member states of ECOWAS than with its sub-regional organization. The findings suggest that until member states have a peace architecture that could prevent and manage conflicts proactively, the little that ECOWAS does at the sub-regional level might not be enough to ensure sustainable peace in the sub-region. The logical implication of this is that as ECOWAS works towards building peace sub-regionally, member states have to double their efforts to establish architecture for peace at a national level. The need for this kind of synergy in conflict prevention and management was underscored by the African Union in 2002, when it observed that "The security of each African country is inseparably linked to that of other African countries and the African continent as a whole" (AU 2002, 2).

One of the possible ways of realizing this objective is for African states to have peace policies that clearly set out how to prevent and manage emerging conflict issues in a collaborative manner. Nigeria and Ghana have taken a leadership role in this respect. While Nigeria's National Peace Policy is ready for approval of the Federal Executive Council (Golwa 2011), the Ghana National Peace Council came into full force in 2011. While awaiting the final approval and implementation of Nigeria's Peace Policy, this paper takes a careful look at the Ghana Peace Council Act of 2011 (Act 818), which is already being implemented.

Framework for Peace Architecture

The first challenge here is to define "peace." The term has been defined as "...the dynamic processes that lead to the relative conditions of the absence of direct and indirect violence, plus the presence of freedom, equality, economic and social justice, cooperation, and harmony" (Sponsel 1996, 98). Peace is a process and not an event. It is many-sided and a never-ending struggle to transform conflict or violence. The theoretical framework for linking peace and state building is the "democratic peace theory", which assumes that peace is a public good and that its provision must be a core duty of a political system. In his pioneering work, Michael Doyle applied the theory (which is sometimes referred to as the "liberal peace theory") strictly to what he called "Liberal states", which he defined as "States with some form of representative democracy, a market economy based on private property rights, and constitutional protections of civil and political rights" (Doyle 1983, 207-208). Hence, the main gist of this theory is that democracies hardly go to war with one another, but make peace. The underlying assumption of this theory is that it is not peace itself that is democratic, but the countries that choose to embrace it (Archibugi 2008). A country embraces peace largely because without it, sustainable development is difficult. To this end, nations are expected to be conflict sensitive in their development planning processes. This goal is easier achieved when the nation has a peace policy in place. By peace policy is meant the formal rules of engagement for conflict prevention and management.

The crafting and implementation of a peace policy needs to respect the principles of Multi-Track Diplomacy, which refers to a synergetic approach to development—particularly peace intervention—across levels, actors and interests. The system was designed by John McDonald and Louise Diamond, who co-founded the Institute for Multi-Track Diplomacy (IMTD) in Washington, in the US. A Multi-Track Diplomacy approach to the task of peace-building revolves around nine tracks, namely: government, professional conflict resolution, business, private citizens, research/training/education, activism, religious funding and public opinion/communication. The conceptual model is well-captured in the following diagram:

Fig.1 Diagram showing the Nine Tracks of Multi-Track Diplomacy

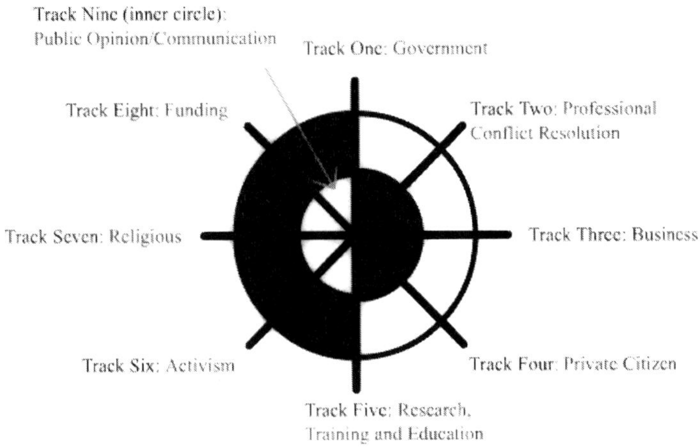

Source: Diamond and McDonald, Institute of Multi-Track Diplomacy (IMTD).

Each of the tracks in the circle refers to particular clusters of stakeholders involved in the peace development process. In the words of the proprietors (Diamond and McDonald) of this model:

> The nine tracks are organized in a circle to suggest graphically the underlying principle of systemic thinking: the whole is greater than the sum of its parts. The components of this system are vastly different from one another, yet somehow they are sufficiently related to, and interactive with, one another to build a synergetic energy that carries their efforts beyond simple listing or summation of one plus one (Diamond and Macdonald, 1996:14).

The lesson of multi-track diplomacy is that the business of making, building, and keeping peace does not reside with the government alone, as assumed by the layman. It is true that this responsibility is fundamental to any government, but other stakeholders are expected to contribute to the process in a collaborative framework. Hence, in the Foreword to a National Association of Social Workers (NASW) publication, *The Global Crisis of Violence: Common Problems, Universal Causes, Shared Solutions* (Van Soest 1997), Josephine Nieves, former Executive Director of NASW, argues that "People acting as a strong, cohesive community can achieve more than individuals." In other words, a good peace policy must establish the collaborative framework for building, making and keeping peace. How adequate is the Ghana National Peace Council in this respect?

Contexts of the Ghana National Peace Council Act

Ghana is generally perceived to be a very peaceful country in a turbulent sub-region. Yet, it has its own types of conflict, which cannot be ignored by any proactive political regime. These conflicts are both external and internal. The external ones derive from the fact that the country's neighbours, most especially Cote d'Ivoire and even Liberia and Sierra Leone, are experiencing different forms of political turbulence which, since the late 1980s, have made refugee and illegal arms flows a major security issue in Ghana. The internal problems, some of which have been exacerbated by the external problems in terms of surplus arms and light weapons from neighbouring states, include chieftaincy crisis, most especially in the northern parts of the country. The peace policy in Ghana is expected to "clean up this mess."

The overall objective of the Ghana peace architecture, according to the country's Minister for the Interior, is "to have a country characterized by a dynamic environment where people can engage in their lawful activities confident that the institutions, mechanisms and capacities for mediating differences and grievance are effective and responsive" (Kan-Dapaah 2006, 1). The minister goes further, identifying the broad policy objective as "to enable and facilitate the development of mechanisms for cooperation among all the relevant stakeholders in peace building in Ghana by promoting cooperative problem solving to conflicts and by institutionalizing the processes of response to conflicts to produce outcomes that lead to conflict transformation, social, political and religious reconciliation and transformative dialogues."

Work started on the Ghana "National Architecture for Peace" in 2005, with a workshop that brought civil society groups, community organizations, professional bodies and faith-based organizations together with governance structures and security agencies into a national framework for anticipating and responding to signs of violent conflict. The architecture for peace was developed following a pilot programme to build peace and mitigate conflict in the Northern Region of Ghana, in response to an intra-clan dispute that led to the death of the king of the Dagombas and 40 of his followers in 2002 (see Albert 2008). At the request of the government in 2003, the UN designed an initial set of interventions to prevent this conflict from undermining the general elections of December 2004 (Bawumia and Ojielo 2007). With additional support from UNDP, the UN

Department for Political Affairs, and the UN Department for Economic and Social Affairs, the government of Ghana decided to establish a national mechanism for the prevention, management and resolution of conflict. All of this opens up space for "community dialogue" on conflict issues, and facilitates processes for resolving them. It also serves as an early warning mechanism on potential conflict, and engages state officials at different levels in ensuring timely response to the issues raised.

The Peace Architecture has Five Related Components

(i) Establishing peace councils at the national, regional and district levels
(ii) Institutionalizing the culture of peace with the introduction of peace education subjects at all levels of education in Ghana
(iii) Promoting and supporting peace media;
(iv) Prevention and control of small arms and light weapons
(v) Building the capacity of executive institutions for effective conflict prevention and management (Kan-Dapaah 2006:2-9).

To consolidate the process, a Peace Building Support Unit was established within the Ministry of the Interior to coordinate support from government agencies, provide mentoring, and organize capacity building in conflict prevention. Another component of the architecture includes support for educational institutions to mainstream peace education in the school curriculum. It was under this process that the University of Cape Coast started an academic Master's degree programme in Peace and Development Studies in 2007 (Albert and Albert 2008).

Contents of the Ghana National Peace Council Act

The Act is broken up into thirty-five sections of six parts. The first part, consisting of eight sections, consists of the establishment, object, functions and governing body of the Act. The other sections of this first part address issues relating to the tenure of the members of the Council, meetings of the Board, disclosure of interest and establishment of committees. The second part relates to the institus, while the third relates to the district peace councils. The fourth part deals with issues of tenure, meetings and allowances of the board members. Administrative and financial issues are addressed in the fifth part, while the sixth addresses miscellaneous matters (Republic of Ghana 2011).

Functions

In line with the three tiers of government in Ghana, the National Peace Council Act of 2011 provides for three categories of peace councils: national, regional and district.

The functions of the National Peace Council (at the national level)

In order to harmonize and co-ordinate conflict prevention, management, resolution, and to build sustainable peace through networking and co-ordination, the following must be done:

(a) Strengthen capacities for conflict prevention, management, resolution and sustainable peace in the country including but not limited to chiefs, women, youth groups and community organizations;
(b) Increase awareness on the use of non-violent strategies to prevent, manage and resolve conflict and build sustainable peace in the country;
(c) Facilitate the amicable resolution of conflict through mediation and other processes including indigenous mechanisms for conflict resolution and peace building;
(d) Promote understanding of the values of diversity, trust, tolerance, confidence building, negotiation, mediation, dialogue and reconciliation;
(e) Co-ordinate and supervise the work of the regional and district peace councils;
(f) Facilitate the implementation of agreement and resolution reached between parties in conflict;
(g) Make recommendations to the government and other stake holders on actions to promote trust and confidence between and among groups, and
(h) Perform any other function which is ancillary to its subjects. (Republic of Ghana 2011:4).

A. The functions of a regional peace council

1) To offer advice to Regional coordinating Council and the regional security council in relation to conflict prevention,

management, resolution and building sustainable peace in the region;

2) To mediate in conflict which is likely to erupt in violence and intervene after law and order is restored by regional security council;
3) To engage in public education and create awareness of conflict indicators within the region and make recommendations to the regional coordinating council and regional security council on how to improve the situation;
4) To facilitate the organizations of activities that build friendship, promote trust, tolerance, goodwill and reconciliation between communities;
5) To initiate and support training and capacity building programs for relevant stake holders in the region;
6) To perform other functions that may be assigned by the regional coordinating council, and
7) To perform any other function which is ancillary to its objectives (Republic of Ghana 2011:7-8)

B. The functions of a district peace council

1) To assist the district Assembly and the District Security Council in peace initiatives;
2) To mediate in inter- and intra-community conflict or conflicts among group within the district, except that where armed violence has broken out, the invitation of the district security council shall be required;
3) To engage in public education and to create awareness on conflict indicators within the district, and to make recommendations to the district assembly on how to improve the situation;
4) To facilitate the organization of activities that build friendship, promote trust, tolerance, goodwill and reconciliation between communities, and that prevent the occurrence of conflict;
5) To initiate and support training and other capacity building programmes for relevant stake holders in the district, and
6) To perform any other function determined by the Regional Security Council and the National Security Co-coordinating Council (Republic of Ghana 2011:9).

Membership of the Governing Board

The Act provides for the governing of the Council at the three tiers of government: national, regional and district. At the national level, the Council has a board, consisting of thirteen eminent personalities across the following four categories:

(a) One representative from each of the following religious bodies nominated by the bodies concerned (Catholic Bishops Conference, Christian Council, Ghana Pentecostal Council, National Council for Christian and Charismatic Churches, Ahamadiyya Muslim Mission, Al-sunnah Muslims, Tijaaniya Muslim Group, and practitioners of African traditional religion);
(b) Two persons nominated by the President, one of whom is a woman;
(c) Two other persons nominated by identifiable groups;
(d) One representative of the National House of Chiefs.

Members of the Regional and District Peace Councils consist of all of the above with slight modifications. Whereas at the national level, it is the President that nominates the two members indicated in (b) above, the responsibility falls on the "Regional Coordinating Council" at the regional level and the "District Assembly" at the District level. Whereas the Act provides for the nomination of a representative of the National House of Chiefs at the national level (d), this position is filled by a representative of the "Regional House of Chiefs" at regional level and "a chief nominated by the Traditional Council in the traditional area of the district."

The Act provides for the "President of the Council" to be appointed by the President in accordance with Article 70 of the Constitution of Ghana.

The tenure of members of the National Peace Council is for four years, and is renewable. The tenure of office for the members of the Regional and District Peace Councils is the same as for those in charge of the National Peace Council. The Councils are allowed to constitute committees that could include non-members as considered necessary from time to time.

Members of the Council at all levels are excluded from participation in politics. A member who has an interest in any matter brought before the Councils is expected to disclose this and such disclosure must form part of the record for consideration on the matter. A member with a vested interest is not permitted to participate in the determination of the matter. Where such an interest is not declared by the member, and this later becomes public knowledge, the affected member would lose his/her membership of the Board.

Meetings of the Board

The quorum of the Board is seven out of thirteen persons. The Board is expected to meet once every three months at locations determined by the chairperson, but an extra-ordinary meeting of the Board could be conducted by the chairperson at the written request of not less than one-third of the membership at a time and location determined by the chairperson. The matter before it shall be determined by consensus, and where this is difficult to achieve, the matter would be determined by voting of the members present. In the matter of equality of votes, the chairperson of the meeting shall cast the determinant vote.

Secretariat of the Council

While the management of the conflicts referred to the Councils is done by the Board, the day to day running of the Councils at the three levels is placed in the hands of "Executive Secretaries", appointed by the President in accordance with Article 195 of the Constitution. These Executive Secretaries are expected to serve as Secretaries to the Boards at national, regional and district levels, and to provide technical advice to the councils on conflict prevention, management, resolution and building a sustainable peace at the national, regional and district levels. They may also be delegated with any other functions by the Boards.

Confidentiality of Information

All members of the Council, as well as all employees of the Council, are expected to treat any information available to them with utmost confidentiality. To this end, all officers of the council are expected to take the Oath of Secrecy, on assumption of duty as specified by the laws of Ghana. However, information may be disclosed when required to do so by a court of competent jurisdiction or under an enactment.

Link with the Ministry of the Interior

The supervising body of the Councils is the Ministry of the Interior, which is mandated to have a Peace building Support Unit, which shall do the following:

(a) Liaise on behalf of the government with the National, Regional and District Peace Councils, and facilitate support from government institutions for the work of the Councils;
(b) Facilitate the implementation of the recommendations of the peace councils addressed to the government or its agencies;
(c) Manage an early warning and analysis sub-unit;
(d) Serve as an advisory body to the Minister for conflict resolution and peacebuilding generally;
(e) Perform other functions that may be assigned by the Minister for the Interior.

Sources of Funding

The Act provides for the establishment of a Peace Fund. While the Act considers it the responsibility of the government of Ghana to be the main source of money for the Fund, it makes provisions for generating additional resources from local private and public organizations and international organizations, foreign governments, revenue generated by the projects done by Councils themselves, and gifts and contributions from any other sources.

A Critique of the Policy

The Ghana Peace Council Act is the first of its kind in Africa, and its structure is very instructive, especially for other African states that might want to establish a similar system in the future. Its source of inspiration is the Resolution of African leaders at the First Standing Conference on Stability, Security and Development in Africa, in Durban in 2002, for each country to establish a national framework for the prevention, management and resolution of conflicts by December 2004.

The implementation of the Ghana Peace Council Act would benefit from some observations made in the following discussion. First and foremost, it has been observed that the Act is not gender-sensitive in the formation of the Boards. From the way the Act is written, only one woman has any chance of being included in the national, regional and district

Boards, making a total of three across the country as a whole. At the national level, the law recommends that "two persons nominated by the President one of whom is a woman" (section 4b). At regional level, it is "two persons nominated by the Regional Coordinating Council one of whom is a woman" (section 9b) and at district level, "two persons nominated by the District Assembly one of whom is a woman" (section 12b). This is nothing but tokenism. What ought to have been done is for a percentage of the seats in the Boards (at least 30%) to have been reserved for women. This means that about four out of the fourteen members in each of the Boards ought to have been women. This recommendation is necessary, not only for affirmative action which is supported by several international agreements, most especially the United Nations Resolution 1325, but more importantly because women have been established, in the extant literature, to be better peacemakers. They have more patience than men in working through peace agreements. The basic problem is that they are barely given the chance to prove themselves in peace work. Similarly, women's related issues in conflict and peace are usually ignored by the patriarchal society in which these women live (Nakaya 2004; UN 2002; UNESCO 2003).

The second observation is that the Ghana Peace Council Act atomizes the role of non-governmental organizations in peacemaking, peace building, peacekeeping and preventive diplomacy. The only part of the Act where anything likely to include NGOs is referred to is section 3(c), 9 (c), and 12(c), where the membership of the Boards is expected to include "two other persons nominated by identified groups." This is a big lacuna in an age where almost all international organizations now speak favourably about the role of NGOs in peace work. For example, Abiew and Keating observe categorically that "NGOs have on occasion overshadowed major UN agencies in peacebuilding activities… There is a considerable body of evidence to suggest that NGOs are increasingly active as a result of the absence of local authorities, the disinterest and fatigue of donor governments, and the limited capacity of international institutions" (Abiew and Keating 2004:95).

In multi-track diplomacy, the state is the first stakeholder in peace work. Security agencies constitute a key player in the game at this level. It is therefore abnormal to observe that the membership of the Ghana National Peace Council does not include anybody representing the security sector. This is a major lacuna that the Council could fill through cooptation or amendment of the Act. By having an "insider" from the security sector, the Councils would find it less cumbersome to investigate and deal with the knotty cases brought before them.

The fourth major gap in the document relates to how the Councils are expected to relate at the national, regional and district levels with the existing security systems at each of these levels. This might appear to be a small problem but, in reality, it could become very significant, given the fact that some of the duties to be performed by the Councils are already being done by some institutions, namely the judiciary and security organisations. How do the Councils build synergy with these existing agencies of law and order? What form of interagency collaboration is required for ensuring the success and sustainability of the work of the Councils? These are practical questions that the implementers of the Act must try to answer.

Conclusion

The main object of the National Peace Council of Ghana, according to the law establishing it (Act 818 of 16 May 2011), is to facilitate and develop mechanisms for conflict prevention, management, resolution, and to build sustainable peace in the country. The contents of the policy are good, but can only produce the desired results if the activities of the Councils are well networked with the existing law and order infrastructures in Ghana. For example, the Councils must work closely with security organizations in the country. It also needs to work closely with those nongovernmental organizations doing peace work at the grassroots level, given the fact that these NGOs have a close working relationship with many of the communities where many of the conflicts in Ghana arise. The councils might not be able to achieve its set goals if it is not adequately funded by the government. In addition to this, officers of the councils must be able to raise addition funds from elsewhere. This requires that the capacity of those working with and for the councils must be built in fundraising and proposal writing. Other African states must follow Ghana's example by building their own architecture for peace. It is only then that the efforts being made by ECOWAS will be able to produce the best results.

References

Adebajo, A. (2002), *Building Peace in West Africa: Liberia, Sierra Leone, and Guinea-Bissau*, Boulder, CO.: Lynne Rienner Publishers.

African Union (2002), Memorandum of understanding on security, stability, development and cooperation in Africa, Heads of State and Government First Standing Conference on Security, Stability, Development and Cooperation in Africa (CSSDCA) 8-9 July 2002

Durban, Durban, South Africa; http://www.africa-union.org/Special_Programs/CSSDCA/cssdca-memorandumofunderstanding.pdf.

Albert, I.O. (2008), "From 'Owo crisis' to 'Dagbon dispute': Lessons in the politicization of chieftaincy disputes in modern Nigeria and Ghana", *The Roundtable: Commonwealth Journal of International Affairs*, Vol. 97 No. 394 pp.47-60.

Albert, I.O. and O. Albert (2008), "Strategies for peace education integration in ECOWAS member states' tertiary school curricula", *Conflict Trends*, Issue 3, pp.11-17.Albert, I.O. (2011), *Practice Guide for Managing Election Disputes in West Africa*, Accra, Ghana: The West African Network for Peacebuilding (WANEP).Archibugi, Daniele, *The Global Commonwealth of Citizens. Toward Cosmopolitan Democracy*, Princeton University Press, Princeton 2008.Bawumia, Abdulai Mumuni and Ojielo, Ozonnia Ojielo, "Building peace in Ghana: Capacity building for conflict prevention", UNDP Ghana, http://www.undp.org/cpr/newsletters/2007_4/article2.htmDiamond, L. and J.W. Macdonald, 1996. *Multi-Track Diplomacy: A Systems Approach to Peace*. New York: Kumarian Press.Doyle, Michael (1983), "Kant, Liberal Legacies, and Foreign Affairs", *Philosophy and Public Affairs*, 205, 207-208.

Draman, R. and D. Carment (2001), "Managing chaos in the West African Sub-Region: Assessing the role of ECOMOG in Liberia," *Occasional Paper* No. 26, The Norman Paterson School of International Affairs, Carleton University, Ottawa, Ontario;

ECOWAS Commission (2010), architecture for peace in Ghana: Concept paper," May; http://www.mint.gov.gh/dmdocuments/A_PEACE_ARCHITECTURE_FOR_GHANA_.pdf.

ECOWAS International Conference on "Two decades of peace processes in West Africa: Achievements, failures, lessons, Monrovia, Liberia, 22-26 March 2010. http://www.comm.ecowas.int/dept/h/h1/en/rapport/Final_Report_Two_Decades_English.pdf.

Golwa, J. (2011), Interview with the Director General of the Institute for Peace and Conflict Resolution, Abuja, April 4.

Kan-Dapaah, Albert (2006), "A national Abiew, F.K. and T. Keating (2004), "Defining a role for civil society", in Tom Keating and W. Andy Knight (eds.), *Building sustainable paece*, Tokyo and Edmunton: United Nations University and The University of Alberta Press pp. 93-118.

Nakaya, S. (2004), "Women and gender equality in peacebuilding", in Tom Keating and W. Andy Knight (eds.), *Building sustainable paece*, Tokyo and Edmunton: United Nations University and The University of Alberta Press pp. 143-166.

Olonisakin, F. (2000), *Reinventing Peacekeeping in Africa: Conceptual and Legal Issues in ECOMOG Operations*, The Hague: Kluwer Law International, 2000.

—. (2008), *Lessons Learned from Peacekeeping in West Africa*, Kofi Annan International Peacekeeping Training Centre.

Republic of Ghana (2011), *National Peace Council Act, 2011 (Act 818)*, Accra: Government Printer Assembly Press.

Sponsel, L.E. (1996). *The natural history of peace: A positive view of human nature and its potential,* in Thomas Gregor, (ed.), *A natural history of peace,* Nashville and London: Vanderbilt University Press pp. 95-125

UNESCO (2003), *Women and Peace in Africa: Case Studies on traditional conflict resolutions practices.* Paris: UNESCO Workshops.

UN (2002), *Women, peace and security*, New York: United Nations.

Van Soest, D. (1997). *The global crisis of violence: Common problems, universal causes, shared solutions.* Washington, DC: *NASW Press.*

CHAPTER ELEVEN

RESTORATIVE JUSTICE AND CRIME PREVENTION: ANTIDOTE FOR PRISON CONGESTION AND IMPROVEMENT OF PRISON CONDITION IN NIGERIA

ANNE AMUCHE OBIORA

Introduction

Prison conditions in Nigeria have deteriorated over the years. Once a person is convicted by the Nigerian courts to serve a prison sentence, such a person is perceived by society to have been sent to hell on earth. Consequently, the poor state of Nigerian prisons has attracted a lot of attention from all and sundry. In order to advance the rights of prisoners in Nigeria and to influence government policy so as to ameliorate the suffering of the prison inmates, there is a need to consider the deplorable prison conditions in Nigeria. In Nigerian prisons, many inmates sleep two to a bed or on the floor in filthy cells. Toilets are blocked and overflowing or simply non-existent, and there is no running water. Diseases are widespread, and successive governments have also demonstrated a less than satisfactory commitment to reforming the laws regulating Nigerian prisons (Ogwezzy, 2011). The administration of the criminal justice system in Nigeria has not helped matters. Frequent and indefinite adjournment of cases in our courts is also a contributory factor to prison congestion.

A prison is supposed to be a place for the reformation of the behaviour of an individual whose life pattern is not in tandem with accepted norms, values or behaviours in wider society, or persons who by omission and commission have violated the criminal laws of the land. The essence of such punishment is to reform and correct the behaviour of such offenders and to serve as a deterrent to would-be offenders against such laws (Ogwezzy, 2011). Nigeria is faced with challenges of prison management, considering the figure of awaiting trial persons (ATPs) which has been put at 36,000, representing over 65% of the estimated total prisoner population of 48,000. Indeed, a large percentage of Nigeria's prison inmates have stayed for five to seven years in detention without trial under deplorable conditions (Ogwezzy, 2011).

This chapter will therefore discuss the programmes of restoration, justice and crime prevention as a remedy for the congestion in Nigerian prisons, which will eventually lead to the improvement of prison conditions in Nigeria.

Explanation of Concepts

Restorative Justice is a way of responding to criminal behaviour by balancing the needs of the community, the victims, and the offenders (UNODC, 2000). There are many terms used to describe restorative justice. These include the following: "communitarian justice," "making amends," "positive justice," "relational justice," "reparative justice," and "community justice" (UNODC, 2000). There is a restorative justice programme and a restorative justice process.

The concept of "restorative justice Programmes" means any programme that uses restorative process and seeks to achieve restorative outcomes. On the other hand, a restorative process is any process in which the victim and the offender—and, where appropriate, any other individuals or community members affected by a crime—participate together in the active resolution of matters arising from the crime, generally with the help of a facilitator (UNODC, 2000). Restorative justice gives as much importance to the process as to the outcome. The individuals involved in this process are referred to as the "parties." The process usually takes the form of "mediation", as distinct from legal adjudication. According to the basic principles, a "restorative outcome" is an agreement reached as a result of a restorative process. The agreement may include: referrals to programmes such as reparation, restitution and community services aimed at meeting individual and collective needs, the responsibilities of the parties involved, and achieving the reintegration of the victim and the offender; a response to crime which is particularly suitable for situations where juvenile offenders are involved and in which an important objective of the intervention is to teach the offenders some new values and skills, and a response that recognizes the role of the community as a prime site of prevention and responding to crime and social disorder.

Underlying Assumptions

Restorative justice programmes are based on the following underlying assumptions:

a. That the response to crime should repair, as much as possible, the harm suffered by the victim;
b. That the offenders should be brought to understand that their behaviour is not acceptable, and that it had real consequences for the victim and community;
c. That offenders can and should accept responsibility for their actions;
d. That victims should have the opportunity to express their needs and to participate in determining the best way for the offender to make reparation;
e. That the community has a responsibility to contribute to this process.

Required Ingredients for a Successful Restorative Justice Programme

There are at least four critical ingredients needed for a fully restorative process to achieve its objectives:

a. An identifiable victim;
b. Voluntary participation by the victim;
c. An offender who accepts responsibility for his/her criminal behavior;
d. Non-coerced participation of the offender.

Most restorative approaches strive to achieve a specific interactive dynamic among the parties involved. The goal is to create a non-adversarial and non-threatening environment in which the interests and needs of the victim, the offender, the community and society can best be addressed.

Features of Restorative Justice Programmes

The following are features of Restorative Justice Programmes:

- A flexible response to the circumstances of the crime, the offender and the victim, that allows each case to be considered individually;
- A response to crime that respects the dignity and equality of each person, builds understanding, and promotes social harmony through the healing of victims, offenders and communities;
- A viable alternative (in many cases) to the formal criminal justice system and its stigmatizing effects on offenders;
- An approach that can be used in conjunction with traditional criminal justice processes and sanctions;
- An approach that incorporates problem solving and addresses the underlying causes of conflict;
- An approach that addresses the harm to and needs of victims;
- An approach that encourages an offender to gain insight into the causes and effects of his or her behavior and to take responsibility in a meaningful way;
- A flexible and variable approach, which can be adapted to the circumstances, legal tradition, principles and underlying philosophies of established national criminal justice systems;
- An approach that is suitable for dealing with many different kinds of offences and offenders, including many very serious offences.

Objectives of Restorative Justice

The objectives of restorative justice programmes have been stated in a number of different ways, all of which contain the following essential key elements:

a. Supporting victims, giving them a voice, encouraging them to participate in the resolution process, and offering them assistance;
b. Repairing the relationship damaged by the crime, in part by arriving at a consensus on how best to respond to it;
c. Denouncing criminal behaviour as unacceptable, and reaffirming community values;
d. Encouraging all concerned parties to take responsibility, particularly offenders. The restorative process is meant to make it easier for offenders to assume responsibility for their

behaviour and its consequences. A restorative process moves from merely assessing legal guilt to attempting to determine responsibility for a conflict and its consequences. Active acknowledgement and acceptance of personal responsibility for the crime and its consequences rather than a mere passive one imposed by others is encouraged;

e. Identifying restorative, forward-looking outcomes. Rather than emphasizing the rules that have been broken and the punishment that should be imposed, a restorative approach tends to focus primarily on the persons who have been harmed. A restorative justice process does not necessarily rule out all forms of punishments (examples include: fines, incarceration, probation), but its focus remains firmly on restorative and forward-looking outcomes;
f. Reducing recidivism by encouraging change in individual offenders and facilitating their reintegration into the community. The past behaviour of individuals and its consequences are clearly a central preoccupation of the restorative process, but so is the offender's future behaviour. An offender's undertaking as it relates to his/her future behavior is usually an essential component of the agreement arrived at through mediation or other restorative process;
g. Identifying factors that lead to crime and informing authorities responsible for crime reducing strategy. The restorative process is an open one, which encourages frank discussion of the background of the offence in a spirit of explanation rather than making excuses. If, for example, this reveals that offenders come from areas with particular deficit, action can be taken to remedy the problem.

Types of Restorative Justiceunderlying assumptions

Following the theoretical discourse on restorative justice above, there are a number of standardized and innovative programmes currently being implemented around the world. These are designed to address the needs of crime victims, respective families, and other community members affected by criminal offending (Don John Otene Omale, 2009). Similarly, in Nigeria there are some cultural and indigenous restorative practices that could be adapted or adopted to suit modern conflict resolution mechanisms, if properly studied and researched. These processes are designed to intervene in the context of the community in which the offending behaviour took place, rather than in the formal and traditionally intimidating atmosphere of the courtroom. The review of Nigerian Indigenous practices is intended to see how these could be mainstreamed into the standard practice models, grouped into the following four main categories: circles, panels, conferences, and victim-offender mediation. However, there are no strict models of restorative justice. This is because they could be customized to suit the indigenous and cultural orientation of the participants.

The standardized restorative justice models below are given as instances of some Nigerian cultural restorative practices that could improve and be complimentary to international models, such as Family Group Conferencing, Circles and panels, for instance. The models complement one another and should not automatically be seen as mutually exclusive. These include:

a. **Victim-Offender Mediation:** Victim-offender mediation practice is designed to bring victims and offenders together face-to-face in safe, structured, facilitated dialogue, that typically occurs in a community-based setting. Before this meeting, it is suggested that a separate pre-conference meeting with both the victim and the offender is held to explain and assess the individual's readiness for the process, and to assist the victim in communicating the physical, emotional and financial impact of the crime to the offender. The meeting should be conducted by a trained mediator or facilitator. The meeting helps the offender to take responsibility for his/her offending behaviour, and allows the victim to receive answers from the offender about "why" and "how" the crime occurred. On the basis of this meeting, the victim and the offender would together determine an appropriate plan to repair the harm to the victim, which may include material and/or non-material compensation. The victim-offender group is a model where several victims and offenders, who have either been affected by or committed the same offence, are brought together in a mediation process. For instance, a number of victims of residential burglary might meet with a similar number of offenders who had committed residential burglary, where these may be their own offenders. It was suggested that this might be a useful way of involving victims who seem likely to benefit from a restorative process when "their" offender has either not been apprehended or is considered totally unsuited to a restorative process.

b. **Family Group Conferencing:** This is the most popular model of restorative conferencing. Family Group Conferencing is based on ancient practices originated by the Maori tradition of New Zealand. In Nigeria, a similar tradition can be found in the use of Umunnas (the use of family members who share lineage in dispute resolution) among the Igbos. The Igbo often do not believe in top-bottom involvement in family disputes. In family group conferencing, it is noted that meetings typically occur following separate face-to-face meetings with the victim and the offender, which may include members of their respective families and any supporters or significant others that the key parties might wish to have present. The conference enables the parties to share their stories, to identify the impacts of the crime on those present, and to collectively determine an appropriate resolution. Recidivism rates decreased for violent offenders, and young offenders who participated in conferences were more likely to say they would obey the law in future than among those who went through the court system; victims also reported that they were better served by conference process than court proceedings.

c. **Circles:** This practice model is sometimes referred to as "sentencing circles," "peace making circles," or community circles. In Nigeria, this practice model of restorative justice can be found in Akwa Ibom, Cross River States, and the Igbos. They are known as the "Ekpo" and "Ekpe" societies respectively. These are dispute resolution groups and they resolve disputes by sitting together in circles in the village square, to mediate between the parties to a crime; a healing sacrifice/ceremony is performed to resolve the conflict and to forestall further resentment among parties. Circles carry particular spiritual significance for many indigenous people. This process is more complicated and time consuming than other restorative models. It may involve up to "five distinct stages"; these are labour intensive, and would demand a considerable amount of commitment to the process from the participants.

d. **Panels:** This model of restorative justice practice has been called several names. These include: citizen panels, neighbourhood boards, diversion boards, youth panels, reparative boards and community boards. This type of restorative justice practice is found among different tribes in Nigeria. Among the Igbos it is called "Ndi-nze" (Committee of red cap chief), the "Ama-ala (The nobles of the land) the "Ba'ale" amongst the Yoruba, the "Mai-ungwo" amongst the Hausas, and the "Madakis" "Gangos" (The eyes of the community) amongst the Igalla tribe in conflict resolution. This model is mainly composed of a small group of citizens who come together to determine what should happen, primarily in a non-violent atmosphere and in cases of offences involving interfering in property, like stealing, etc. However, in Nigeria, this model could be used for serious crimes, provided it is in the interest of the parties and the communities concerned. Panel members meet face to face with offenders to discuss the nature of the offence, its implications, and the appropriate reparative action. If the victims are absent, they might be consulted for input prior to the panel meeting: alternatively, a delegation of representatives of the victims might be consulted. If present, panel members typically determine the reparative outcomes, but might involve the offender in generating conditions of agreement and the time frame for completion. The panel members also monitor the completion of the agreement, and might report to the court, the police or other statutory body to indicate the conclusion of the matter (if the matter was withdrawn from court or the police, for example). The essence of this method is to promote citizen's involvement in and ownership of the justice process, and to offer the community and the offender the opportunity to come together to deal with the offending behaviour constructively.

Each of the above four methods of restorative justice, if conducted effectively, are democratic means of conflict/dispute resolution. They would equally contribute in no small measure to the decongestion and improvement of prison condition in Nigeria.

Limits of Restorative Justice Programmes

Reeves (1989) notes that restorative justice has been the subject of much criticism, despite the progress it has made. Organizations that support victims and advocate for their rights also have reservations and questions about the model. According to Roach (2000), some of the pitfalls of restorative justice include the following:

a. Mediation programs apply in a minority of cases compared to the total volume of crimes commited, and mainly target property offences and young first-time offenders. Many experts feel that these measures help cast a wider penal net in areas that are not normally within the jurisdiction of the courts, and more often than not are detrimental to disadvantaged groups (Walgrave L., 1993). They are seen more as ways for offenders to avoid the criminal process.
b. Unfortunately, victims are left on the sidelines in the very programs designed to give them a more central role (Fatta E., 1998). Whether the chosen method is mediation, family conferences or some other practice, too many victims are relegated to the role of facilitator or intermediary, or are used as a pretext for pursuing an educational initiative for offenders (Dognan J., 2003). Victims are sometimes not involved because they are not invited or could not be reached, or because indirect mediation was chosen in order to reach a quicker resolution, to provide financial compensation, or to keep the procedure from becoming unduly complicated.
c. Some of the criticisms of restorative justice also relate to the ways in which conditions aimed at fostering the participation of victims and offenders are set. Too often, the victims and the offenders' status are not carefully assessed and/or their needs do not undergo a comprehensive analysis. Time is not always spent providing victims with information, preparing them psychologically, or allowing them to familiarize themselves with the process and its objectives (Hudson B., 2003). In addition, some studies have shown that victims were pressured into taking part in mediation or meeting circles (Dognan J. & Cavadino, 1996). They may also become involved at a time when they are not prepared to do so.
d. There is also a tendency to forget that restorative action in its various forms is rarely motivated by the wishes of the victims themselves or victim support organizations. Most of the time, the action centers on the offender. It is often set in motion by services

that work with offenders—both minors and adults —in the context of probation, alternatives to incarceration or parole. The role of mediator is then assigned to stakeholders whose first mandate is to aid the rehabilitation of offenders. Although responding to the needs of victims is not absent from their concerns, it is not in the forefront. Many such stakeholders are uncomfortable dealing with the victims, in terms of being prepared to meet their expectations, being taken off guard by their reactions, and feeling that they are playing conflicting roles and are poorly equipped.

e. Given that a significant number of stakeholders have little or no experience with victims and rely heavily on volunteers in the community, it is important to remember the importance of improving their knowledge and skills. The implementation of programmes that focus on meetings between victim and offender entails a long period of preparation at each stage, and repeated contact with the parties involved (LaPraoroe C., 1995).

Although some of the pitfalls of restorative justice have been discussed, this doesn't mean that it has stopped being an important remedy to prison congestion in Nigeria. It is very relevant.

Crime and the Police

Black (1990) defined a crime as any act committed in violation of those duties which an individual owes to the community, and for the breach of which the law has provided that the offender shall make satisfaction to the public, or omitted in violation of a law forbidding or commanding it, and to which is annexed, upon conviction, one or a combination of the following punishments:

a. Death;
b. Imprisonment;
c. Fine;
d. Removal from office;
e. Disqualification to hold and enjoy any office of honour, trust or profit.

A crime (offence) is an act or omission which renders the person doing the act or making the omission liable to punishment under the code or under any order in council, ordinance, or law or statute (Section 1, Criminal

Code Act, 2004) is called an offence. Section 36 (12) (Constitution, 1999) provides that:

> Subject as otherwise provided by this constitution, a person shall not be convicted of a criminal offence unless that offence is defined and the penalty therefore is prescribed in a written law…

It then follows that each crime has a corresponding prescribed penalty (punishment). Therefore, every criminal offence has a penalty or punishment attached to it.

Elements of an Offence

There are two elements of an offence, namely the *actus reus* and the *mens rea.* All offences require the two to ground conviction. An offence is the criminal act or an unlawful omission of an act. Therefore, a person cannot be convicted for thinking criminal thoughts. There must be an action. It is difficult to talk about or discuss crime without the police, whose principal duty is to prevent crime. The following sections in the Criminal Procedure Act (CPA, 2004) have empowered the police to arrest suspects and then prevent the commission of crime.

Section 53 of the Criminal Procedure Act provides thus:

> *Every police officer may interpose for the purpose of preventing, and shall to the best of his ability prevent the commission of any offence.*
>
> *A police officer may of his own authority interpose to prevent any injury attempted to be committed in his view to any public property, movable, or immovable, or the removal of or injury to any public landmark or buoy or other mark used for navigation.*

Section 54 of the Criminal Procedure Act provides thus:

> *Every police officer receiving information of a design to commit any offence shall communicate such information to the police officer to whom he is subordinate, and to any other officer whose duty it is to prevent or take cognizance of the commission of any such offence.*

Section 55 of the Criminal Procedure Act provides as follows:

> *Notwithstanding the provisions of this or any other written law relating to arrest, a police officer knowing of a design to commit any offence may arrest without orders from a magistrate and without a warrant, the person*

> *so designing, if it appears to such officer that the commission of the offence cannot otherwise wise be prevented.*

Having established that the police are connected with the prevention of crime, it is appropriate to discuss the role of the police in crime prevention.

Police and Crime Prevention

Section 4 of the Police Act provides thus:

> *The police shall be employed for the prevention and detection of crime, the apprehension of offenders, the preservation of law and order, the protection of life and property and the due enforcement of all laws and regulation with which they are directly charged....*

The police cannot prevent crime if they do not detect the crime. Therefore, crime prevention and detection will now be discussed.

Crime prevention and Detection

It must be borne in mind that you can only prevent the commission of a crime if you detect its anticipatory steps early enough, before the commission of the crime. However, prevention, as used in the Police Act, refers to situations where crimes are discovered and thus prevented before commission. On the other hand, crime detection refers to the investigatory power of the police to discover the commission of crime at any point in time and to be able to identify the *personae criminis* involved in the commission of the crime. You can only prevent a crime if you know of its existence and anticipate it, and you know of the existence of a crime without being a party to it if you detect it. Thus, the prevention of a crime can be and usually is preceded by detection of the acts of committing a crime.

The task of the police in preventing the commission of crime can be carried out through any or all of the following mechanisms:

- **Beat Patrols:** A beat is the area which a particular constable or groups of constables is detailed to patrol during a single tour of duty. It may be a precinct in a city or town, embracing an area as small as a couple of streets or roads, or be as large as a kilometer in radius, depending on the density of the population.

The known crime rate and the economic or administrative importance of the establishments or buildings in the area will be familiar to the police. In rural areas, it may be a collection of villages or hamlets, or a stretch of kilometers along national borders. The aim is to make sure that an offender is immediately apprehended, which will be a strong deterrent to potential offenders.

- **Anti-Vice Squads:** This is a surveillance squad operating in disguise and carrying out intelligent surveillance of areas that are potential breeding grounds for various vices such as gambling, rioting, etc. They operate at large gatherings of people, public places, motor parks, etc., where theft and affray have been found to be rampant. The objective of the squad is to gather information and to provide proactive measures preventing the commission of crime and, where this fails, to at least immediately apprehend the criminals at the point of commission of the offence (Police Act, 2004).
- **Detain and Search:** By virtue of the power conferred by the provisions of section 29 of the Police Act, a police officer on duty is expected to be vigilant, and when his suspicion is aroused, is entitled to detain and search any person whom he reasonably suspects of having in his possession or conveying in any manner anything he has reason to believe has been stolen or unlawfully obtained, or with reference to which an offence has been committed (CPA, 2004). This method contributes greatly to the prevention of crime.
- **Special Escort:** These are armed policemen guarding large sums of money, valuables or explosives in transit. This is a service rendered free of charge to governmental and quasi-governmental agencies, but on payment of fees to private organizations and individuals
- **Static Guards:** This is an anti-crime prevention model adopted in the advanced world and partially in Nigeria during the colonial era and the first republic. Through this model, police guards are provided at public institutions and places to check ingress and exit of customers and clients etc. They prevent crime in such establishments.
- **National (Internal) Security:** The police, in collaboration with the relevant state security agencies, also provide a surveillance network on the activities of persons considered to be a security

risk, in order to prevent sabotage and subversion of the nation and its established institutions.

- **Regulating Assemblies, Processions, etc.** The police are empowered to prevent likely breaches of the peace and to contain any tendency towards inciting and provocative acts etc., by any persons initially gathered for a lawful purpose, or such acts by others towards a lawful gathering and or possession.
- **The Supervisee System:** This system enables the police to keep an eye on the movement and activities of criminals who, on conviction, are sentenced to police supervision. The term of the order of supervision directs the supervisee to report to a police officer in his area of residence once a month. The police are afforded the opportunity of monitoring the activity and movements of known and habitual offenders, in order to prescript and anticipate their next or potential crime manoeuvers:

The following are some of the ways crime can be prevented, and the upsurge of people into the Nigerian prisons can be halted or minimized.

Community Responsibility for Crime Prevention

Individuals and communities within society have a singular responsibility to themselves and to the state to be conscious of their preventive rights. This right is best exemplified when you try to anticipate and prevent yourself from being harmed by the actions of others. By doing so, you are carrying out the civil and legal duty of crime prevention in the society (Police Act, 2004). This task of crime prevention is not achieved through retaliatory actions or preemptive violence, but by promptly reporting such incidents or facts to the law enforcement agency in your neighbourhood. Therefore, all hands must be on deck to achieve the task, and we all have a responsibility and a role to play in the crime prevention task.

Apart from the self-preventive duty of members of the community to prevent the commission of crime by reporting the same to the police, the law imposes a duty on members of the community to assist the police on their crime preventive function.

By virtue of the provision of section 34 (b) (CPA, 2004):

> [...] every person is bound to assist a ... police officer reasonably demanding his aid in the preventive or suppression of a breach of the peace

or in the prevention of any injury attempted to be committed to any telegraph or public property.

Members of the community are also expected to assist a police officer in the course of her/his duty. Therefore, everybody is bound to prevent the commission of crime as statutorily required. This may explain or suggest why there are vigilante groups in villages.

Prison Conditions in Nigeria

In Nigeria, four out of every five prisons were built before 1950 (Amnesty International, 2008). Many need renovation. The infrastructure is old. Many buildings can no longer be used. In others, the ceilings are about to collapse, the buildings in use as workshops are inadequate, and sanitary facilities have broken down. The prisons have problems with their electricity supplies, and most often have no water supply. Several prisons do not have a modern drainage system, and use open drains that create a serious health risk for inmates and staff alike. Most cells have only small windows for ventilation, and considering our hot weather this can be very inconveniencing. Inmates on death row and prisoners awaiting trial face even worse conditions. Death row inmates are held in cells that are tiny, dark and filthy with almost no ventilation. They are allowed outside their cells during the day for a limited period of time along with other convicted inmates. The same is true for most prisoners awaiting trial, who are generally held in much more overcrowded quarters.

A General Statistics of Prison Inmates in Nigeria (Nigeria Prison Service, 2013)

Total capacity: 47.284

	Male	***Female***	***Total***
Awaiting Trial Persons (ATPs)	***37,519***	***833***	***38,352***
Convicted Persons (CPs)	***15,593***	***211***	***15,804***
Inmate Population	***53,112***	***1,044***	***54,156***

B Breakdown of Convicted Prisoners

	Male	*Female*	*Total*
Number of death row	***983***	***19***	***1,002***
Number on life sentence	***448***	***7***	***455***
Number on long term sentence (>2years)	***6,852***	***97***	***6,949***
Number on short term sentence	***7,310***	***88***	***7,398***

In Peter Nemi versus the Attorney General of Lagos State (1996), Uwaifo JCA (as he then was) stated, in a judgment he delivered at the Court of Appeal, that prisoners' rights remain intact except when they are deprived of them by law. Even a condemned prisoner awaiting execution still has his rights, until he is properly executed by the due process of law.

Prisons register the date of entry and exit of each prisoner. The administration of inmates is very outdated: each day, prison directors register who has been looked up on a blackboard near the prison gate, and report to the zonal offices, who, in turn, report to the headquarters in Abuja. Few computers are used. Amnesty International observed that the prison headquarters were unable to provide data on the prison population. It is estimated that there are almost 45,000 inmates in Nigeria's 144 prisons, and 98 additional specialized facilities. Approximately 25,000 are awaiting trial, and some 784 are on death row. The total number of staff is almost 25,000.

This is just "the tip of the iceberg" concerning what Nigerian prisons look like. I am of the view that if restorative justice and crime prevention techniques are applied, this will go a long way to reducing the number of prison inmates, especially those awaiting trial. Invariably, the conditions of prison inmates will improve, because when prisons are decongested via restorative justice and crime prevention, the existing facilities will be able to better accommodate the lower numbers of prison inmates.

Recommendations

- There should be workshops and seminars to make people aware of the need and importance of restorative justice.
- The condition of life in Nigerian prisons should be the concern of everybody and all hands must be on deck.

- It is the responsibility of all and sundry to be involved in the prevention of crime and to contact the police whenever the need arises.
- Human rights should be extended to those in prison custody.

Conclusion

This chapter started by discussing the condition of Nigerian prisons, which have been deteriorating over a long period of time. The purpose of establishing prisons was also mentioned: among other things, prison is a place for the reformation of the behaviour of an individual whose life pattern is not in consonance with the accepted norms and values of wider society. The failure of the criminal justice system of Nigeria to meet the challenges of handling prison matters appropriately was mentioned, as a contributory factor in prison congestion. Restorative justice and crime prevention, both recommended in order to decongest prisons, were extensively discussed, as were statutory provisions. The police were identified as principal actors in the prevention and detection of crime. Finally, some human living conditions in the Nigerian prisons were highlighted, and recommendations were made. Statistical data on prison inmates in Nigeria was provided.

References

Amnesty International (2008).*Prisoners' Rights Systematically Flouted.* Al Index; Amnesty International Publications, Nigeria. Assessed March 10, 2013 at 9:00a.m

Black (1990). Black's Law Dictionary (6th edition). Constitution of the Federal Republic of Nigeria 1999 (as amended) Criminal Procedure Act Cap.C41Laws of Federation of Nigeria 2004 (as amended)

Dignan J., (2003). *Towards a Systemic Model of Restorative Justice: Reflections on the Concept, its Context and the Need for Clear Constraints* in Von Hirsh, A. Roberts, J. Bottoms, A Roach, K. Schiff, M (ed) Restorative Justice and Criminal Justice.(Oregon).

Dignana J. & Cavadino (1996).*Towards Framework for Conceptualizing and Evaluating Models of Criminal Justice from a Victim's Perspective.*International Review of Victimology.

Don John Otene Omale, (2009). *Restorative Justice As An Alternative: Dispute Resolution Model: Opinions Of Victims Of Crime, And Criminal Justice Professionals In Nigeria.* (P.hD Thesis, De Montfort

University)Retrieved: https://www.dora.dmu.ac.uk/bitstream/handle/2086/2411/

Fatta E., (1998). *A Critical Assessment of Two Justice Paradigms: Contrasting Restorative and Retributive Justice Models*. In Fattah, E., Peters T., (ed), Support for Crime Victims in a Comparative Perspective. Leuren University Press.

Hudson B. (2003).*Victims and Offenders*, In Von Hirsh, A. Roberts, J. Bottoms, A. Roach, K. Schijj, M (ed), Restorative Justice and Criminal Justice.(Oxford and Poland).

La Prairie, C. (1995). *Altering Course: New Directions in Criminal Justice Sentencing Circles and Family Group Conferences*. In The Australian and New Zealand Journal of Criminology (Canada).

Ogwezzy, M.C, (2011). *From Reformation to Deformation: An Approach Towards Sustainable Development of Effective Prison System in Nigeria*. Journal of Sustainable Development in Africa.

Peter Nemi v Attorney General of Lagos State (1996). 6NWLR (1996) (Pt.452) at 42.

Police Act Cap.P19 Laws of Federation of Nigeria 2004 (as amended).

Reeves H., (1989). *The Victim Support Perspective*. In Martin Wright & Burt Galawa (ed.) Mediation and Criminal Justice, Victims, Offenders and Community. Article Published in the Proceedings of the Symposium of the Ecole Nationale De La Magistrature, Paris: Edition, 2005 retrieved from http:///www.victimsweek.gc.ca/pub/pdf/restorative _justice.pdf.

Roach K., (2000). *Changing Punishment at the Turn of the Century: Restorative Justice on the Rise*, Du Chatiment a la Justice Reparatrice: Une Evolution? Canadian Journal of Criminology

Section 10 Criminal Procedure Act Cap C 41. Laws of Federation of Nigeria 2004 (As amended).

Section 2 Criminal Code Act.Cap.C38 Laws of Federation of Nigeria 2004 (As amended).

Section 24 (1) of Police Act Cap.P.19 Laws of Federation of Nigeria 2004 (As Amended).

Section 35 CPA Criminal Procedure Act Cap C 41. Laws of Federation of Nigeria 2004 (as amended).

The Nigerian Prisons Service (2013).*Statistical Information of the Prisons in Nigeria*. Retrieved from http://www.prisons.gov.ng/about/statistical-info.php.

United Nations Office on Drugs and Crime (UNODC), (2000).United National Publication, Vienna International Centre.

Walgrave L. (1993). Au-delà de la Rétribution et de la Réhabilitation: la Réparation Comme Paradigme Dominant dans Intervention Judiciaire. Confre la delin quinze (des jeunes)? (1993). LeGazeau, J.F Peyre, V., (ed*) La justice Réparatrice et les jeunes, IXe Journées Internationales de Criminologie Juvénile. Centre de Recherche Interdisciplinaire de Vaucresson.*

EPILOGUE

ADR AND PEACE STUDIES IN AFRICA, FIFTEEN YEARS LATER: LESSONS AND FUTURE DIRECTIONS BEARING WITNESS TO THE ADR, CONFLICT RESOLUTION AND PEACE BUILDING MOVEMENT IN GHANA

MARTIN A. B. K. AMIDU

It gives me pleasure, great as my content to be here before you on this auspicious occasion of the celebration of fifteen years of Alternative Dispute Resolution and Peace Studies in African at the invitation of the Ghana Association of Certified Mediators and Arbitrators, to take part in this conference on the theme: "ADR and Peace Studies in Africa: Lessons and Future Directions."

When I received the invitation from the GHACMA, (and give me the privilege of calling you by this acronym, if you have not been calling the association by it already), signed by Professor Quashigah, my mind went immediately to Mr. Fui Tsikata, the former unassuming and distinguished teacher at the Faculty of Law of the University of Ghana, who facilitated the agreement that was signed between Ghana and the United States of America to facilitate ADR practice in Ghana. It was Mr. Fui Tsikata who in 1996 approached me, as Deputy Attorney General and Minister of Justice at the time, to seek the approval and support of the Ministry of Justice and the Government of Ghana to enable the Faculty of Law, as lead facilitator with the Bench and the Bar, to enter into an agreement with the Center for African Peace and Conflict Resolution of the California State University, Sacramento, for the implementation of an agreed programme for Alternative Dispute Resolution in Ghana. The Government of the United States of America, pursuant to this agreement, was to make a grant to the Center which would in collaboration with the Government of Ghana and Bench, Bar and faculty of Ghana develop and implement ADR mechanisms and processes that would answer Ghana's needs for easing the delays in the administration of justice and expedite the speedy disposal of cases in the courts. If my memory serves me right, Mr. Fui Tsikata had been approached by Mrs. Henrietta Mensah-Bonsu (now Associate Professor) to lead the Bench, Bar and Faculty to seek the endorsement of Government through the Ministry of Justice and Attorney General's Department for the project. I signed the Agreement on behalf of the Government of Ghana. Professor Uwazie, who still heads the Center, signed for the Center. It was pursuant to this Agreement that a delegation consisting of a Justice of the Superior Court, a member of the Ghana Bar Association, and a lecturer of the Faculty of Law University of Ghana, undertook a study tour of a number of States in the United States of America, to acquaint themselves with the working of the ADR system in the Unites States of America, in July 1996.

The study tour was to assist the country and the Judicial Service in particular to reduce to a considerable extent the case load of the courts by facilitating the speedy dispensation of justice and humanizing the otherwise adversarial system. The return of the delegation of three trainee/trainers saw the beginning of the advocacy for the Alternative Dispute Resolution Movement in Ghana in earnest. The basic philosophical and practical application of the concepts, frameworks and module of ADR was learnt, internalized and objectified as a social reality by this first batch of Ghanaian trainees of trainers who started the propagation of its ideal. The then Chief Justice of Ghana, the Honourable Justice Archer, who was well acquainted with the benefits of Alternative Dispute Resolution for the judicial system in Ghana, bought into the ADR system proposed by his representative who went on the study tour. Chief Justice Archer thus became the first Chief justice to lead the movement for judicial reform using ADR to obtain substantial and speedy justice, whose outcome may be owned by the parties in dispute with the help of a third party facilitator.

It was easy for Government and the Ministry of Justice to accede to the request to enter into the agreement with the California State University Center for African Peace and Conflict Resolution, because the Ministry of Justice was in the process of overhauling the Arbitration Act, 1961 (Act 38). I was then also a student of conflict resolution and I had returned from an Asian African Legal Consultative Committee meeting in New Delhi with a textbook on the subject, to be read by Mrs. Ofori-Boateng, the then Director of Legislative Drafting and myself, to aid us in making proposals for the new ADR Bill. But let me confess today that the involvement of

Mr. Fui Tiskata was the main assurance for me to sign the agreement for the project.

It has been said that when the elements of nature favour an event, it cannot fail. The ADR Movement was destined to begin and succeed in Ghana, so Government readily granted approval, the delegation made the study tour and returned to begin the campaign for speedy and relational justice through ADR. The judicial system incorporated ADR into the justice delivery system administratively and later under the High Court (Civil Procedure) Rules. The elements of nature disfavoured the replacement of the Arbitration Act with a new Alternative Dispute Resolution Act consolidating ADR mechanisms and processes with formal arbitration frameworks. Consequently, even though the Alternative Dispute Resolution Bill was drafted and debated at a number of conferences and forums, the Bill remained in the wilderness and never saw Parliament until the year 2010. Some of you would remember that we held a grand conference of stakeholder (bench, bar Faculty, and Business) in Elmina. Mrs. Betty Mould Iddrisu, who was the programme director and coordinator for the ADR conferences eventually, saw to the enactment of the ADR Bill into law in 2010 when she became Minister of Justice and Attorney General in 2009.

Ghana has now reached the stage where there is in existence an Alternative Dispute Resolution Act, 2010 (Act 798) that governs not only the mechanisms and processes of ADR in Ghana but its practice as well. I have no doubt that GHACMA is by now well acquainted with the Act 798 and that it will guide your practice.

In the interim, the wisdom of the Faculty of Law in leading and coordinating the movement for ADR yielded fruits when the Judicial Service continued the institutionalization of the ADR concept. The Bench, Bar and Faculty have institutionalized the holding of an annual ADR Day to educate and advocate on the benefits of ADR. The consistent education and advocacy undertaken particularly by the Judicial Service under various Chief justices is the most patent and overt advertisement over the years of the ADR concept. The real practice of the process in the courts has enhanced the learning process for both litigants and facilitators. Let me mention, before I forget, that in tandem with the developments in the judicial service of ADR, the Ghana School of law incorporated some ADR training in its Advocacy and Legal Ethics course. The lecturer of the Advocacy course was, fortunately, one of the pioneer delegates on the study tour of 1996. That pioneer, many of you know, is our own Nene Amagatcher, Esq.

The Legon Center for International Affairs (LECIA) of the University of Ghana was established around the same period in collaboration with the Ministry of Foreign Affairs, and offered training for nation's Foreign Service Officers. Dr. Obed Asamoah, who was Minister of Foreign affairs and Acting Attorney General, was the key facilitator of its establishment. The LECIA Master of Arts in International Relations has a course component in Conflict Resolution. The efforts of the Ghana Armed Forces in peacekeeping worldwide were rewarded by the establishment the Kofi Annan Peace Keeping Center in 2005. A number of tertiary institutions in Ghana and Africa also began offering modules in Conflict Resolution and later Peace Studies. The University Of Cape Cost, and the University of Development Studies are a few I can recall. Indeed, there are today in Africa several institutions of higher learning offering programmes in Conflict Resolution and Peace Studies. One can say today that ADR, conflict and peace studies, and conflict resolution and peace building practice have become part of our academic and professional lives.

My perspective is that Ghana did not start the study of ADR as part of Peace Studies or to resolve intractable interpersonal or group or community conflicts. The urgency for ADR at the time was how to remove the delays and expedite the justice delivery system and to humanize it by giving ownership of the outcomes of conflict or dispute to the parties in conflict, in such a manner as would foster the maintenance of relationship, if the parties so desired.

Ghana was certainly concerned about the several destructive and intractable conflicts in Liberia, Sierra Leone, Rwanda, Burundi, the Democratic Republic of the Congo, Guinea Bissau, Angola Namibia, South Africa, Mozambique, etc. Our respected Ghana Armed Forces were playing critical roles in conflict resolution and peace keeping in some of these countries. Indeed, Ghana had her own internal violent pre-independence conflicts and post-independence unification conflicts. These conflicts have taken various shapes and forms, depending on the circles of the conflict and its dominant theme at a particular epoch: ethnic chieftaincy, chieftaincy and land, land, religious, environmental, and political conflicts, or what I term "the right to govern the nation," etc. Of course, you know that these conflicts cannot be separated into compartments in the real world as I have attempted to do, because they intermix and influence each other. The African conflicts and internal intractable conflicts might account for the later developments of Conflict Resolution and Peace Studies by NGOs, Universities and other tertiary institutions of learning but not, in my respectful view, for the ADR movement in Ghana.

I must at this stage recognize one of the early advocacy groups in Ghana for Peace and Conflict Resolution, the West African Network for Peace-building, WANEP. That was one of the first organized conflict resolution and peace building network groups that started to engage and intervene in internal intractable and violent conflicts outside the judicial system in Ghana. I should also salute the various Non-Governmental Organizations who engaged in some aspects of peace-building and conflict resolution in their work of alleviating poverty and promoting development in Ghana. In those early days, before the UNDP highlighted the interrelationship of small arms, poverty, conflict and development, the operations of these NGOs had led them to make that connection and addressed those linkages. I have in mind Action Aid International, Ghana, Oxfam, Catholic Relief Service, ADRA, etc. who operated in Northern Ghana.

This conversation with you, on my bird's eye view of the history of ADR and Peace Studies in Africa, fifteen years later would be incomplete for Ghana if I did not mention the fact of the effect of the escalation and implosion of the Dagbon Chieftaincy Affair on official Government policy on conflict Resolution, peacemaking and national security. It may be recalled that on 25th March 2002, a fight broke out in Yendi between the two supporters of the rival factions in the Yendi Skin Affairs, resulting in the death of several fellow citizens including the King of Dagbon. The Government of the day (as one of the ways of dealing with the matter) collaborated with the United Nations through its United Nation Development Programme to find ways of reducing the proliferation of small arms in Dagbon and other conflict areas of Ghana. The immediate result was the establishment by law of the Ghana National Commission on Small Arms.

As part of implementing the recommendations of the UNDP team of experts and as a means of diffusing the tension in Dagbon to enable the 2004 elections to take place in that area, the Government accepted and implemented administratively the establishment of a Northern Region Peace Advisory Council to peace making in Ghana. Those who lived through the 2008 Presidential elections and know the role of the National Peace Council at the last and critical stages of that election would appreciate the role the National Peace Council played in making peace for a successful election.

This is why, with my background in conflict studies and conflict resolution, I saw the urgency as the Minister of the Interior with additional responsibility for Intelligence Services for finalizing the National Peace Council Bill, obtaining Cabinet approval and submitting same to

Parliament for enactment into law before my transfer to the Ministry of Justice. I am also happy to say that in spite of my transfer I still had the privilege to move the Bill through the Committees of Parliament and also through all the enactment stage of Parliament. I can proudly say that Ghana now has a National Peace Council Act, 2011 (Act 818).

Ghana's ADR, conflict and peace studies, conflict resolution and peace-building architecture has come a long way since the modest efforts of the Bench, Bar and Faculty in 1996. We now have a sizeable number of citizens trained in these disciplines either as educators, educator/practitioners, practitioners, or advocates etc.

I have tried within the proceeding conversation with you to show that Ghana has within the last fifteen years established a firm foundation for the academic study and practice of ADR, conflict and peace studies, and conflict resolution and peace building. The existence of the Ghana Association of Certified Mediators and Arbitrators and other like associations in this discipline shows how far we have come. Ghana is also the only country which has institutionalized the concept of a National Peace Council by law. Zimbabwe is in the process of enacting its National Peace and Reconciliation Council Bill into law soonest. On 22nd November 2010 I was invited by the UNDP to speak to select members of the UN Permanent Representative of donor countries at the United Nations Head Office in New York at a lunch on Ghana's National Peace Council Bill. The next day, I spoke to a group of UNDP officers around the world, who happened to be at the UN Head Office but could not attend the previous day's conversation with the selected UN Permanent Representatives. It was here that I learnt that there were about 22 twenty-two countries who were trying to learn from Ghana's efforts at ADR, and conflict resolution and peace building efforts to craft their own peace agenda. Ghanaians, therefore, ought to be proud of the nation's achievements and to maintain our place as a stable and peaceful nation.

The question I wish to ask is: how can we keep Ghana's pioneering achievement in the ADR, conflict and peace studies field refined and reinforced into the future? We are in a multi-disciplinary field of studies and professional practice. The field encompasses religion; sociology; anthropology; history; psychology; political science; medicine; nursing; military or security studies; communication studies; law; social work, etc. Indeed, today's world in almost every academic discipline has an aspect of conflict and peace studies. What is it that we in this multidisciplinary field, who hold ourselves out as educators, practitioners, or advocates of conflict resolution, do that is different from that which our illiterate forbearers did in facilitation of conflict resolution and peace building?

A few years back it was enough to recite the myths in our field that as facilitators of ADR, conflict Resolution or Peace Making we are independent and neutrals. We only control the ADR, and peace making process while the parties control the outcome by the agreement they reach with our help. But this myth of our independence and neutrality has been overtaken by the findings of empirical research from several disciplines in this field including the physical sciences. The findings are that as third party facilitators we become part of the conflict interaction and affect the conflict dynamics from the moment of our intervention. As the recognized experts in the field the parties may abdicate their self-determination of the outcome to us and take cues from us as to what outcome they may accept. This is why in this discipline facilitators are classified according to whether they are perceived to be directive; prescriptive; elicitive; controlling; transformative or transforming etc. in their interventions. I am looking forward to the day when professionals in conflict, peace and ADR research and practice will all become reflective practitioners and know when they are dictating the outcome for the parties in the conflict and not vice versa. It is important to me that I own up to what I do with the parties in conflict at a facilitation session as I can consciously ensure that my contribution to the outcome may be benign and not malignant.

Are you a facilitator, whose business in guided by the framework of problem solving, settlement, transforming conflicts by promoting self-determination, recognition, and empowerment? If you are transformative mediators which of the schools do you function from? Or do you combine aspects of all the perspective depending on the issues of conflict? Do you see yourselves purely as umpires who facilitate dialogue and discourse by ensuring that the ground rules are respected during the discourse? Do we see peace making and conflict resolution to include therapy, and redemption from the hereafter? What is the influence of our fees and salaries on the work we do as peace makers and conflict resolvers?

Are we developing artistry in this field or are most of us still content to be only craftsmen in ADR, conflict resolution and peacemaking? To be artists, we need constant reflective thinking using journal entries to keep track of our progress and innovations as professional mediators. Is this part of our practice?

Before I take my seat I would like to underscore one important fact in the field of conflict resolution and peace making. The basic foundation of a conflict determines the outcome of its resolution. This is because of the recognition of the fact that there are multiple social realities and multiple truths in the social world. It is therefore unfair and oppressive for any individual to determine for parties in conflict what outcome they must accept. This is why conflict resolution theory particularly sees arbitration and adjudication as being directive, controlling, and at times oppressive of the parties in dispute. The foundation on which the legal system and adjudication is based is the theory in the social world that one can with due diligence and patience discover the one and only one true answer or solution to any question or problem. The function of the arbitrator or the judge is to find that one truth, correct answer or solution to any problem posed by conflict. Quantum theory killed the Newtonian physical laws of nature which postulated one correct answer or solution long ago. Conflict resolution has moved in tandem with the new philosophical developments.

It is for this reason that I would urge those who have taken up the new profession of mediators or facilitators to know exactly what they have undertaken to sell to the public. If you choose to mediate, let the parties determine their own version of the truth by their own agreement. Do not do it for them. I look forward to a growing and vibrant ADR and peace building profession and practitioners in Ghana governed by sound professional ethics in this field.

I thank GHACMA for offering me this opportunity to share my perspectives and to bear witness to the ADR, Conflict Resolution and Peace building field in Ghana (15) fifteen years after its inception. I wish all of you fruitful deliberations. Thank you sincerely for giving me audience.

APPENDIX

THIRD INTERNATIONAL AFRICA PEACE AND CONFLICT RESOLUTION (PCR) CONFERENCE COMMUNIQUÉ

JULY 26 - 28, 2011, ACCRA, GHANA

Webpage: www.csus.edu/org/capcr
www.ghacma.org/conference.html

FOR IMMEDIATE RELEASE!

Communiqué Issued at the End of the 3rd International Africa Peace and Conflict Resolution Conference Held in Accra, Ghana from July 26 to 28, 2011

Conference Theme: "Alternative Dispute Resolution (ADR) and Peace Studies in Africa, 15 years later: Lessons and New Directions."

The delegates at the 3rd international Africa Peace and Conflict Resolution Conference organised by the Centre for African Peace and Conflict Resolution (CAPCR) of California State University, Sacramento, USA and the Ghana Association of Certified Mediators and Arbitrators (GHACMA) give regard to the fact that conflict in its varied forms and manifestations is inevitable in our communities, business places and in our governance systems;

They acknowledge the downward conflict trend and increasing level of democratization in Africa as positive developments that demand more robust, sustained efforts at ADR and peace studies;

They find paucity of evaluation data and best practices on peace and conflict resolution in Africa;

They are concerned about the negative effects of conflicts on the African continent, especially the ones that result in the loss of millions of precious lives;

They recognise the importance of engaging governments, the business community, religious organisations, traditional authorities, civil society and other stakeholders on peacemaking and peace building initiatives;

They are conscious of the need to educate the public about issues of peace and conflict resolution, as well as sensitization on issues of social justice that aggravate violence;

They are aware of the gap that exists in the number of dispute resolution practitioners and peace makers across the world and Africa in particular;

They appreciate the special workshop on complex/multiparty mediation, facilitated by Mr. Daniel Yamshon;

They are committed to educating the public and highlighting issues of peace and social justice, as well as training and building the capacity of peace makers and dispute resolution practitioners and institutions;

They recall the challenge faced by ADR and peace building institutions in accessing funding to promote peace initiatives and institutionalize ADR;

They acknowledge with gratitude and promise the new enabling legislations on Alternative Dispute Resolution (ADR) in several African countries, in Ghana and Uganda in particular;

They realise the indigenous appeal of Alternative Dispute Resolution within the African context;

They are mindful of the call to institutionalise Dispute Resolution training and practice at critical levels of society and nation;

They are satisfied by the resolve of academia to introduce or expand the teaching of Alternative Dispute Resolution (ADR) as a degree programme at the graduate or undergraduate level;

They embrace the critical appraisal of the role of technology in dispute resolution and its facility in the form of online dispute resolution (ODR);

They commend the efforts being made to mainstream ADR in the judiciary, thereby improving upon the justice delivery system, without recreating or exacerbating the problems that necessitated ADR;

They are convinced of the immense potential of ADR in increasing access to justice, decongesting the courts of a backlog of cases, and providing justice in a manner that is speedy, cost effective and which satisfies the interests of disputing parties;

They are determined to empower the youth and women in peace initiatives and in dispute resolution practice and leadership;

They know that the youth are not only the most affected in any conflict but are also our most effective means of transferring knowledge and continuing a conscious culture of peace and effective dispute resolution;

Therefore,

1. They commit themselves to work to prevent conflicts in Africa and, where it has already occurred, to work to resolve the conflicts in a timely and effective manner;
2. They accept the challenge to institutionalise the training and practice of Alternative Dispute Resolution at critical levels, including expansion of peace and conflict studies curricular in secondary and university education;
3. They call on the rest of Africa to follow the examples of Ghana and Uganda to enact appropriate ADR legislations;
4. They request the Bar and the Bench to adopt proactive measures in mainstreaming ADR in Africa;
5. They encourage organisations and institutions engaged in peace building and dispute resolution to empower the youth and women in their efforts aimed at making the world a more peaceful place to live in;
6. They entreat African traditional authorities to maintain the African appeal of their dispute resolution processes while embracing ADR;
7. They invite religious leaders and religious organisations to emphasise peaceful co-existence to their congregants;
8. They call on ADR and peace building institutions to adopt measures aimed at attracting funding for their purposes;
9. They call on governments, the business community and donor agencies to support the course of ADR and peace building institutions;

10. They recommend the development and implementation of evaluation instruments for macro level assessment of the success of peace and conflict resolution projects and activities, and
11. They further agree on the need for the creation of a sustainable peace and conflict resolution network of peace, and to hold the international peace and conflict resolution conference every 3 years; and resolved to hold the next conference in South Africa.

Delegates expressed their immense gratitude to the Ghana Association of Certified Mediators and Arbitrators (GHACMA) as well as its staff for successfully hosting the conference and for giving them a feel of the Ghanaian hospitality and also to the Centre for African Peace and Conflict Resolution (CAPCR) for instituting the conference. They also expressed their gratitude to Her Ladyship the Chief Justice of the Republic of Ghana, Justice Georgina T. Wood for delivering the concluding keynote address; Hon. Martin Amidu, Attorney-General and Minister of Justice for delivering the opening keynote address; Prof. Ernest Uwazie for the conference opening address; Lt. Gen. Arnold Quainoo, Executive Director of the Centre for Conflict Resolution (CENCOR) for chairing the opening ceremony and for hosting the welcome reception and the workshop on Multi-Party/Complex Dispute Resolution at CENCOR; His Lordship Mr. Justice S.A. Brobbey, Justice of the Supreme Court of Ghana for participating in the Town Hall Discussion on ADR and Peace Studies in Africa; Mr. Justice Bawa Akamba, Justice of the Appeal Court of Ghana and Director of the Judicial Training Institute for gracing the opening ceremony; Nana Dr. S.K.B. Asante, Chairman of the Ghana Arbitration Centre for his participation and offering important insights in the practice of Arbitration; Dr. Robin Carter, Associate Dean of the College of Health and Human Services of California State University for chairing a paper presentation panel; Mr. Austin A. Gamey, Chief Executive Officer of Gamey and Gamey Group for chairing a paper presentation panel; Mrs. Chris Dadzie, Lawyer and former senior staff member of the Ghana Commission on Human Rights and Administrative Justice (CHRAJ) for chairing a paper presentation panel; Dr. Sylvester Bowie, Chair of the CAPCR Board and Associate Professor of Social Work at California State University, Sacramento, USA for chairing a paper presentation panel; Mr. Martin C. Nwosu, General Secretary of Ghana Association of Certified Mediators and Arbitrators (GHACMA) for chairing a paper presentation panel; Miss Joyce N.N. Oku for serving as Rapporteur General at the conference; Mr. Saeed Musah-Khaleepha for ably coordinating the conference planning and arrangements, and kind remarks and presents from the California delegation through Prof. Uwazie and Ms. Ellen Taylor of the California Lawyers for the Arts.

The delegates also commend and appreciate the visionary leadership and landmark ADR contributions of Prof. Ernest Uwazie, Director of Center for African Peace and Conflict Resolution (CAPCR) of California State University, Sacramento, USA; and Professor Kofi Quashigah, President of Ghana Association of Certified Mediators and Arbitrators (GHACMA).

They acknowledge presenters at the conference for providing enlightenment through their respective presentations and interactions with the audience:

Prof. Ernest Uwazie
Mr. Daniel Yamshon
Rev. Sr. Barr. Ijeoma Njoku
Mr. J.S.T. Abbossey
Miss Ijeoma Ononogbu
Dr. Ephraim S. Essien
Miss Joy O.S. Ogaji
Dr. Chniyere Comfort Ani
Mr. Ahmed Baba Yahaya
Mr. Adebgoyega Adebayo Karim
Mr. Segun Arinze
Rev. Dr. Cletus Obasi
Dr. Sunday Ogbodo
Mr. Saeed Musah-Khaleepha
Dr. Jose Pascal da Rocha

They further acknowledge the following organisations and their representatives:

1. Center for African Peace and Conflict Resolution (CAPCR), California State University, Sacramento, USA
2. Ghana Association of Certified Mediators and Arbitrators (GHACMA)
3. African Centre for the Constructive Resolution of Disputes (ACCORD), South Africa
4. Lagos Multi-Door Courthouse, Lagos, Nigeria
5. California Lawyers for the Arts, California, USA
6. Nigerian Institute of Advanced Legal Studies, Lagos

7. Ashaiman ADR Centre, Ghana
8. The Judicial Service of Ghana
9. Ghana Ministry of Justice and Attorney-General's Department, Ghana
10. Centre for Conflict Resolution (CENCOR), Ghana
11. Ghana Arbitration Centre
12. Afripeace & Development Foundation, USA
13. Justice and Peace Commission, Ghana
14. El-Shiloh Foundation, Ghana
15. Catholic Secretariat, Ho, Ghana
16. Assemblies of God, Assin Fosu, Ghana
17. Young mediators and Negotiators of Nigeria
18. Spiritan Int. School of Theology & Evangelism, Ghana
19. University of Cape Coast, Ghana
20. International Islamic University, Malaysia
21. Creative Advantage International
22. Centre for Peace and Strategic Studies, Univ. of Illorin, Nigeria.
23. School of Law, Warwick University, UK
24. Christ Mission Foundation, Ghana

Contacts

USA: uwazieee@csus.edu
Ghana: saeed@ghacma.org

CONTRIBUTORS

Isaac Olawale Albert is a Professor of African History, Peace and Conflict Studies at the University of Ibadan, Nigeria. In 2006, he won the Peace Education award of the Centre for African Peace and Conflict Resolution, California State University, Sacramento (USA). He is a Fellow and Board Chairman of the Society for Peace Studies and Practice (SPSP) and a Regional Board Member of the West African Network for Peacebuilding (Accra, Ghana).

Martin Amidu has a longstanding political career in Ghana, having served in various party and political roles since the nineteen-eighties. He was a foundation member of the National Democratic Congress. He has held several regional and national positions in Ghana, including roles in Local Government and Rural Development; Industries, Science and Technology; the Interior and Justice Ministries respectively, as well as the Attorney-General's Office, having once served as the Attorney General and Minister of Justice. He stood as Vice Presidential candidate alongside Prof. John Evans Atta Mills in the NDC's 2000 election campaign. Amidu currently serves as a Private Legal and Conflict Resolution Consultant.

Chinyere C. Ani holds a Ph.D. in Public Law from the University of Lagos, Nigeria. She is the head of the ADR unit of the Nigeria Institute of Advanced Legal Studies, Lagos. She is also a member of the Chartered Institute of Arbitrators, UK, and the Nigeria Bar Association. She has participated in several ADR training workshops, and is a certified mediator and serves on the panel of neutrals of the Lagos Multidoor Courthouse. Currently, she is conducting research on the "Rights of Juvenile Offenders Undergoing Institutional Treatment in Lagos State, Nigeria.

Robert Dibie, Ph.D. is a Distinguished Professor of Public Policy and Public Management, and Dean of the School of Public and Environmental Affairs at Indiana University Kokomo Unites States. He is the author of several books, book chapters, and more than 80-peer reviewed journal articles relating to public policy, environmental issues and sustainable development. Professor Dibie has consulted for NGOs and universities in several Africa, and Caribbean countries, United States, and Canada. He is the current editor of the *Journal of International Politics and Development*

Steven Gatembu Kairu is a judge of the Court of Appeals, Nairobi, Kenya. He was admitted as an Advocate of the High Court of Kenya in 1985, formerly a partner in Kairu & McCourt Advocates. He retired from the firm to go into full time arbitration and mediation work under the firm name of Arbitration & Mediation Chambers. He is a trainer of trainers in Alternative Dispute Resolution and has facilitated workshops in Kenya, Ethiopia, Tanzania and Seychelles. He has also taught at the School of Law, University of Nairobi, since 1990. He holds law degree from the University of Nairobi and a master's degree in law from Boston University.

Adegboyega A. Karim holds a Ph.D in Peace and Development Studies from University of Ilorin, Ilorin, Nigeria. He is an active member of many academic and professional bodies including Society for Peace Studies and Practice (SPSP), Nigerian Institute of Management (NIM) among others. He has attended many academic conferences and presented scholarly papers on electoral violence, conflict, terrorism, religious crisis and inter-faith relations.

Saeed Musah-Khaleepha is a young dispute resolution professional with five years working experience. He works with Gamey and Gamey Group, an Employment Dispute Resolution and Labour Consultancy firm in Accra, Ghana. He served as Programmes Manager for Ghana Association for Chartered Mediators and Arbitrators (GHACMA). His areas of interest are professionalising dispute resolution, systems design, employment, commercial, land and environmental disputes.

Carol Ijeoma Njoku (Reverend Sister) is a practicing attorney and teaches at the University of Nigeria, Enugu Campus. She is the coordinator of the Human Rights Association of Peace and Dispute Resolution, Nigeria (HRAPADRON). Her publications include: *Shackles in God* (Chimavin Publisher, Owerri), 2002; and *Together in God: A Critical Analysis of the Three Major Religious Sects in Nigeria* (Gostalk Publishers, Enugu), 2005.
E-mail: njokucaroli@gmail.com

Anne Amuche Obiora is a nun with the Congregation of the Handmaids of the Holy Child Jesus. She is a Lawyer by training and a lecturer in the faculty of Law of Anambra State University, Igbariam campus, Nigeria. She has written books on Arbitration and Law of contract and published articles in both local and international journals.

Joy Ogaji holds an LLM in Environmental law from Demontford University, Leicester UK. Her PhD from Warwick University, UK focused on the Viability of Applying Alternative Dispute Resolution Processes in Nigeria. Joy Ogaji currently works with the Regulatory and Transactions Monitoring Unit of the Presidential Task Force on Power in Nigeria as a Senior Technical Adviser. Engaged in the transaction monitoring, evaluation and facilitation for the completion and handover of the vertically unbundled PHCN Assets to private owners.

Ijeoma Ononogbu is a dual qualified lawyer, having been admitted in Nigeria 2004, and England & Wales 2008. She has a Master in Laws (LLM) from Queen Mary, University of London in 2011, where she specialised in International Dispute Resolution. She is a member of Chartered Institute of Arbitrators, and London Court of International Arbitration. A practising solicitor in London with interests in International Dispute Resolution. Her conference presentations on Online Dispute Resolution have been well received. Ijeoma has chaired mediation competitions. A Fellow of the National Center for Technology and Dispute Resolution

Georgina T. Wood is the Chief Justice of Ghana, the first female Judge to head Ghana's Judiciary, an institution to which she has devoted nearly forty years of her life. Since becoming Chief Justice in 2007, she has initiated several judicial reform programmes to promote access to justice, particularly Alternative Dispute Resolution (ADR) and the creation of specialized courts, including Commercial Courts, to ensure speedy resolution of cases. Since her ADR training in the US with CAPCR in 1996, she has remained a leader in promoting ADR in the judiciary, legal profession and traditional institutions in Ghana.

Daniel Yamshon, Esq. is a lead trainer for the Center for African Peace and Conflict Resolution. He serves on the Commercial, Construction and Large, Complex Case panels of the American Arbitration Association as an arbitrator and mediator, is an arbitrator for the Financial Industry Regulatory Authority and others. Mr. Yamshon is the chair *emeritus* of the

California State Bar Association ADR Committee's International Subcommittee. He is a co-author of the book *Construction ADR* published by the American Bar Association. Mr. Yamshon has provided various ADR services in eleven countries, including several in Africa.

INDEX